BEYOND CLASSICAL PEDAGOGY

Teaching Elementary School Mathematics

STUDIES IN MATHEMATICAL THINKING AND LEARNING
Alan H. Schoenfeld, Series Editor

Artzt/Armour-Thomas • *Becoming a Reflective Mathematics Teacher: A Guide for Observations and Self-Assessment*

Carpenter/Fennema/Romberg (Eds.) • *Rational Numbers: An Integration of Research*

Cobb/Bauersfeld (Eds.) • *The Emergence of Mathematical Meaning: Interaction in Classroom Cultures*

English (Ed.) • *Mathematical Reasoning: Analogies, Metaphors, and Images*

Fennema/Nelson (Eds.) • *Mathematics Teachers in Transition*

Fennema/Romberg (Eds.) • *Mathematics Classrooms That Promote Understanding*

Lajoie (Ed.) • *Reflections on Statistics: Learning, Teaching, and Assessment in Grades K–12*

Lehrer/Chazan (Eds.) • *Designing Learning Environments for Developing Understanding of Geometry and Space*

Ma • *Knowing and Teaching Elementary Mathematics: Teachers' Understanding of Fundamental Mathematics in China and the United States*

Martin • *Mathematics Success and Failure Among African American Youth: The Roles of Sociohistorical Context, Community Forces, School Influence, and Individual Agency*

Reed • *Word Problems: Research and Curriculum Reform*

Romberg/Fennema/Carpenter (Eds.) • *Integrating Research on the Graphical Representations of Functions*

Schoenfeld (Eds.) • *Mathematical Thinking and Problem Solving*

Sternberg/Ben-Zeev (Eds.) • *The Nature of Mathematical Thinking*

Wilcox/Lanier (Eds.) • *Using Assessment to Reshape Mathematics Teaching: A Casebook for Teachers and Teacher Educators, Curriculum and Staff Development Specialists*

Wood/Nelson/Warfield (Eds.) • *Beyond Classical Pedagogy: Teaching Elementary School Mathematics*

BEYOND CLASSICAL PEDAGOGY

Teaching Elementary School Mathematics

Edited by

Terry Wood
Purdue University

Barbara Scott Nelson
Education Development Center, Newton, Massachusetts

Janet Warfield
Purdue University

 LAWRENCE ERLBAUM ASSOCIATES, PUBLISHERS

2001   Mahwah, New Jersey   London

The camera ready copy for this book was supplied by the editors.

Lawrence Erlbaum Associates, Inc., Publishers
10 Industrial Avenue
Mahwah, NJ 07430

Cover design by Kathryn Houghtaling Lacey

Library of Congress Cataloging-in-Publication Data

Beyond classical pedagogy : teaching elementary school mathematics
/ edited by Terry Wood, Barbara Scott Nelson, Janet Warfield.
    p. cm.
Includes bibliographical references and index.
    ISBN 0-8058-3570-9 (cloth : alk. paper)
    ISBN 0-8058-3571-7 (pbk. : alk. paper)
    1. Mathematics—Study and teaching (Elementary) I. Wood, Terry
Lee, 1942– . II. Nelson, Barbara Scott. III. Warfield, Janet.
    QA135.6 .B49 2001
    372.7—dc21
                                                    2001016100
                                                         CIP

Books published by Lawrence Erlbaum Associates are printed on
acid-free paper, and their bindings are chosen for strength and durability.

Printed in the United States of America
10 9 8 7 6 5 4 3 2 1

Contents

Preface

The emergence of the National Council of Teachers of Mathematics (NCTM) *Curriculum and Evaluation Standards* in 1989, and the research that preceded it, have sparked a sea change in thought about the nature and quality of mathematics instruction. In the decade since the publication of the original NCTM *Standards* and the 2000 revised *Standards* many teachers, teacher educators, and researchers have worked to understand what teaching designed specifically to support mathematical sense-making among students would be like. This book reports on the current state of our knowledge about the forms of teaching that have evolved from these efforts.

There is, at this point, a substantial body of research that examines the processes by which teachers make transitions from traditional instruction to instruction that focuses on mathematical sense-making (e. g., Fennema & Nelson, 1997; Schifter, 1996). Yet relatively little is known about the characteristics of such teaching itself. This book aims to fill that gap for mathematics instruction in the elementary grades. It provides descriptions and analyses of the teaching that has evolved in mathematics classrooms of teachers who have been forerunners in this effort. Nationally known scholars and promising young researchers report on the insights they have gained from their investigations into elementary mathematics teaching and, in some cases, their own experience as teachers. The book focuses on teaching in elementary school mathematics classrooms, where the majority of the *Standards*-based efforts have occurred. Such classrooms are a rich and revealing source for understanding the complexity involved in teaching, teachers' learning, and the impact of both on children's learning.

Research and insights from three disciplinary perspectives are presented: (a) the psychological perspective, which focuses on such teaching as a process of teachers learning; (b) the mathematical perspective, which focuses on the nature of the mathematical knowledge that teachers need in order to engage in teaching for mathematical sense-making; and (c) the sociological perspective, which focuses on the interactive process of meaning construction as teachers and students create intellectual communities in their classrooms.

Because it presents an analysis of teaching from three different disciplinary perspectives, this book will be useful for scholars in mathematics education and teacher education more generally. It also can serve as a text for graduate courses in mathematics education, teacher education, elementary mathematics teaching methods, and methods of research in mathematics education. Further, the images of teaching presented in this book, while not intended to be prescriptive, will be enlightening for teacher educators, staff developers, and many teachers.

ORIGIN AND ORGANIZATION OF THE BOOK

This book grows out of a state-of-the-art conference on mathematics teaching held at Purdue University in October 1998.[1] Each of the presenters at that conference has prepared a chapter for this book, presenting their past and current thinking about teaching mathematics in the elementary grades. Although these chapters are research based, they also present rich images of classroom teaching for the consideration of the mathematics education community at large. The authors often write in personal, rather than academic voice, providing access to the stories of their own development as teachers and researchers, and how their ideas about the nature of mathematics teaching have evolved.

Part I includes the editors' Introduction and a chapter by Deborah Loewenberg Ball, which sets the stage by providing illustrative examples of facilitative teaching as it occurs in her teaching practice. These examples raise issues that are encountered in this form of pedagogy. The remainder of the book is divided into four sections. Parts II, III, and IV present research and insights on teaching for mathematical sense-making from the disciplinary perspectives of psychology, mathematics, and sociology. Each of the sections

---

[1] The participants were Thomas Carpenter, Elizabeth Fennema, Megan Franke, Barbara Jaworski, Betsy McNeal, Barbara Scott Nelson, Deborah Schifter, Miriam Sherin, Martin Simon, Janet Warfield and Terry Wood.

concludes with commentary by Barbara Jaworski, who served as a responder at the Purdue conference. Her reflections on each set of papers address questions and issues that were raised by those papers at the Purdue conference. Part V pulls together and contextualizes the work described in the preceding chapters.

Part II consists of three chapters written from a psychological perspective, which focus on teaching as a process of teachers' own learning. In their chapter, Thomas Carpenter, Ellen Ansell, and Linda Levi set the basic context for this perspective by arguing that teaching, that takes as its goal the development of students' mathematical understanding, needs to proceed from an understanding of what students already understand rather than from a preestablished and decontextualized instructional program, such as a curriculum or a lesson plan. Megan Loef Franke and Elham Kazemi build on this position, arguing that such teaching requires that teachers engage in continuous learning about the development of children's mathematical understanding in general, and the mathematical understanding of the children in their own classes in particular. Franke and Kazemi examine the several professional contexts in which such teacher learning occurs. Part II concludes with a chapter by Miriam Gamoran Sherin, who argues that in order to engage in instruction that supports mathematical sense-making, teachers need to attend increasingly to the mathematical thinking of the students in their classes, rather than primarily to the effectiveness of their own pedagogical moves.

Part III consists of three chapters written from a mathematical perspective, which focus on the nature and role of teachers' mathematical knowledge and ideas about the nature of mathematics, as they engage in teaching that supports students' mathematical thinking. The section begins with a chapter by Deborah Schifter, who lays out several different kinds of mathematical knowledge that are entailed in teaching for mathematical sense-making. This chapter is followed by one by Janet Warfield, who illustrates what teaching for mathematical sense-making has to gain from both the teacher's mathematical knowledge and her knowledge of how students' mathematical problem-solving strategies develop. Finally, Martin Simon provides a chapter in which he describes teaching for mathematical sense-making as driven by successive working hypotheses on the part of the teacher about what students are understanding, mathematically. Simon emphasizes that students and teacher may inhabit very different mathematical worlds, and that inherent in teaching for mathematical sense-making is the necessity for the teacher to understand the *students'* mathematical world.

Part IV consists of two chapters written from a sociological perspective, in which the focus is on interactive processes of meaning construction as teachers and students create intellectual communities in their classrooms. Terry Wood and Tammy Turner-Vorbeck present a theoretical framework that links the nature of the discourse between students and teacher with the kind and degree of complexity of student thinking and the locus of responsibility for mathematical thinking. Betsy McNeal describes the dilemmas of a teacher who is trying to balance her conviction that her teaching should support the development of mathematical sense-making on the part of her students with the expectations of other teachers and the community that students achieve certain skills at certain grade levels. This brings to a full circle the issue raised initially in the chapter by Carpenter, Ansell and Levi.

Following the three disciplinary sections the two chapters in Part V synthesize and situate the work described in the book. A synthesizing chapter by Barbara Scott Nelson identifies points of convergence on what is known about teaching for mathematical sense-making and what is still in contention. Nelson traces what the analyses from three different disciplinary perspectives have in common and where they are in conflict. She also identifies a number of issues that are raised by the set of chapters and require more work. A chapter by Virginia Richardson critically examines this entire body of work and situates it in the larger context of research on teaching. Richardson reviews some 30 years of research on teaching and situates the work presented in this book in that historical sweep. She identifies the work as largely postmodern, in the sense that the authors explicitly identify the conceptual and theoretical frames they are using for their work and see that acknowledging such frames is an integral part of the work. Richardson also comments on the shift in research on teaching toward subject-matter-specific studies, of which this book is an example.

Finally, concluding remarks by Wood, Nelson, and Warfield argues that research on mathematics instruction, as a whole, needs to focus more on the development and testing of theories of pedagogy if it is to move forward.

We would first like to express our thanks to Elizabeth Fennema and Barbara Jaworski, who were responders to the papers during the Purdue conference, and whose astute commentary gave the conference much of its shape. Appreciation is also due to Alan

Schoenfeld, editor of this series for Lawrence Erlbaum Associates, whose keen editorial pen helped us keep to the intellectual core of this discussion about elementary mathematics teaching.

We would like to express our thanks to Karen Hearn for providing professional assistance to the editors and authors of this book. Without her help, this volume would still lie in pieces on the editors' desks.

The preparation of the book was supported by funding from the National Science Foundation, through the Research on Teaching and Learning program [RED 9254939] to Wood, Cennamo, Lehman, and Warfield. Other support for the book's preparation was provided by the School Mathematics and Science Center, School of Education, Purdue University and by the Center for the Development of Teaching at the Education Development Center in Newton, Massachusetts. Some preparation was accomplished while the first editor was an Academic Visitor in the Department of Educational Studies, University of Oxford. All opinions are those of the authors. And finally, to Robert and Christine, may the ideas about teaching portrayed in this book be another response to the thorny question you asked in 1989.

> *— Terry Wood*
> *— Barbara Scott Nelson*
> *— Janet Warfield*

Part I

SETTING THE STAGE AND RAISING ISSUES

OVERVIEW

In chapter 1, we provide background for the chapters presented in this book. Then, in order to set the stage for the chapters to come, we asked Deborah Loewenberg Ball to provide illustrative examples from her own teaching of third grade mathematics. In her chapter, she offers initial vignettes that vividly characterize the nature of her teaching, which is illustrative of the pedagogy described by the authors in the forthcoming chapters. Ball's examples, along with her comments, highlight a number of major issues teachers' encounter when teaching in this manner and for the field of mathematics education more generally. The major concerns that she raises from the perspective of one teaching echo throughout the book, providing a common thread for connecting the issues raised in each of the individual chapters.

1

Introduction

Barbara Scott Nelson
Education Development Center, Newton, MA

Janet Warfield
Terry Wood
Purdue University

In their 1986 chapter for the *Third Handbook of Research on Teaching,* Romberg and Carpenter summarized the status of research on children's learning in mathematics, the nature of research on the teaching of mathematics, and the relation between the two (Romberg & Carpenter, 1986). They noted that although the emphasis in research on learning had changed dramatically in the previous 15 years, reflecting the turn in the field of psychology toward cognitive science, work on the instructional implications of these theories of learning was at a nascent stage, and much of the research directly addressing questions of teaching remained untouched by the revolution in cognitive science. Romberg and Carpenter argued that theories of instruction needed to be consistent with what we know about how children learn and think.

The chapters presented in this book represent the work of a number of scholars to develop frameworks and describe practices of teaching that are compatible with a constructivist theory of learning.[1]

---

[1] We note that there are many different theoretical versions of constructivism (Phillips, 1995; Prawat & Peterson, 1999) and we make no attempt to delineate them here. Our purpose is merely to establish a basic orientation toward learning that unites the authors of chapters in this book, leaving it to them, in their respective chapters, to specify the aspects of constructivist theory that they are adopting.

Although there are differences in emphasis and orientation among these scholars, they all take as basic tenets of a constructivist theory of learning that children actively construct mathematical knowledge for themselves through interaction with the social and physical environment and through extension and reorganization of their own mental constructs. Children are not passive recipients of such knowledge; they generate it, put structure into it, assimilate it in light of their own mental frameworks, and revise existing mental frameworks to accommodate new experience. Further, such mathematical thinking does not begin in school. Children begin life as active mathematical thinkers and come to school with rich networks of informal mathematical ideas already in place.

Such basic ideas about the nature of learning have been supplemented by ideas from several fields of study. From information-processing psychology and cognitive science have emerged ideas about the organization of knowledge in memory, including the notions that structure is imposed on concepts when they are stored in long-term memory and that the richer the structure, the more accessible the concepts (Chi, Glaser, & Rees, 1982; Romberg & Carpenter, 1986). From the field of mathematics come ideas about the nature of the discipline itself. Mathematics is not taken to be only a static, bounded discipline with a rich record of knowledge to be transmitted, but a humanistic field that is continually growing and being revised and that consists of "ideas created by human beings, existing in their collective consciousness" (Hersch, 1997, p. 19). Doing mathematics or learning to think mathematically is valued as highly as knowing the facts and procedures that have been developed earlier. From sociocultural theory and sociology has come the idea that communities of knowers share the construction of beliefs or knowledge. What is accepted as knowledge at a given time by a set of people is created through discursive processes and negotiation of meaning carried out in accord with the norms of the group (Harré & Gillett, 1994; Kuhn, 1970; Prawat & Peterson, 1999). In this view, classrooms are mathematical communities writ small, and key reform documents envision the classroom as a mathematical culture governed by roughly the same norms of argument and evidence as govern discourse within communities of scholars in the disciplines themselves (Lampert, 1990; Thompson & Zeuli, 1999).

The National Council of Teachers of Mathematics' (NCTM) *Curriculum and Evaluation Standards for School Mathematics* (1989) and the research that lay behind it created a vision of mathematics instruction that took seriously the fact that children construct their mathematical knowledge. In this view, teaching would no longer be a matter of viewing students' minds as blank slates and getting them to internalize the correct mathematics. Rather, the work of teaching would consist of developing instructional contexts in which students could move from their own, intuitive, mathematical understandings to those of conventional mathematics. The goal of instruction also changed. Rather than aiming for content mastery alone, the goal now included having students see mathematics as a sense-making activity. Mathematical processes such as problem solving, reasoning, making connections among mathematical ideas, and communicating mathematical ideas were highlighted. In sum, mathematics teaching was envisioned as teaching for mathematical sense-making, with a focus on both content and process.

At the time the NCTM Standards were released, research on mathematics teaching had been addressing the processes by which teachers changed their knowledge, beliefs, and instructional practices so that their teaching would emphasize mathematical sense-making on the part of their students. Four basic positions had developed, each with somewhat different theoretical roots (Nelson, 1997). These are now elaborated.

Carpenter, Peterson, and Fennema, with their roots in cognitive science, suggested that change in teaching was brought about by changes in the content and structure of teachers' knowledge, specifically their knowledge about the development of children's mathematical thinking. They claimed that teacher change occurred when teachers learned about research-based information on children's mathematical thinking, organized this information into a framework that related to the thinking of the children in their own classes, and used that framework to make decisions about teaching (Carpenter, Fennema, Peterson, & Carey, 1988; Carpenter, Fennema, Peterson, Chiang, & Loef, 1989; Peterson, Carpenter, & Fennema, 1989). A second position, taken by Schifter and Simon, along with Fosnot, was a Piagetian, developmental one, in which it was held that change in teachers' ideas about the nature of learning and mathematics was necessary and required a process of disequilibration of prior ideas, the resolution of which resulted in the reconstruction of more powerful ideas (Schifter, 1996a, 1996b; Schifter & Fosnot, 1993; Schifter & Simon, 1992). The third position, taken by Cobb, Wood, and Yackel (1990) started from a radical constructivist position but soon coordinated this view with a sociological perspective influenced by symbolic interaction and enthnomethodology. They posited that, as teachers and their students renegotiated the norms of the classroom to legitimate students' construction of mathematical concepts and discussion of mathematical ideas, teachers encountered and resolved conflicts between their prior beliefs about learning and what they observed happening in their classrooms (Cobb et al., 1990; Wood, Cobb, & Yackel, 1991). Finally, Ball and others, drawing on Shulman's concern for reconceptualizing the nature of teaching, argued that the nature of teachers' mathematical knowledge was critical. They contended that the character of many teachers' mathematical knowledge needed to change, becoming less algorithmic and more conceptual, if teachers were to understand their students' mathematical thinking, develop representations of mathematical ideas for use with their students, and facilitate mathematical discourse in their classrooms (Ball, 1988; McDiarmid & Wilson, 1991; Shulman, 1986, 1987).

In the intervening 10 years, many teachers, teacher educators, and researchers have been exploring what constitutes teaching for mathematical sense-making. The authors of the chapters in this book bring to this question many of the same underlying assumptions, theoretical orientations, and research methodologies that characterized their work a decade ago. Coming from different orientations, the authors of the chapters in this book put somewhat different emphases on the importance for teaching of the elements of the cognitive and social constructivist positions. They make different interpretations of such basic elements as what it means for children to be in interaction with the environment, what is meant by the reorganization of mental constructs, what kind of structure children put onto their knowledge, and what the role of the social environment may be. Such differences in focus and orientation have important implications for the emergent views of mathematics teaching that these scholars propose and raise important questions for future research.

This book provides views of the nature of teaching for mathematical sense-making in relatively mature forms. That is, chapters in this book are not primarily about how teachers learn to teach in this way but rather about the nature of the teaching itself when done by experienced practitioners. Although there is substantial research on earlier, more traditional forms of mathematics teaching and on the processes by which teachers make transitions from traditional pedagogy to teaching for mathematical sense-making (Fennema & Nelson, 1997), relatively little is known yet about the characteristics of this teaching itself, teaching that has been evolving in many classrooms over the past 10 years. This book aims to spark a conversation in the field about the nature of teaching for sense-making and how to study it.

REFERENCES

Ball, D. L. (1988). *Knowledge and reasoning in mathematical pedagogy: Examining what prospective teachers bring to teacher education.* East Lansing, MI: Michigan State University.

Carpenter, T. P., Fennema, E., Peterson, P., & Carey, D. (1988). Teachers' pedagogical content knowledge of students' problem-solving in elementary arithmetic. *Journal for Research in Mathematics Education, 19,* 385-401.

Carpenter, T. P., Fennema, E., Peterson, P., Chiang, D., & Loef, M. (1989). Using knowledge of children's mathematics thinking in classroom teaching: An experimental study. *American Educational Research Journal, 26,* 499-531.

Chi, M. T., Glaser, R., & Rees, E. (1982). Expertise in problem solving. In R. Sternberg (Ed.), *Advances in the psychology of human intelligence* (pp. 7-75). Hillsdale, NJ: Lawrence Erlbaum Associates.

Cobb, P., Wood, T., & Yackel, E. (1990). Classrooms as learning environments for teachers and researchers. In R. Davis, C. Maher, & N. Noddings (Eds.), *Constructivist views on the teaching and learning of mathematics* (pp. 125-146). (Journal for Research in Mathematics Education, Monograph No. 4). Reston, VA: National Council of Teachers of Mathematics.

Fennema, E. & Nelson, B. S. (1997). *Mathematics teachers in transition.* Mahwah, NJ: Lawrence Erlbaum Associates.

Harré, R. & Gillett, G. (1994). *The discursive mind.* London: Sage.

Hersch, R. (1997). *What is mathematics, really?* Mahwah, NJ: Lawrence Erlbaum Associates.

Kuhn, T. S. (1970). *The structure of scientific revolutions* (2nd ed.). Chicago: University of Chicago Press.

Lampert, M. (1990). When the problem is not the question and the solution is not the answer: Mathematical knowing and teaching. *American Educational Research Journal, 27,* 29-63.

McDiarmid, G. W., & Wilson, S. (1991). An exploration of the subject matter knowledge of alternate route teachers: Can we assume they know their subject? *Journal of Teacher Education, 42,* 93-103.

National Council of Teachers of Mathematics (1989). *Curriculum and evaluation standards for school mathematics.* Reston, VA: Author.

Nelson, B. S. (1997). Learning about teacher change in the context of mathematics education reform: Where have we come from? In E. Fennema & B. S. Nelson (Eds.), *Mathematics teachers in transition* (pp. 3-18). Mahwan, NJ: Lawrence Erlbaum Associates.

Peterson, P., Carpenter, T., & Fennema, E. (1989). Teachers' knowledge of students' knowledge in mathematics problem solving: Correlational and case analyses. *Journal of Educational Psychology, 81,* 558 - 569.

Phillips, D. C. (1995). The good, the bad, and the ugly: The many faces of constructivism. *Educational Researcher, 24,* 257-262.

Prawat, R. S., & Peterson, P. L. (1999). Social constructivist views of learning. In J.
    Murphy & K. S. Louis (Eds.), *Handbook of research on educational administration* (2nd
    ed., pp. 203-226). San Francisco, CA: Jossey-Bass.
Romberg, T. A., & Carpenter, T. P. (1986). Research on teaching and learning
    mathematics: Two disciplines of scientific inquiry. In M. C. Wittrock (Ed.),
    Handbook of research on teaching (3rd ed., pp. 850-873). New York: Macmillan.
Schifter, D. (Ed.). (1996a). *What's happening in math class: Envisioning new practices
    through teacher narratives.* (Vol. 1). New York: Teachers College Press.
Schifter, D. (Ed.). (1996b). *What's happening in math class: Reconstructing professional
    identities.* (Vol. 2). New York: Teachers College Press.
Schifter, D., & Fosnot, C. T. (1993). *Reinventing mathematics education: Stories of teachers
    meeting the challenge of reform.* New York: Teachers College Press.
Schifter, D., & Simon, M. (1992). Assessing teachers' development of a constructivist
    view of mathematics learning. *Teaching and Teacher Education, 8,* 187-97.
Shulman, L. S. (1986). Those who understand: Knowledge growth in teaching.
    Educational Researcher, 57, 4-14.
Shulman, L. S. (1987). Knowledge and teaching: Foundations of the new reform.
    Harvard Educational Review, 57, 1-22.
Thompson, C. L. & Zeuli, J. S. (1999). The frame and the tapestry: Standards-based
    reform and professional development. In L. Darling-Hammond & G. Sykes
    (Eds.), *Teaching as the learning profession: Handbook of policy and practice.* San
    Francisco: Jossey-Bass.
Wood, T., Cobb, P., & Yackel, E. (1991). Change in teaching mathematics: A case
    study. *American Educational Research Journal, 28,* 587-616.

Teaching, With Respect to Mathematics and Students

Deborah Loewenberg Ball
University of Michigan

For over 20 years, I have been trying to teach elementary school mathematics in ways that honor and are rooted in concerns for the integrity of mathematics as a discipline and that attend to and make serious use of students' thinking. Although these may be laudable aims, exploring what this might mean has presented interesting intellectual and practical problems. On one hand, possible mappings between the construction of knowledge in the discipline and school learning are far from simple or obvious. And, on the other hand, for any defensible instantiation of such practice, too little is known about what it takes for teachers and students to work in these ways in school. Hence, my work has entailed both invention and investigation. I use my teaching to explore what these ideas might mean in practice. I study the resulting teaching and learning — both mine and my students' — in order to explore the problems and demands of such practice (see, for example, Ball, 1993a, 1993b, 1997; Ball & Wilson, 1996).

Because the mathematics education community has been so active in seeking to improve the teaching and learning of mathematics in this country, mathematics reforms are often perceived as having widespread impact. In fact, many of the current debates are rooted in the assumption that mathematics teaching and learning have shifted from an emphasis on skills to a soft exploration of ideas. But this impression may be more myth than reality. Most evidence suggests that mathematics teaching that focuses on understanding as well as skill, that involves children in significant mathematical reasoning, and that strives for high standards of progress and accomplishment, is not commonplace.   In most classrooms, skill practice still dominates. Teachers explain and children follow. Explanations are based on rules and steps more often than on mathematical structure and reasoning.   And student learning continues to be low, distressingly stratified by race, gender, and class.

Why is there so little change in the direction of what seems to be a well-articulated vision? Some point the finger at teachers, citing their weak knowledge of mathematics. Others blame the lack of alignment among textbooks, tests, and professional development (Smith & O'Day, 1990).   Still others call for research that would identify effective practices. Certainly, all of these matter. However, recruiting mathematically sophisticated teachers, changing teacher education, aligning tests and textbooks, or producing knowledge about effective practices would not automatically enable teachers to teach for understanding. My work has been based on the premise that what is needed in order to improve any of these critical systemic supports for the improvement of mathematics education is detailed knowledge about mathematics teaching and learning, as well as means of contending with its inherent challenges. In this chapter, I offer an example of mathematics teaching and learning and briefly identify and explore three endemic problems central to teachers' work.   I argue that understanding the nature of these problems and of what is involved in dealing with them is crucial to developing skilled practice.

My work as a teacher is framed within multiple commitments that are at times in tension with one another.[1] I aim to create a practice that is rooted in mathematics as a discipline in intellectually honest ways (Ball, 1993b; Bruner, 1960; Lampert, 1992).   As I hear my students exploring important mathematical ground (Hawkins, 1974), perspectives on mathematical activity help me to guide their work (e.g., Kitcher, 1984; Lakatos, 1976).   My recent work with mathematician Hyman Bass has provided additional direct opportunities to consider how the practice of learning and doing mathematics and the practice of teaching mathematics might be connected (e.g., Ball &

---

[1]   My perspective on teaching practice as a matter of managing dilemmas rooted in multiple and competing commitments has been influenced by my ongoing work with Magdalene Lampert (see also Lampert, 1985). Her current book (Lampert, 2000) explores and represents essential teaching problems.

Bass, in press, 2000). What are big ideas of the discipline and how are they linked across the familiar school curriculum? How is mathematical knowledge constructed? How is it justified within a community? At the same time that I seek to be sensitive to and informed by mathematics as a discipline, I also aim to create a practice that is responsive to students' ideas, interests, and lives. I strive to hear my students, to work with them as they investigate and interpret their worlds. I want to respect who they are, as well as who they can become. As a public school teacher, I am also concerned with "covering" the mandated curriculum so that students are prepared for the next grade and for the standardized tests used to chart their progress. And while I want to redefine what "covering the curriculum" might mean (Lampert, 1992, 2000), caring for my students means also being responsible to current definitions (Delpit, 1988). Moreover, my concerns transcend students' mathematical learning. I aim to create a classroom community in which differences are valued, in which students learn to care about and respect one another, and in which commitments to a just and democratic society are embodied and learned (Dewey, 1915/1956; Schwab, 1976).

In the next section, I provide a narrative segment of mathematics teaching and learning, drawn from my own classroom. The purpose of this segment is to take the reader inside the detail of some of the complexity of practice as my students and I work on problems of doing and understanding mathematics. In the third section of the chapter, I probe this complexity analytically by identifying four recurrent problems of practice with which teachers contend who aim for mathematical integrity and attention to students' thinking. The segment of teaching and learning provides a common ground for the consideration of these problems.

PROBLEMS IN DOING, REASONING ABOUT, AND JUSTIFYING MATHEMATICS

This segment centers on the third graders' work on subtraction of multidigit numbers, learning the conventional place value algorithm, and also trying, using, evaluating, and comparing other procedures. Near the beginning of class, the students are discussing solutions to the simple problem that they had worked on for homework:

> Joshua ate 16 peas on Monday and 32 peas on Tuesday.
> How many more peas did he eat on Tuesday than he did on Monday?

The lesson is about more than finding the answer to this single problem. This is November of third grade, and virtually all of the children can use the standard algorithm for multidigit subtraction. They can effectively solve:

$$
\begin{array}{r}
\cancel{3}\,{}^{2}1\,2 \\
-\,1\;6 \\
\hline
1\;6
\end{array}
$$

However, the language in which they couch their explanations suggests a mechanical grasp of the procedure: "the three becomes a two and the two becomes a 12," "cross out the three and make it a two, put a little line above the two," and so on. I know that this way of talking often reflects a lack of substantive understanding of the algorithm. In fact, sometimes they make errors because their grasp of the procedure is fragile. It is not because their second-grade teachers did not explain the algorithm and did not engage them with thoughtful use of concrete representations. I have learned not to assume that what has been taught has been learned. In this series of lessons, my intention is to build understanding underneath their competence with the written algorithm, linking other explanations and representations with the procedure they already know to execute.

At the beginning of class, several solutions are offered. After a somewhat abbreviated explanation of what he thinks the problem is asking, Sean says he used the number line. He goes to the board and, pointing at each number on the number line, he counts up from 16 to 32.

> I went sixteen . . . one, two, three, four, five, six, seven, eight, nine, ten, eleven, twelve, thirteen, fourteen, fifteen, sixteen and I ended up on thirty-two.

Lucy volunteers, and says that she agrees with him, because she "got the same answer and did it the same way." Riba concurs, and offers to "prove that his answer is right." She explains:

Riba: Because a half of . . . a half of thirty-two would be sixteen.

Ball: Uh huh. And how does that prove that his answer is right?

Riba: I . . . because . . . it's . . . it's a half of thirty-two. Sixteen is a half of thirty-two. That proves his answer.

Not exactly sure what to do with Riba's idea, I say, "Interesting," rather feebly. Sean calls on Betsy.

Betsy, speaking mostly to Sean, says that she "did the same thing as you" but that she used beansticks[2] to solve the problem and that she has gotten 15. She goes up to the overhead projector and lays out representations of 16 and 32:

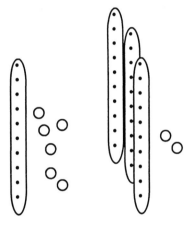

She begins matching individual beans, and then trades a beanstick for 10 loose beans. She continues matching individual beans with others and then one beanstick from each group. She explains,

> Okay, so there's sixteen, and here's thirty-two. And what I did is I went like this and I matched them together. And see . . . then I couldn't match anything else together but these two. So, I took one of these and I traded it in for ten beans.

Mei objects to Betsy's method of representing both 16 and 32 beans on the overhead. "I disagree," she announces. "With the method?" I ask. "Yes," continues Mei. "If you do that you'll . . . if

---

2   Beansticks are a base-ten model, constructed with 10 dried beans glued to a popsicle stick to represent tens, and loose beans to represent units. Ten "ten-sticks" can be glued side by side on a cardboard square to represent hundreds. The children were working only with tens and ones in this lesson.

you want to do thirty-two take away sixteen or something like that, you'll need to take away only sixteen and . . . and you shouldn't be putting on thirty-two *and* sixteen up there."

Betsy tries to explain. She counts out her beans and sticks saying that the sixteen was "what he ate on Monday" and the thirty-two was what he ate on Tuesday. Then she tries to justify her method.

> So, what I'm doing is I'm seeing how much more he ate by putting them together. And when you put them together, you're matching it up just like . . . just about the same way Shea would. But, see instead of adding them together, I'm putting them together like this. And then, since it has a match, I'm putting it down here. So that means you don't count these ones because those are the one that have a match. So, I keep . . . I did this and then see I can't take four away from ten. So, what I do is take this in for ten beans and then I match these together. Then, I counted how many I had.

Mei seems unconvinced. Betsy goes through her solution again. With the teacher's help, she narrates the placement of beansticks and what they represent. She explains the processes she is using to compare the two amounts.

> See, I'm taking these two beans and matching them with *these* two beans. I'm taking these two beans and matching them with these two beans. These two beans and matching them with them.

After doing it, slowly, with explanations, Betsy arrives at the correct answer, 16, which she recognizes is inconsistent with her original answer, 15. Experiencing, in front of the class, as well as in her own mind, the disequilibrium of this contradiction, she proceeds, with the invitation of her teacher and indulgence of her classmates, to reenact carefully the matching of the 16 beans with part of the 32 beans, and, once again, finds that 16 beans remain unmatched. At this point she places (a still slightly tentative) confidence in the answer, 16. Moreover she retracts her earlier notion that her solution is like the method of "counting up" on the number line used by Sean. The class goes on to see yet another solution, presented by Cassandra, hers using the conventional subtraction algorithm. This prompts Sean to offer

$$\begin{array}{r} {}^{1}16 \\ + 16 \\ \hline 32 \end{array}$$

for another approach. The class watches him explain this procedure:

> I went sixteen plus sixteen equals . . . (He writes the problem on the board.) Then, I went six plus six is twelve. Then I put down the two, carried the one. Then I went one plus one is three . . . One plus one is two plus one more is three.

Several children assent. A couple say they did the same thing. Thinking about the separation among the various solutions, and about beginning to investigate them side by side, I ask whether anyone can come up and use the beansticks to "follow" what Sean wrote. I refer to this as "proving."

> I would like to ask if someone can come up and prove the sixteen plus sixteen one on the left, the red one, with bean sticks. Would someone come up and prove that and make it come out, make it follow?

Lucy volunteers and I tell the class to "watch closely and see if what Lucy does *matches* what Sean wrote—not just the answer, but *how* she does it." The children watch her at the overhead. Riba asks Lucy to speak louder.

> Lucy: You have a ten stick. So you have to add six. So, you have one, two, three, four, five, six, so you have sixteen, right there. You have sixteen right there. Then you get another sixteen. One, two, three, four, five, six. Then, you put them together. Put these together, that equals twenty. Then you add one plus one equals three . . . one plus three . . . one plus two equals three. Three plus one equals four, then five, six, seven, eight, nine, ten. So, then that's thirty, and you have thirty-two.

Thinking about my request that someone use the beansticks to "follow" what Sean wrote, I press her.

> I don't quite understand how that matches what Shea wrote, because Shea doesn't have twenty and twelve and that's what you have. You have two tens and you have twelve, and that's not . . . I agree that you have thirty-two all together, but I don't quite understand how that matches what he wrote. Do you see it? Can you help me with it?
>
> Lucy: I don't . . . could you say that again?

I try again.

My question is, If Sean has three tens and two ones, and Lucy has two tens and twelve ones, and I wanted to know if we could make the bean sticks match.

As the lesson continues, I press the students to connect the different solution methods. By the end of class, the students seem able to consider and evaluate the independent validity of the different approaches and representations, but they are still holding them somewhat separate.

PROBLEMS OF TEACHING WITH RESPECT FOR MATHEMATICS AND STUDENTS

Interesting as this segment may be, it is replete with challenges for the teacher. I name and explore briefly three problems, which, at their root, emerge from the inherent effort to reconcile, in practice, respect for mathematics and students. These problems reappear across lessons and their management is a critical part of teaching.

One endemic problem arises in the course of trying to figure out what students understand[3] as they work on mathematical problems, do written work, and offer their methods and solutions. Children represent their ideas in ways often unfamiliar to adults, with idiosyncratic language and unusual syntax. Their pictures are not transparent and their representations not immediately obvious. Seeking to hear what students mean and considering the mathematical consequences of their ideas, teachers must re-purpose their own mathematical knowledge to serve as a resource. Even a short lesson segment such as this is filled with such small mysteries, too often mistaken or missed. When Riba offers to prove Sean's solution is "right," what does she think it means to prove something? When Betsy says that she has gotten 15, what has happened? When she says she "did it like Sean," on what is she focusing? Later she retracts this suggestion, before I recognize to probe what she had in mind. I miss her initial insight, some connection she had made between her "compare" representation with beansticks, and his "counting on" strategy on the number line.

Whether working from students' written work or in the context of class, teachers face problems of seeing and interpreting mathematics

---

[3] This section is based on conceptual distinctions and analyses developed in Ball (1997).

across divides of age, culture, and experience. If teachers "fill in" and overinterpret what students know and can do, they may inappropriately credit students with a "right" answer. Consequently, they may attribute to students an understanding that students have not yet reached. If, however, teachers cannot hear "below the surface" features of children's talk and representations, they may miss the mark by considering a student wrong who has in fact an interesting idea or is carrying out a nonstandard procedure, but one with mathematical promise. Suspending one's desire for students to get answers right and thinking mathematically about what a child might mean are among the most difficult problems of teaching.

Second, and not unrelated to the first, are problems of managing and using multiple representations and solutions generated in the course of the work (Ball & Bass, 2000). These multiple representations arise both from mathematics and from students. Students, because they think differently from one another, see problems in a range of ways, and represent and solve them in multiple ways. In this lesson segment, Sean used the number line and counted the number of steps up from 16 to 32. Betsy used beansticks to represent 16 and 32 and constructed a one-to-one correspondence of the 16 with part of the 32 to figure out how many more 32 was than 16. Riba took advantage of the particular numbers to see 16 as half of 32. Sean adds, using the conventional place value algorithm, and Lucy adds with beansticks. The mathematics we teach can also be represented in a variety of ways. For example, Mei challenged Betsy, saying that, in order to represent $32 - 16$, she should not put both the 32 and the 16 "up there." She was thinking of "take away" whereas Betsy was working with comparison, both significant interpretations of subtraction. And, in fact, most teachers believe that showing and exploring content through multiple representations is important in order to reach a wide diversity of students.

At the same time, a classroom in which students generate such a range of mathematical ideas can easily produce not mathematical clarity and depth, but cacophony. Each child has his or her own way, and children may even become confused by listening to one another. Children do not necessarily reconcile the different approaches, but often hold them separate. If, as is often the case, these methods produce common answers, the children see the multiplicity as evidence that certain answers are true (more ways to get the same answer makes them more confident that their answer is right), but do not consider the correspondences among the representations. Without this, the generation of multiplicity has unclear pedagogical merit, and falls short of the mathematical import of investigating and reconciling multiple solutions, representations, methods, and algorithms. Finding ways to engage students in comparing multiplicities that arise in class is a challenge of teaching with respect for both mathematics and students.[4]

Third, and emerging from the first two, are more general problems of engaging a wide range of students in productive individual and collective mathematical work. Teachers face classes that, like this one, include children from a wide range of backgrounds and experiences. How to manage the group's mathematical progress in ways that give space to individual students' ideas and questions while moving the mathematical curriculum along is a nontrivial problem of practice. Take this lesson segment as an example. One by one, different children offer alternative ways to solve the problem. Most think that the answer is 16, and just have different ways to get it. For the lesson to be more than a drawn out "show and tell" of the different methods requires the composition of a mathematical discussion that takes up and uses the individual contributions. Consider Betsy, who gets the floor because she claims that the answer is 15 with the beansticks. A great deal of time is given over to the examination of her solution and its method. For this to be worthwhile is a problem of making available one child's thinking for the rest of the class to work on. How can this be more than an opportunity for Betsy to discover what the other children already know — that is, that the answer is 16, not 15? What do other children have to learn from Betsy's thinking? It is on questions such as these that strategies for managing this work in class can be built.

Learning to Teach with Respect for Mathematics and Students

My purpose is not to make unnecessarily complex the work of teaching with respect to mathematics and students. Instead, the chapter is predicated on the assumption that learning to teach (and developing one's teaching) depends on understanding and learning to contend with recurrent problems of practice. Making visible and probing these problems can offer resources for the development of

---

[4] The problem of investigating correspondences among multiple mathematical representations, answers, solutions, and methods, mapping across and reconciling multiplicities, has become a central focus of our work on the mathematical entailments of elementary teaching. See Ball and Bass (in press, 2000).

practice[5]. Instead of romanticizing mathematics teaching, the study of such problems affords knowledge of the work that can enable its development and improvement.   Teachers can develop an appreciation for the roots of these problems, insights important to identifying them in the course of the work, and a repertoire of ways to respond to and contend with them in practice. Although this brief chapter does little more than sketch a set of such endemic problems, work on these and others is a worthy agenda for the development of professional knowledge and practice.

ACKNOWLEDGMENTS

This work is supported, in part, by the Spencer Foundation for the project, "Crossing Boundaries: Probing the Interplay of Mathematics and Pedagogy in Elementary Teaching," (MG #199800202). This paper draws on my collaboration with Hyman Bass and other members of the Mathematics Teaching and Learning to Teach Group: Mark Hoover, Jennifer Lewis, Ed Wall, Raven Wallace, Merrie Blunk, Deidre LeFevre, Geoffrey Phelps, Katherine Morris, Heather Lindsay.

REFERENCES

Ball, D. L. (1993a). Halves, pieces, and twoths: Constructing representational contexts in teaching fractions. In T. Carpenter, E. Fennema, & T. Romberg, (Eds.), *Rational numbers an integration of research* (pp. 157-196). Hillsdale, NJ: Lawrence Erlbaum Associates.

Ball, D. L. (1993b). With an eye on the mathematical horizon: Dilemmas of teaching elementary school mathematics. *Elementary School Journal, 93*, 373-397.

Ball, D. L. (1997). What do students know? Facing challenges of distance, context, and desire in trying to hear children. In B. Biddle, T. Good, & I. Goodson (Eds.), *International handbook on teachers and teaching* (Vol. II, pp. 679-718). Dordrecht, Netherlands: Kluwer Press.

Ball, D. L., & Bass, H. (in press). Interweaving content and pedagogy in teaching and learning to teach: Knowing and using mathematics. In J. Boaler (Ed.), *Multiple perspectives on the teaching and learning of mathematics*. San Francisco, CA: JAI/Ablex.

Ball, D. L., & Bass, H. (2000). Making believe: The collective construction of public mathematical knowledge in the elementary classroom. In D. Phillips (Ed.), *Constructivism in Education*, (193-224). Chicago: University of Chicago Press.

---

[5] I thank Jennifer Lewis for discussions about "making teaching visible" and about the contributions that the study of instruction can make to teacher education and professional learning.

Ball, D. L. & Wilson, S. (1996). Integrity in teaching: Recognizing the fusion of the moral and the intellectual. *American Educational Research Journal, 33,* 155-192.

Bruner, J. (1960). *The process of education.* Cambridge, MA: Harvard University Press.

Delpit, L. (1988). The silenced dialogue: Power and pedagogy and other people's children. *Harvard Educational Review, 50,* 280- 298.

Dewey, J. (1956). *School and society.* Chicago: University of Chicago. (Original work published 1915)

Hawkins, D. (1974). Nature, man, and mathematics. In D. Hawkins (Ed.), *The informed vision: Essays on learning and human nature* (pp. 109-131). New York: Agathon.

Kitcher, P. (1984). *The nature of mathematical knowledge.* New York: Oxford University Press.

Lakatos, I. (1976). *Proofs and refutations: The logic of mathematical discovery.* Cambridge: University of Cambridge Press.

Lampert, M. (1985). How do teachers manage to teach? Perspectives on problems in practice. *Harvard Educational Review, 55,* 178-194.

Lampert, M. (1992). The practice and problems of teaching and learning authentic mathematics in school. In F. Oser, A. Dick, & J. Patry (Eds.), *Effective and responsible teaching: The new synthesis* (pp. 295-314). San Francisco, CA: Jossey-Bass.

Lampert, M. (2000). *Teaching problems.* Manuscript in preparation.

Schwab, J. J. (1976). Education and the state: Learning community. In R. M. Hutchins & M. J. Adler (Eds.), *Great ideas today* (pp. 234-271). Chicago: Encyclopedia Britannica.

Smith, M., & O'Day, J. (1991). Systemic school reform. In S. Fuhrman & B. Malen (Eds.), *The politics of curriculum and testing: The 1990 Yearbook of the Politics of Education Association,* (pp. 233 – 267). New York: Falmer Press.

TEACHING VIEWED FROM A PSYCHOLOGICAL PERSPECTIVE: TEACHING AS ENTAILING TEACHERS' LEARNING

OVERVIEW

We characterized the chapters in this section as coming from a psychological perspective, by which we mean that characteristics of students' mathematical thought are of primary interest. Rather than children's understanding of particular mathematical ideas or the social characteristics of learning and teaching, themes of chapters in Part II and Part III, in this section the emphasis is on students' strategies and ideas as they learn mathematics. Although the three disciplinary categories are not mutually exclusive (most authors in this book treat all three categories to some degree), they do represent the basic orientation of most chapters in this section. Also, beforehand, it was the grouping used at the Purdue Conference in which the papers were first presented and from which the discussion questions presented in the commentaries arose in response to the presentation of this cluster of papers. So we have chosen to maintain it in this book.

The psychological perspective as represented in this book makes a critical contribution to our knowledge of teaching by suggesting that it is the strategies children's use to solve mathematical problems that reveals their mathematical thought, which is of utmost importance to teaching. Progress is not defined in terms of whether or not a student can solve particular problems; rather it is defined in terms of the strategy each student uses to solve a problem and the understanding the child holds in order to use that strategy. Each of the three chapters discusses the necessity of redirecting teachers' focus to students' strategies rather than their teaching actions. Pedagogically, teachers must possess and continue to develop substantial knowledge about the development of their students' mathematical strategies for solving problems.

An Alternative Conception of Teaching for Understanding

Case Studies of Two First-Grade Mathematics Classes

Thomas P. Carpenter
University of Wisconsin-Madison

Ellen Ansell
University of Pittsburgh

Linda Levi
University of Wisconsin-Madison

Learning with understanding is central to reforming mathematics education because it provides a basis for students to apply their knowledge to learn new ideas and to solve new and unfamiliar problems. When students do not understand, they perceive each topic as an isolated skill, and they cannot apply their skills to solve problems not explicitly covered by instruction, nor extend their learning to new topics. As a consequence, unless students learn with understanding, whatever knowledge they acquire is likely to be of little use to them outside of school.

It is generally accepted that understanding is not an "all or none" phenomenon. Virtually all complex ideas or processes can be understood at a number of levels and in quite different ways, and it is more appropriate to think of understanding as emerging or developing rather than presuming that someone either does or does not understand a given topic or idea. Carpenter and Lehrer (1999) characterized understanding, as used in mathematics education, in terms of individual mental activity that contributes to the development of understanding rather than as a static attribute of a person's knowledge. They identify five forms of mental activity from which mathematical understanding emerges: (1) constructing relationships, (2) extending and applying mathematical knowledge, (3) reflecting about experiences, (4) articulating what one knows, and (5) making mathematical knowledge one's own.

This analysis is not prescriptive; it provides a frame for examining specific contexts of learning and instruction to consider how instruction does or does not afford learning with understanding. However, many different patterns of instruction can support learning with understanding, and the critical story lies in the details of how these forms of activity are instantiated in specific contexts.

In this chapter, we use this frame to consider a model for mathematics instruction that differs in significant ways from traditional conceptions of instruction in mathematics classes. In traditional instruction, individual lessons have particular objectives. Students are expected to learn a specific concept or skill, and the next lesson moves on to a new objective for which the concept or skill learned in the preceding lesson may be a prerequisite. This hierarchical view of learning and instruction is most clearly articulated in Gagne's (1977) discussion of learning hierarchies. Although current curriculum generally is not based explicitly on Gagne's notions of behavioral task analysis, most instruction is based on implicit assumptions that certain concepts and skills have to be learned before others, and lessons are planned to teach specific concepts and skills that form the basis for learning concepts and skills that are taught in subsequent lessons. Recent analyses of videotapes of mathematics lessons in Japan, Germany, and the United States documents that this pattern characterizes instruction in all three countries (Siegler & Hiebert, 1998). In these classes, learning objectives are defined in terms of being able to solve particular problems. In some classrooms, students may be afforded the opportunity to use a variety of strategies to solve a given problem, but the goal remains that the strategies used by each student demonstrate understanding of the specific concepts or skills that are the focus of the lesson.

In classes taught by teachers participating in Cognitively Guided Instruction [CGI] (Carpenter, Fennema, & Franke, 1996; Carpenter, Fennema, Franke, Levi, & Empson, 1999; Fennema, Carpenter, Franke, Levi, & Empson, 1996) and in other similar programs (Hiebert et al., 1997), we observed a quite different pattern of instruction. Lessons are not designed with a goal that all students meet the same objective at the same time. Students may solve the same or similar problems, but they solve them using strategies that represent very different levels of understanding of the basic concepts involved. As a consequence, the lessons have very different objectives for different students, and progress is not defined in terms of solving particular problems; rather progress is defined for each student in terms of the strategy the student uses to solve the problem and the concepts and skills that underlie the strategy.

Although students learn major concepts and skills at different times during the year, this perspective on instruction should not be perceived as lacking structure or purpose. In fact just the opposite is true. When this form of instruction is successful, it is precisely because the teachers have a very clear understanding of the learning trajectories for the specific content they are teaching, the activities and supports that elicit students' thinking at different levels within the trajectories, and the scaffolding students need to move to higher level concepts and procedures. This knowledge provides a basis for teachers to orchestrate instructional activities that afford access to students at all levels of achievement to participate in meaningful ways, and the knowledge also provides a basis for teachers to interact with students in ways that support learning. The teachers are not just engaging students in interesting activities. The tasks, the tools that students use to solve activities, and the forms of interaction that students engage in are carefully selected to facilitate conceptual growth of students by building on what they generate. This is structure; it is just not the kind of structure that is represented in most descriptions of mathematics instruction.

Our portrayal of mathematics instruction is based on year-long case studies of two first-grade classes, although similar patterns of instruction have been observed in a wide variety of classes of kindergarten through grade-five teachers participating in the CGI project (Fennema et al., 1996). In the case studies we observed how the two teachers helped children build on their informal mathematical thinking to develop understanding of multidigit concepts and operations. The lessons in the two classes were not organized around a hierarchy of objectives, with each lesson dedicated to meeting a particular objective. Students often solved the same problem, but the different strategies they used represented very different points in the evolution of their understanding of multidigit concepts and operations. The concepts that some students were developing in October other students were learning in December or February.

Some students progressed further than other students. The goal was not that every student reaches a certain point but that each student extends his or her knowledge as far as possible. What was critical was that each extension in a student's knowledge represented a deepening understanding, that each new strategy could be related in a meaningful way to concepts and strategies that the student already understood.

Students in the two classes demonstrated remarkable levels of understanding of basic addition and subtraction concepts and procedures. By the end of the year, the majority of the students in both classes were facile with calculations that generally are expected of second- and third-grade students. Furthermore, they had not acquired rote computational procedures; their calculations involved nonstandard procedures that were grounded in an understanding of base-ten number concepts and operations.

In this chapter, we focus concurrently on student learning and classroom processes. Although this book is about facilitative teaching, it is our position that we cannot talk about teaching without talking about student thinking. Consistent with the approach advocated by Cobb and Yackel (1996) and Yackel and Cobb (1996), we are interested in understanding the reflexive relation between the development of individual students' understanding and their participation in class interactions. The focus of CGI has been to reframe discussions of teaching to emphasize the development of student thinking. Our interactions with teachers are not about their teaching practices but about the mathematical thinking of the students in their classes. We try to help teachers change their teaching practices not by talking about what they do; instead, we try to reframe teachers thinking about their teaching so that the emphasis is on the development of student thinking rather than on teacher actions. For us and for the two teachers in the case studies discussed in this chapter, talking about teaching entails talking about the development of student thinking in the context of classrooms.

In the two case studies, we followed the mathematics instruction of two first-grade teachers, Ms. Gehn and Ms. Keith, over the course of a school year. The data include detailed field notes for approximately 100 mathematics classes for each teacher together with accompanying protocols transcribed from audio recordings of the classes, four videotapes of mathematics lessons of each teacher, and four interviews of all of students in each class.

MS. GEHN

Ms. Gehn's class had well-established norms for mathematics instruction. Almost all instruction involved students in solving word problems, which generally were written around a theme for the day. (For a discussion of the role of word problems in CGI classes, see Carpenter et al., 1996, and Carpenter et al., 1999.) Ms. Gehn almost never showed students how to solve a problem or modeled a particular strategy. Typically, the class would solve and discuss three or four problems during the mathematics lesson, which usually would last about 1 hour. Ms. Gehn would read a problem several times and write the numbers given in the problem on the overhead projector at the front of the room. The students then were given about 10 to 15 minutes to work on the problem. Most students initially worked on a problem individually. When a student completed a problem, he or she was expected to solve the problem another way or compare his or her strategy with another student.

When almost all children had solved the given problem, three or four children would be called on to share their strategies with the class. The emphasis was on the strategies that the students used to solve the problem rather than on the answer, and volunteers were asked to share strategies that were different from the strategies that other students had already shared. Thus, for each problem, students saw a variety of different solutions. During the sharing, Ms. Gehn would ask clarifying questions but she generally would let the students do most of the explaining. The norms for sharing were clearly established. The students understood that they were expected to describe their strategies completely when they shared them with each other, with Ms. Gehn or another adult, or with the entire class. As a consequence, the students became increasingly proficient in explaining their strategies throughout the year.

Entering Knowledge

The 18 students in Ms. Gehn's class had been in a kindergarten class in which they had solved a variety of word problems by modeling with counters. At the beginning of the year, all of the children could solve at least some problems by modeling, and about half showed some limited knowledge of base-ten number concepts. During individual interviews conducted at the beginning of the year, 8 students consistently solved a variety of addition, subtraction, multiplication, and division problems using modeling or counting strategies. (See Carpenter et al., 1999 for a discussion of these strategies.) All 8 of these students could count collections of 10 by counting by tens, but only 2 of these 8 students, Dave and Alice, used the base-ten materials to add 24 and 10, and they counted the total by ones. Another cluster of 8 students solved a range of problems by modeling with counters, but showed no knowledge of tens groupings.

In the Beginning

The students started solving word problems the first day of class. Ms. Gehn first put a pile of counters on each group of desks and asked the children to each count out various numbers of counters ranging from 12 to 25. From watching the children count, she determined that all children could construct and count sets of counters up to at least 25, so she started them off that day with problems involving relatively large numbers. One problem was based on the lunch count taken earlier in the day (13 children are eating hot lunch, and there are 18 children in the class. How many children are not eating hot lunch?). Several problems involved comparing the numbers of children who traveled to school in different ways that day. Ms. Gehn told the children they could solve the problems any way they wanted and could use whatever materials they wanted (counters, the number line on their desks, their fingers); she did not demonstrate a method for solving the problems or tell the children how to use the materials. During the rest of the first week, the children solved a variety of word problems involving joining, separating, comparing, grouping, and partitioning (see Carpenter et al., 1999). Most of the numbers in the problems were in the teens or 20s, and most of the children directly modeled the problem with individual counters.

At the beginning of the second week, Ms. Gehn passed out 10 base-ten bars to each child, and asked them to count the little cubes in the bars. After everyone agreed that each ten bar was made up of 10 cubes, she asked the class how many little cubes there were in all 10 ten bars. About half the class counted the individual cubes one by one, and the other half counted by tens. Both strategies were shared with the class, and a discussion ensued about which way was easier. All but one student thought that counting by tens was easier than counting by ones, but many students had not demonstrated they understood how to count by tens. Thus, there was a great deal of variability in the children's knowledge, and there was little evidence that even the most advanced children had more than limited notions about base-ten number concepts.

Students were provided mathematics tools that would afford solutions of problems using base-ten principles, but beyond establishing that there were 10 cubes in each ten bar and counting the number of cubes by ones and by tens several times, little emphasis was placed on base-ten number concepts per se. Rather, following the introduction of the base-ten bars, Ms. Gehn gave the children problems that might be solved using these materials.

Over the next month and a half, almost all the experiences that the children engaged in involving base-ten concepts were imbedded in solving word problems involving addition, subtraction, multiplication, or division of multidigit numbers. Progress in the use of base-ten concepts and materials was slow and irregular as children began to use a variety of strategies to solve problems with larger numbers. During this time, no single strategy prevailed at any point in time. Different children used quite different strategies, reflecting different conceptions of base-ten number concepts and of addition, subtraction, multiplication, and division. Individual children also used different strategies to solve different problems, depending on the numbers in the problem, the operation, and the materials available. During the first week of school, virtually all of the problems Ms. Gehn gave involved at least 1 two-digit number in the teens or 20s. What made this choice possible was that, unlike the traditional curriculum programs, Ms. Gehn did not expect students to use abstract methods to calculate. Students were able to use counters to model the problems, and as long as they could count to 30 or more, they could solve problems involving numbers in the 20s. By the beginning of October, students were solving problems with numbers in the 40s and 50s. By December and January, they were dealing with numbers in the hundreds. Ms. Gehn reported that she progressed quickly to the larger numbers because she thought that the larger numbers forced the students to reflect more explicitly on the operations and deal with base-ten concepts more than the smaller numbers did.

The Evolution of Students' Strategies

During the first month of school, only Dave and Alice used base-ten materials to solve problems, and their use of the materials initially was somewhat limited. As they discussed their solutions and shared them with the class, their solutions became more efficient and flexible; and other children began to use the base-ten materials. Thus, although Ms. Gehn did not model the use of the base-ten materials herself, Dave and Alice provided the other students with models of how the materials could be used. The other students did not, however, immediately follow their lead. The evolution of use of base-ten materials was gradual, and there was a great deal of diversity within the class throughout the year. By the beginning of October, five students in the class were using base-ten materials to model and solve problems. By the end of November, all but two of the students could use base-ten materials to model and solve problems, and the remaining two students could identify a number represented with base-ten blocks without counting the individual units. Individual students' use of base-ten materials emerged gradually. At first, they could count units of ten, but did not use the base-ten materials to represent numbers in problems. When they started using base-ten blocks to solve problems, most of them initially would construct two sets representing the addends in a given problem but would count the total by ones. Throughout the year, students could use any appropriate strategy or materials, and it was not expected that students adopt a particular strategy once it had been introduced. However, Ms. Gehn regularly probed individual students to determine whether they could use more advanced strategies, and she encouraged discussion of the more advanced strategies and the efficiency they provided. One of the ways she did that was through what she called "piggybacking." This involved asking students if they could build on a strategy that another student had just presented and make it more efficient. For example, on September 23, Barbara used base-ten blocks to add 24 + 37. She constructed sets of blocks representing 24 and 37 counting the tens as units (10, 20, 21, 22, 23, 24), but when she calculated the answer, she counted the individual units by one counting on from 24 (25, 26, 27, 28, 29, 30, 31, . . . 59, 60, 61). Ms. Gehn then asked if someone could piggyback off Barbara's strategy. Elise came up and used Barbara's blocks but with support from Ms. Gehn counted the tens (10, 20, 30, 40, 50, 51, 52, . . . 61).

As the rest of the class learned the concepts and procedures required to use the base-ten materials to represent multidigit numbers and solve problems, Alice and Dave began to abstract the strategies involving the base-ten materials and solve problems without them. The invented algorithms that Dave and Alice started to use were abstracted from the blocks procedures and in fact students' verbal descriptions of blocks procedures sounded very much like the invented algorithms that they came to use. [For a discussion of invented algorithms, see Carpenter, Franke, Jacobs, & Fennema, (1998) and Fuson et al., (1997)].

The following exchange that took place on November 4th, illustrates a child going through a transition from a strategy using blocks to a more abstract invented algorithm. Alice was solving an addition problem involving the sum 30 + 45. She first demonstrated a solution with the base-ten blocks. When she had finished she said,

> I don't need these [pointing to the 3 ten blocks representing the 30]. I can just go 30 (pause), 40, 50, 60, 70, 71, 72, 73, 74, 75 [pointing to the blocks representing the 45 as she counted on from 30] . . . I don't need these at all [pushing aside the blocks representing the 45]. I can do 30 (pause), 40, 50, 60, 70, 75 [keeping track of the counts of the 4 tens on her fingers].

This example illustrates another feature of the class that may have played a role in the transition from modeling to more abstract invented algorithms. Not only did different children use different strategies, each child was encouraged to find multiple ways of solving a given problem. If a child finished solving a problem before the other students were ready to discuss the solutions, Ms. Gehn's standard response was to ask the student to solve the problem in a different way. We hypothesize that searching for multiple solutions potentially contributed to the kind of abstraction reflected in the sequence of strategies just described by Alice.

Dave and Alice started using invented algorithms in October and November, but neither of them used them consistently until the beginning of December. In the interview at the end of November, they were the only two students in the class who could use invented algorithms to solve problems that involved regrouping. Three other students could use them to solve problems involving a multiple of 10 (24 + 10), and about half the class could add two multiples of 10 (20 + 30) without materials of any kind.

Widespread use of invented algorithms emerged slowly, and it was not until February that a number of other students began to use them with any regularity. At that time, Ms. Gehn decided to do a unit on money because she thought that a number of children were ready to start to use invented algorithms, and their familiarity with combinations of coins would allow them to think about numbers more abstractly without the support of the blocks or other physical materials. This turned out to be the case. The use of invented algorithms involving money became more common. As more students started to use invented algorithms, the discussion of those algorithms and their relation to strategies based on manipulations of blocks or other materials became more frequent. This encouraged more students to begin using invented algorithms.

The following episode from a sharing session illustrates the variety of strategies students used near the beginning of the unit on money. It also illustrates some students' flexibility in using materials. Students were solving problems related to a planned trip to a local restaurant. They were sharing strategies for a problem in which they were to find the difference in price between a steak sandwich that cost $5.95 and a corned beef sandwich that cost $4.55. The first student, Rhonda, used base-ten blocks to represent each price. She then matched the blocks in the two piles and wound up with $1.40. The second student shared the following strategy:

> Barbara: I only need to look at this [She indicated the $5.95 and the $4.55 written on the overhead projector with the $4.55 written above the $5.95.] There's the $5. If I took $4 away from that, it would be $1. [She crossed out the 4 and the 5 and wrote a 1 next to were she crossed out the 5.] If I took away 5 [crossing out the 5 cents in the steak sandwich price] because of this 5 [crossing out the 5 cents in the corned beef price], That would be 90. And I did some on my fingers. I got to take away 50, so 90, 80, 70, 60, 50; there's 40 left . . . $1.40.

> Ms. Gehn: Could you say that one more time. It was a neat way.

> David: And it was fast.

Barbara repeated her solution in much the same way she had presented it initially.

> Ms. Gehn: Did anyone solve it a different way? Craig.

> Craig: I matched up the coins. I took 25 and a 5 and 25. That would be 55. [He put plastic see-through coins on the overhead projector representing quarters and a nickel]. Then I took a 25 and 25, that's 50 [putting two quarters in a different pile on the overhead]. Then 60, 70, 80, 90, 5 [adding dimes and one nickel to the pile as he counted].

> Ms. Gehn: Okay. So tell me why you did this.

Craig: Well I did that so I would know how to do it because this is the 95 and this is the 55.

Ms. Gehn: Where are the dollars?

Craig: I just used my fingers for the dollars. [He then matched the quarters and nickels in the two piles]. Then I would have 40. And with the $4 taken out of the 5 . . . that's $1.40.

Ms. Gehn then engaged the class in a discussion of how Craig's way and Rhonda's way were alike and different.

When the students in the class were individually interviewed in May, 13 of the 17 students could use invented algorithms to add two-digit numbers that required regrouping (38 + 26) and 10 could use an invented algorithm to add three digit numbers (256 + 178). Of the remaining 4 students, 3 could use an invented algorithm to add 57 + 30, and the other one used base-ten blocks to solve a variety of addition, subtraction, multiplication, and division problems. Most students had more difficulty using invented algorithms to subtract. Only 3 students correctly used invented algorithms to subtract two-digit numbers on the final interview, and none did so for three-digit numbers. However, 10 students correctly used an invented algorithm for a subtraction problem involving money ($4.00 -- 1.86), and 8 students used an invented algorithm to multiply (6 x 42). When students did not use invented algorithms, they generally modeled with base-ten materials.

MS. KEITH

The second case shares many similarities with the first, and we will not dwell on the specifics of the case in quite as much detail, focusing instead on differences that illuminate the variety in the contexts in which learning with understanding can occur.

Perhaps the most critical difference in the two classes involved the use of notation to represent solution strategies for word problems. In the second week in November, Ms. Keith introduced a notation to represent children's solution strategies when they used an invented algorithm. Up to that time, the few children who used invented algorithms did them mentally, and there was no record of what they had done. As one child, Jerome, explained his solution to a problem involving the sum 52 + 28, Ms. Keith wrote the following:

$$50 + 20 \rightarrow 70 + 8 \rightarrow 78 + 1 \rightarrow 79 + 1 = 80.$$

She did not tell Jerome that he should use this notation, she simply used it to record what he had done. In the ensuing weeks, Ms. Keith continued to use the notation when students presented invented algorithms.

Later in the year, Ms. Keith introduced another notation, which the students called the *pull down method*. Whereas the arrow notation was effective in representing solutions in which calculations in which a running total was kept, the pull down method allowed numbers to be combined in a variety of ways. In the example in Fig. 3.1, tens and ones are first combined separately and then the two sums are combined.

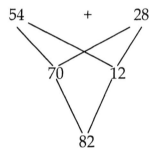

FIG. 3.1. Pull-down notation for the sum 54 + 28.

These notations provided a frame of reference so that everyone could see how numbers had been combined. This facilitated discussion and comparison of alternative strategies. Over time, the students began to appreciate that the notation could provide them with a record of what they had done so that they could share it more easily with the class. It also provided a record of the numbers they had combined so that they could check their work. Over the next few months, students began to adopt the notations to record their work.

Entering Knowledge

Most of the students in Ms. Keith's class also had been in a kindergarten class in which they had solved a variety of word problems by modeling with counters. But there was more variability among the students than was the case in Ms. Gehn's class. On a baseline interview at the beginning of the year, 6 of the 16 students in the class consistently solved a variety of addition, subtraction, multiplication, and division problems by modeling or counting. All 6 counted groups of 10 by counting tens, but only one could use ten groupings to add 10 to 24. Five additional students solved a variety of problems by modeling the problem structure with counters, but they showed no knowledge of tens groupings. One student had difficulty solving problems by modeling but demonstrated some knowledge of base-ten concepts. Four students had limited knowledge of modeling. Three could solve a simple joining problem (3 + 4), but the fourth had difficulty counting a set containing more than 8 objects. As did Ms. Gehn, Ms. Keith learned about her students' knowledge as they solved problems during instruction.

Developing Students' Multidigit Concepts

Like Ms. Gehn, Ms. Keith did not demonstrate strategies for solving problems, and throughout the year, to solve any given problem, the students used a variety of strategies. Ms. Keith also did not focus explicitly on activities designed to promote knowledge of place value and base-ten number concepts. Most discussions of base-ten number concepts occurred in the context of solving problems, as illustrated in the following exchange that took place during the last week in September as a student was describing to the class her method of subtracting 27 − 4.

Kim: The answer is 23.

Ms. Keith: Oh, and how did, wait a minute. Are we going to let her just give the answer?

Students: No!

Ms. Keith: What are we going to say to her?

Students: How did you figure it out?

Kim: I figured it out with the [linking] cubes.

Peter: But how?

Kim: I'll show you. [Goes to get the cubes].

Ms. Keith: Wait, wait, we want you to use words. It's very hard to put into words, some things, but it's a very good thing to do.

Kim: Okay. Well I had two sets of 10 and that made 20, and then I added a 7 to that.

Ms. Keith: Okay, you guys understand so far?

Students: [Some say yes and some no].

Ms. Keith: Listen so you understand. She had two sets of 10, which would make her have [pause].

Students: Twenty.

Ms. Keith: Twenty, and then she had 7 more in a set.

Kim: And then I took away 4 on the 27.

Ms. Keith: On the 7 stack or on the 20 stack?

Kim: On the 7 stack.

Ms. Keith: Okay. Then what happened?

Kim: And then I got 23.

Ms. Keith: Did you go back and count how many?

Kim: Yes.

Ms. Keith: And when you counted, what did you do? How did you count?

Kim: One 2, 3.

Ms. Keith: You didn't use your tens?

Kim: Cause I had 20. Okay. 10 and 10 make 20, and then 1, 2, 3.

This exchange took place early in the year when base-ten number concepts were tenuous for most students. Ms. Keith helped Kim make explicit the relation between groups of ten and ten individual units and that units of ten can be counted. By having Kim explain what she did without the blocks, Ms. Keith encouraged Kim and the rest of the students to reflect on the numbers and the operations rather than just manipulate blocks. In this exchange, we also see Ms. Keith's efforts at making explicit class norms in which students are expected to explain their thinking. She continually probed to insure that Kim was explicit in explaining the steps in her strategy, and she talked to the class about listening so that they would understand what Kim did.

Over the course of the year, the development of students' multidigit concepts and procedures followed much the same course that it did in Ms. Gehn's class. Initially a few students started using base-ten materials and subsequently invented algorithms, and over time, other students followed their lead. In individual interviews in May, 11 of the 16 students in the class could use invented algorithms to add two-digit numbers that required regrouping (38 + 26) and 7 could use an invented algorithm to add three-digit numbers (256 + 178). Of the 11 students who used invented algorithms for addition problems, 6 used invented algorithms to subtract two-digit numbers, 4 to subtract three-digit numbers, and 5 to multiply 6 x 42. All 11 students successfully used base-ten materials when they did not use invented algorithms. Of the remaining 5 students, 1 used an invented algorithm only with multiples of ten and modeled the other problems with base-ten materials. The other 4 students, who had limited problem-solving skills at the beginning of the year, solved addition and subtraction problems with base-ten materials but had difficulty using base-ten materials with other types of problems. However, these students solved a variety of problems by modeling with individual units. The student who had difficulty counting sets larger than 10 at the beginning of the year, made substantial gains during the year and solved a variety of problems by modeling the problems with single counters, but he was the one student in either class who demonstrated little knowledge of base-ten number concepts.

COMMON FEATURES OF THE TWO CLASSES

Although there were fundamental differences in the organization and operation of the two classes, they had much in common. In both classes, instruction was orchestrated to help students build on their existing knowledge. The focus on building on each student's thinking was reflected in the multiplicity of strategies that different students used at any given point throughout the year.

Neither teacher demonstrated or modeled target problem-solving strategies that they expected students to learn. Rather, they immediately started with word problems that the students could solve using informal modeling and counting strategies. Throughout the year, students solved problems that were similar to the word problems that they solved at the beginning of the year. The numbers changed somewhat as the year progressed, but the problems were essentially the same and could be solved with the same modeling strategies that students used at the beginning of the year. What characterized learning in these classes was the evolution of the strategies that students used to solve the problems. The evolution was characterized by the adoption of progressively more efficient strategies that drew on increasingly sophisticated multidigit number concepts. The transition from using single counters to using base-ten materials represented not only a more efficient way to represent large numbers, it was based on at least an implicit understanding that units of ten could be counted and the relation of collections of units of tens and ones to the number names used to designate them. The development of invented algorithms meant that students were able to reflect on the operations on the blocks to the point that they could abstract them. These transitions were made throughout the year for different students at different points in time.

Student Learning

By the end of the year, most students in both classes demonstrated emerging understanding of base-ten number concepts and operations. Over half of the students in each class could use invented algorithms to solve a variety of problems. Most of the rest could use invented algorithms for some problems and modeled the rest using base-ten materials. There was almost no evidence of students using either symbolic procedures that they did not understand or manipulating physical materials in ways that did not make sense to them.

To put these results in context, most traditional instructional programs do not include addition or subtraction with regrouping by the end of the first grade, and many do not include adding three-digit numbers in the second grade. Multiplication generally is not introduced until the end of the second grade or the middle of the third grade. Although the students in these classes did not use standard algorithms, the majority of them were facile with calculations that are expected of second- and third-grade students. Furthermore, they had not acquired rote computational procedures; their calculations were grounded in an understanding of base-ten number concepts and operations. What they had developed was an understanding of basic number concepts and operations that was evidenced in their ability to invent strategies for solving problems. We should point out that neither teacher's goal was to teach efficient computational procedures. Their goals were to develop understanding of concepts and operations that would serve as a basis for learning procedures; the procedures came as a byproduct of developing that understanding.

SUPPORTING LEARNING WITH UNDERSTANDING

We conclude by revisiting the five forms of mental activity from which learning with understanding emerges (Carpenter & Lehrer, 1999) and considering how these two classes afforded student engagement in them.

Forging Connections

One of the benchmarks for assessing whether instruction is promoting the development of understanding is to be able to characterize how it provides for the construction of critical connections that give meaning to the newly learned ideas. The strategies that students developed represented reasonably natural extensions of existing strategies and were perceived as such. Using base-ten materials to solve problems was another form of modeling using objects collected into groups of 10; invented strategies were abstractions of the strategies using base-ten materials. Because of the range of problems that students solved, they frequently moved back and forth from modeling with tens to using invented strategies for different problems, and they also were encouraged to solve problems in more than one way. Thus, when students adopted more advanced strategies, they did not forget about the more basic strategies to which new strategies were related. Furthermore, because different students in each class used different strategies, strategies were continuously juxtaposed and compared as the students shared their strategies.

Extending and Applying Knowledge

In both classes, learning new concepts and procedures was taken as a problem-solving activity in which children constructed new concepts and procedures by extending their knowledge of basic number concepts and procedures. All tasks were posed in problem contexts. As a consequence, children did not learn computational procedures that they later applied to solve problems; they learned procedures in the context of and for the sake of solving problems.

Reflection and Articulation

Reflection played a major role in the development of children's mathematical thinking. By reflecting on manipulations of physical materials, children developed more mature symbolic procedures for adding and subtracting. One of the primary motivations for children to reflect was the class norm that they consistently articulate their solution processes. By regularly explaining how they solved problems and negotiating how solutions were alike and different, children became more reflective and more articulate in explaining their thinking. Sharing strategies appeared to play a critical role in students' developing more advanced strategies and connecting them to existing strategies. One important consequence of sharing was that the more advanced students modeled strategies for other students. Too often, demonstrations of procedures by teachers or students focus on the external behaviors involved in carrying out a procedure and mask the underlying cognitive processes and decisions involved in the solution. Collins, Brown, and Newman (1989) hypothesized that making underlying cognitive processes visible is a critical feature of successfully modeling problem solving. This was what happened in the sharing sessions in these classes. Students not only shared their answers; they made their thinking involved in solving the problem visible.

Another important aspect of sharing strategies was that the necessity of articulating their solution processes appeared to encourage students to reflect on their solutions. In fact the articulation of strategies often became a form of public reflection as is illustrated in Ms. Keith's interaction with Kim. We hypothesize that this reflection played a critical role in the transition to using invented algorithms and in maintaining connections between invented algorithms and the operations on base-ten materials on which they were based.

Ownership

Students in both classes were personally involved in constructing their own solutions to problems. Neither teacher demonstrated procedures for children to imitate. In constructing their own procedures for solving problems, students were expected to take personal responsibility for their own learning.

HOW DOES THIS KIND OF TEACHING DEVELOP?

The kind of teaching described in this chapter was developed by teachers focusing explicitly on student thinking so that lessons were conceived in terms of student thinking, not in terms of teacher activity or curriculum objectives. Although almost all teachers in a four-year study of CGI classrooms (Fennema et al., 1996) followed many of the principles just outlined, not all reached the level of instruction represented in these 3 classes. The levels represented in these two classes developed through teachers engaging in practical inquiry directed at deepening their understanding of student thinking. The frame that we have applied to analyze how instruction in these two classes afforded student learning with understanding can also be applied to considering teachers learning with understanding. These ideas are described in more detail in Franke, Carpenter, Fennema, Ansell, and Behrend (1998) and Franke, Carpenter, Levi, and Fennema (1998) and are elaborated in Franke and Kazemi (this volume).

ACKNOWLEDGMENTS

The research reported in this paper was supported in part by a grant from the National Science Foundation (MDR-8955346) and a grant from the Department of Education Office of Educational Research and Improvement to the National Center for Improving Student Learning and Achievement in Mathematics and Science (R305A60007-98). The opinions expressed in this paper do not necessarily reflect the position, policy, or endorsement of the National Science Foundation, the Department of Education, OERI or the National Center.

REFERENCES

Carpenter, T. P. Fennema, E., & Franke, M. L. (1996). Cognitively Guided Instruction: A knowledge base for reform in primary mathematics instruction. *The Elementary School Journal, 97*, 3-20.

Carpenter, T. P. Fennema, E., Franke, M. L., Levi, L. W., & Empson, S. B. (1999). *Children's mathematics: Cognitively guided instruction*. Portsmouth, NH: Heinemann.

Carpenter, T. P., Franke, M. L., Jacobs, V., & Fennema, E. (1998). A longitudinal study of invention and understanding in children's multidigit addition and subtraction, *Journal for Research in Mathematics Education, 29*, 3-20.

Carpenter, T. P., & Lehrer, R. (1999). Teaching and learning mathematics with understanding. In E. Fennema & T. A. Romberg, (Eds.). *Classrooms that promote mathematical understanding* (pp. 19-32). Mahwah, NJ: Lawrence Erlbaum Associates.

Cobb, P., & Yackel, E. (1996). Constructivist, emergent, and sociocultural perspectives in the context of developmental research, *Educational Psychologist, 31*, 175-190.

Collins, A., Brown, J. S., & Newman, S. (1989). Cognitive apprenticeship: Teaching the crafts of reading, writing, and mathematics. In L. Resnick (Ed.), *Knowing, learning, and instruction: Essays in honor of Robert Glaser* (pp. 453-494). Hillsdale, NJ: Lawrence Erlbaum Associates.

Fennema, E., Carpenter, T. P., Franke, M. L., Levi, L. W., & Empson, S. B. (1996). A longitudinal study of learning to use children's thinking in mathematics instruction. *Journal for Research in Mathematics Education, 27*, 403-434.

Franke, M. L., Carpenter, T.P., Levi, L., & Fennema, E. (1998, April). *Teachers as learners: Developing understanding through children's thinking.* Paper presented at the annual meeting of the American Educational Research Association, San Diego.

Franke, M. L., Carpenter, T. P., Fennema, E., Ansell, E., & Behrend, J. (1998). Understanding teachers' self-sustaining, generative change in the context of professional development. *International Journal of Teaching and Teacher Education, 14*, 67-80.

Fuson, K., Wearne, D., Hiebert, J., Human, P., Murray, H., Olivier, A., Carpenter, T. P., & Fennema, E. (1997). Children's conceptual structures for multidigit numbers and methods of multidigit addition and subtraction. *Journal for Research in Mathematics Education, 28*, 130-162.

Gagne, R. M. (1977). *The conditions of learning* (3rd ed.). New York: Holt, Reinhart & Winston.

Hiebert, J., Carpenter, T. P., Fennema, E., Fuson, K., Human, P., Murray, H., Olivier, A., Wearne, D. (1997). *Making sense: Teaching and learning mathematics with understanding.* Portsmouth, NH: Heinemann.

Siegler, J., & Hiebert, J. (1998). *Back to teaching.* Unpublished manuscript.

Yackel, E., & Cobb, P. (1996). Sociomathematical norms, argumentation, and autonomy in mathematics. *Journal for Research in Mathematics Education, 27*, 458-477.

Teaching as Learning Within a Community of Practice

Characterizing Generative Growth

Megan Loef Franke
University of California, Los Angeles

Elham Kazemi
University of Washington

Teaching as learning is a simple concept yet one that is potentially overused and little understood. Understanding teaching as learning and how it manifests itself in teachers' professional lives provides a basis for characterizing the teaching of mathematics. Drawing from our prior research and our ongoing work with teachers, we believe that the teachers whose students learn the most mathematics are those who engage in practical inquiry. We describe those teachers as engaged in "generative growth" (Franke, Carpenter, Levi & Fennema, in press; Franke, Fennema, Carpenter, Ansell & Behrend, 1998). Not only do teachers engaged in generative growth learn in the context of their classrooms, but they also create communities of learners for themselves that include their students and colleagues.[1] Although we may believe that we can identify these teachers, we have yet to articulate what it looks like for generative teachers to learn in the context of their ongoing practice.

---

[1] Clearly others in the field discuss teaching as learning and articulate its meaning. Our understanding emerged as an amalgamation of their work, our experiences and research and we do not attempt to separate those ideas here.

Although we have been interested in teachers' professional communities in our work with Cognitively Guided Instruction (CGI)[2], we have to this point focused more on the cognitive aspects of teacher learning. This chapter builds on the existing notions of generativity but frames them such that teacher learning is seen as a community activity. Our intent is to provide a way of thinking about generativity that accounts for how teacher learning occurs within sites of practice that include classrooms and professional communities. We draw from our previous work, our current research and the perspectives of those in the field writing about learning within communities of practice.

The chapter begins with a description of generativity as we conceived of it in our earlier work. We lay out the characteristics of generativity and provide examples of what these characteristics look like for teachers in classrooms. We then outline the work that drives our conception of sociocultural theory and teacher learning. This work provides the basis for our reconceptualization of generative growth. Examples from our current work with teachers illustrate our elaboration of generativity. Specifically, we describe how a sociocultural perspective influences our conceptions of generativity and of ways to create opportunities for generative growth.

DEVELOPING UNDERSTANDING: GENERATIVITY

Prior CGI work provides evidence that student learning in mathematics is fostered as teachers themselves engage in ongoing learning or what we call generative growth (Fennema et al., 1996; Franke, Fennema & Carpenter, 1997). This CGI research drew both on the development of student understanding in mathematics to conceptualize ongoing teacher learning and other conceptions of teacher learning including Carpenter's ideas of teaching as problem solving. Our current ideas of generativity extend Carpenter's original conceptions by focusing on aspects of growth; that is, how teachers develop in their understanding of teaching and learning. Our goal is to create a set of principled ideas that enable us to conceptualize ongoing teacher learning (see Franke et al., in press, and Carpenter et al.'s chapter in this volume for a more complete description of the development of our conception and use of generativity). In our

---

[2] For an overview of Cognitively Guided Instruction, see Carpenter, Fennema & Franke, 1996.

earlier CGI work, we closely examined teachers' knowledge, beliefs, and practice. We created levels of development to characterize the integration of teachers beliefs, knowledge, and practice; however, this model did not provide the basis for understanding what enabled teachers to not only sustain their practice after professional development ended, but what enabled teachers to continue to learn (see Franke et al., 1998).

In order to focus on characterizing teachers' ongoing growth, we focused on how teachers sustained their practices and how this differed from generativity. We found that some teachers were able to sustain their practices and that many of the same beliefs and knowledge that supported their practices at the end of professional development were still in existence years later. However, these teachers had not continued to learn beyond the notions they developed in professional development. Although we find it quite impressive that the teachers could sustain their classroom practices, we were interested in understanding what it would require for teachers to add to and adapt their understandings about the teaching and learning of mathematics after the professional development ended.

In studying CGI, teachers both throughout the professional development (over 4 years) and then 4 years later, we came to see generativity as encompassing three main characteristics: (1) detailed knowledge, (2) knowledge rich in structure and connections, and (3) a view that knowledge is one's own to adapt and create.[3] We illustrate each of these characteristics in mathematics teaching by drawing on examples from the study of teachers 4 years after their engagement with the CGI project (Franke et. al., in press).

Detailed Knowledge

The teachers engaged in generative growth could articulate detailed knowledge of their students' mathematical thinking. They provided step-by-step descriptions of the strategies a student used to solve a given problem and routinely talked about where that strategy fit into a particular developmental trajectory. When teachers at this level were asked about their students, they detailed multiple students'

---

[3] We recognize that this is potentially a limited list and one specifically tied to our CGI work. Yet, it serves as an initial set of principled ideas by which we can challenge ourselves and deepen our own understanding.

thinking. To illustrate, Ms. Andrew,[4] a first grade teacher, could describe in detail the strategies different students used as they solved a given problem. When reflecting on a lesson in which she posed the problem, 124 + 137, she described the different ways children solved the problem using their knowledge of hundreds, tens and ones.

> Well, I saw a couple of different ways of adding on. Allison said, "Well, I had two hundred and fifty and seven more was two hundred and fifty-seven." And then she counted up four more. Okay? Then I had another child do that . . . it was two hundred and fifty and eleven more. "Well, I know there's another ten in eleven. So that was two hundred six."

Teachers' detailed knowledge about their students' strategies was also seen in how the teachers interacted with their students. Ms. Andrew used her knowledge to consistently probe her students' thinking. She wanted to know more than just the surface features of whether the students got a correct answer, drew a picture, or did it in their heads. In the following excerpt, note how Ms. Andrew continually questions Kevin about how he was thinking about the problem in order to acquire detailed knowledge of his particular strategy. When she completes her questioning of Kevin, Ms. Andrew knows in detail how he counted up and how he kept track of his count.

> Ms. Andrew: [speaking to the class] Remember to try these [word problems] two ways. [Goes to Kevin] Can you tell me how you did that? [pointing to student's work on a word problem with the structure of 34 + 80 = ____] I'd like to have you tell me how you did that, Kevin [pointing to the answer of 113 that is written on his paper].
>
> Kevin: I did it with my fingers.
>
> Ms. Andrew: How did you do that with your fingers?
>
> Kevin: I counted like. I counted up the 30 or 80 and then I had, and then I counted out . . . 34 more and [telling, not showing].
>
> Ms. Andrew: And how did you do that?

---

[4] All teachers' and students' names are pseudonyms. In the case of our current work we have chosen to use teachers' first names to most closely represent how the teachers addressed each other and us.

Kevin: I counted [holds up one finger for each count] 1, 2, 3 . . . 11, 12 [alternating from hand to hand] 21, 22 . . . 34, and then I counted 80 more. 1, 2, [starts counting fingers again] 3, 4 . . .

Ms. Andrew: [Interrupts] How did you count 80 more?

Kevin: 12, 13, 14, [counts by ones holding up a finger for each number and alternating hands] . . . 80. And I came up with 113.

Ms. Andrew: I don't understand though how you got from 80 to 113 when you were counting by ones. Can you explain how you got up there? I didn't hear you get up to 113.

Kevin: I just counted to 80, and then I counted this many more [pointing to the 34].

Ms. Andrew: Could you show me how you did that? You said you counted 80. Did you actually count up to 80 or did you start with 80.

Kevin: I just started with 80, and then I put that many more [pointing to 34] with 80 and came up with this [pointing to 113 answer].

Ms. Andrew: Okay, could you show me how you started with 80 and did that many more? I'd like to see that.

Kevin: 80, 81 [starting counting on his thumb], 82, 83 [holding up a finger for each number and alternating hands as he counts -- it is not apparent that he is keeping track of 10s] . . . 113.

Ms. Andrew: And how many more was that, then? You've got 1, 2, 3 and it was 34 more. So, you're really close aren't ya? If it's (pause) you counted 30. I saw you count 30 with your fingers, but then you needed 34 and you counted 31, 32, 33 [pointing to Kevin's fingers starting with thumb, Kevin counting along] 34. So do you know what that would be? You were up to 113. What would that be if you had one more?

Kevin: 114.

Ms. Andrew: See, the first time I was really confused, but now I see what you did.

Here Ms. Andrew supported Kevin in describing his thinking and showed him, through her persistence, how important it is for him to detail his thinking so she can understand. Knowing that he used his fingers was not enough; Ms. Andrew wanted to know in detail how he used his fingers. She wanted to know if he used a counting strategy and if so what type of counting strategy he used so that she could develop a sense of what Kevin understood about addition and place value.

Structured Knowledge

We found that teachers engaged in generative growth viewed their knowledge of children's thinking as organized or structured. A major tenet of CGI has been that teachers structure their knowledge of children's thinking in ways that allow them to understand the principles supporting it. That is, the analysis of the mathematics of children's thinking involves more than lists of problems and strategies; the analyses involve an integrated perspective based on relationships between mathematical problems and strategies for solution.

The teachers engaged in generative growth perceived the relationships among the problem types and strategies as critical to understanding what they would do with the knowledge. For example, Ms. Sage commented about how she uses a framework based on what she learned from CGI:

> I need a framework. I definitely think there's a framework with CGI that's made a big difference for me. Strategies have been identified, there's definitely a hierarchy . . . I mean, a lot of curriculum materials have problem solving. A lot of them do. But you don't know what to do with it. I mean, how do you decide why problems would be more difficult than others for children to solve? You know, what makes this problem difficult? And with CGI, that has been researched, and I think accurately researched, and it enables me to know why certain kids are struggling, what I can do to facilitate that. . . . I want to know where I'm going and where I'm taking them. So I need that framework.

In all cases, the generative teachers talked about how they organized their knowledge of children's thinking to facilitate decision making. One teacher talked about the CGI framework as having "slots" that helped her think about where her students were and what problems to pose next. Another teacher talked about the CGI structure as providing general guidance that she could then build on and "fill in the details" for herself. In each of these cases, the teachers noted relationships among the ideas about children's thinking highlighted in CGI and used these relationships as a way to organize their thinking. They often started with the structure provided by CGI and then adapted and added to it to create their own working model.

Knowledge as One's Own

The teachers engaged in generative growth focused on structure and detail in talking about their knowledge of children's mathematical thinking. Yet, they did not see their knowledge as static. They saw knowledge of children's mathematical thinking as their own to create and adapt. The teachers were consistently curious about how their children would solve problems; they regularly tested and revised their knowledge. They thought about what the students did, and they struggled to make sense of it. Every teacher engaged in generative growth talked in detail about how much they learned with each student interaction and how that knowledge informed other interactions. As Ms. Baker commented, "And so every time you interact with a child, you're gaining more knowledge of how to interact with other children. Every time they show you, and tell you, what they're doing and thinking, you just learn more about what's going on in their head."

The generative teachers also reported that the substance of what they knew about children's thinking had changed. Ms. Sullivan not only spoke in general terms about how her knowledge had changed, she described specific changes in her fundamental understanding of children's thinking. She used her knowledge about individual students to elaborate and extend the conceptual frames she used to understand children's thinking. As a consequence, she had much more detailed and complex schemes for analyzing children's thinking than the ones that were discussed during the CGI professional development program. The workshops and readings had focused on distinctions between several primary classes of strategies that children invented for adding multidigit numbers. Ms. Sullivan not only identified more fine-grained distinctions among strategies; she integrated them into a coherent framework that provided for her a more complete picture of the development of children's mathematical thinking. She states,

I'm definitely more aware of how [the children] start out at the beginning of the year with modeling and how that modeling very much influences the types of invented strategies that they're going to use. . . . I'll see some kids count all the tens, and then they'll go to the ones, and then I'll see other kids who do 46, 56, 66, 76, and then pick up the ones. So for me there is a little bit of a distinction there that I want to clarify because it helps me know what they're probably going to do with it next. Do they do all the tens and then go to the ones? Or do they do a mixture? Because I really will see more kids use a tens and ones invented strategy when they do that [count tens then ones when modeling] versus more of an incremental strategy when they do the other one [count on by tens].

Summary

The follow-up study with CGI teachers 4 years after the end of the professional development provided evidence that the link between developing elaborated and interrelated understandings of children's thinking and making knowledge one's own was critical to understanding generative change in CGI teachers (Franke et al., in press). Teachers who developed a framework for analyzing students' mathematical thinking used that structure as they assimilated what they heard from students. The framework helped teachers know what to listen for and how to connect that to other knowledge they had about students' strategies. Teachers who viewed knowledge as something they could add to and change, could use the framework as a basis for beginning to understand how to create connections across students' thinking, mathematics and pedagogy in a way that allowed the knowledge to provide a basis for continued learning

COMMUNITIES OF PRACTICE

Sociocultural Theories and Generativity

Drawing on the work of Lave, Wenger, Cobb, Wertsch, Rogoff, and others, we have adapted our thinking about teacher learning and generativity to highlight learning within a community of practice. Lave and Wenger (1991) defined a community of practice as a set of relations across people and activity, over time, and, in relation with other communities of practice and learning as "changing participation in changing communities of practice" (Lave, 1996, p. 150). Shifts in participation do not merely mark a change in a participant's activity or behavior. Shifts in participation involve a transformation of roles and the crafting of new identities, identities that are linked to new knowledge and skill (Rogoff 1994, 1997). Lave (1996) stated: "crafting identities is a social process, and becoming more knowledgeably skilled is an aspect of participation in social practice . . . who you are becoming shapes crucially and fundamentally what you know (p. 157)."

Although Lave, Wenger, and Rogoff have provided a way to think about teacher learning as shifting participation and the reforming of identity, Wertsch (1991, 1998) offered a way to frame and capture these shifts. Wertsch (1998) drew on the work of Vygotsky and highlights learning as occurring through mediated action. The mediation occurs between the individual and the sociocultural setting where action is at the center of the analysis. Mediated action involves a tension between an active agent and a cultural tool. The cultural tools afford or constrain learning or change. Wertsch's conceptualization highlights the critical nature of tools and artifacts that serve to mediate the action within communities of practice.

The sociocultural perspective for us highlights the taken-as-shared knowledge that teachers appropriate and the ways in which cultural artifacts afford or constrain their participation. A number of researchers within mathematics education have adapted this sociocultural perspective as they characterize and study teachers, students and classrooms. For example, Stein and Brown (1997) used Lave and Wenger's (1991) work on legitimate peripheral participation, and Tharp and Gallimore's (1988) work on assisted performance to describe teacher learning. Cobb (1999) brought a particular mathematical focus to thinking about communities of practice and shifts in participation. He analyzes shifts in classroom mathematical practices that "focus on taken as shared ways of reasoning, arguing, and symbolizing established while discussing particular mathematical ideas" (p. 9). In his work, the mathematics itself plays a central role in understanding the changing community. Although research and work with teachers are being designed and analyzed in ways that incorporate a sociocultural perspective, we still know little about how this perspective can enable us to better describe, document and understand mathematics teaching.

As we come to understand these perspectives in the context of our current work, we have had to both reframe our work and rethink professional development and teacher learning. We became interested in understanding the shifts in participation and the development of teachers' identities as they engaged in particular communities of practice centered on mathematics and the ways in which tools supported or constrained the practices and reasoning of those participating (Saxe, 1991; Wertsch, 1991). In doing so, the sociocultural lens has advanced our understanding of generativity. The advances have been both substantive in characterizing generativity and methodological in how we come to understand generativity.

From this sociocultural perspective, we see that we cannot separate learning from the context in which it occurs and that we need to capture the evolutionary character of teacher learning rather than the more static characteristics described previously. Generativity then becomes more about ongoing shifts in practice within a given community that form a participant's identity as a mathematics teacher. Taking a sociocultural perspective has influenced our thinking about generativity in three significant ways. We (1) reformulated how we think about our work with teachers, (2) elaborated on what it means for teachers to know the details of children's mathematical thinking and why this is important for generativity and (3) enriched the idea of teachers' knowledge as seen as their own by examining and characterizing the development of identity.

OUR CURRENT WORK WITH TEACHERS

We could not begin to understand generativity from a sociocultural perspective without first rethinking our work with teachers. As we began to formulate our new 2-year professional development project, we took the sociocultural perspectives described earlier and redesigned our interactions with teachers. Specifically, we designed opportunities for the creation of a community of learners, we developed a means for artifacts to structure interactions, and we created ways to develop relationships with the participating teachers.

Communities of Learners

We wanted to create opportunities for teachers to come together to create a community in which they could learn together about the teaching and learning of mathematics.

Our intent was to create space, for teachers to share, challenge, and create ideas about the development of children's mathematical thinking. Our work groups were intended to be, as Lave (1996) and Cochran-Smith and Lytle (1999) described, a place where teachers can shape their identities and take on a "stance."[5] Specifically, our goal included supporting teacher workgroup communities in which teachers came together to share and make sense of their students' mathematical thinking. In some sense, it was an opportunity, as Lave described, for teachers to make public their private acts of teaching. We wanted to provide teachers the forum to develop relationships and create a community of practice not separate from their classrooms but one that could mirror the interactions and identities developed there.

Identification of Artifacts

We wanted to create opportunities for teachers to engage in conversation around particular artifacts. We saw the use of artifacts as a way to focus the conversation, bring teachers' rich experiences and histories into the conversations, and create connections between professional development and other aspects of teachers' work. We also needed to choose an artifact that allowed for deep discussions about the mathematics and one that linked to teachers' classroom practice.

We chose to use student work from the teachers' classes as the focus for the workgroup meetings. We proposed a monthly mathematical problem that all teachers would pose to their students. Our intent was to choose a problem that allowed conversation to develop around similar mathematical ideas and permitted a range of entry points to accommodate different mathematical understandings.[6] The teachers' task during the workgroup was to share their students' work, create a group list of elicited strategies, and then rank the list according to sophistication of students' mathematical understanding. All of the conversation revolved around the particular mathematical problem that was solved—whether it be about the students' mathematical thinking, the mathematics in the problem itself, the usefulness of particular

---

[5] Cochran-Smith and Lytle (1999) defined stance as the "ways we stand, the ways we see and the lenses we see through" (p. 49).

[6] As the sessions evolved, the teachers participated in decision making about the tasks to pose to their students.

strategies, the ways to move students' mathematical thinking forward, or the details of student strategies.

Developing Relationships

We saw the formation of relationships among the teachers and the researchers, both within the workgroup and outside the workgroup as critical to the development of communities of learners, to our learning about generativity, and to the potential for this work to become sustaining. We wanted the teachers to see us participating with them in learning about the development of students' mathematical thinking and its classroom use. We wanted the teachers to see from the start that they were also experts in the group.

To this end, the workgroups always began and ended with informal conversations. We visited teachers' classrooms at least once in between workgroup meetings. The visits were not structured formal observations, but rather informal visits during which we documented students' thinking. We did not want the teachers to view us as having answers but as having questions and being in a position of continually learning about their children's mathematical thinking. We also wanted to become a part of the broader school community. We spent time in the lunchroom and on the play yard, we wandered through the school and talked with the administrators and staff. We shared our histories and our personal lives. We wanted the opportunity to learn about the different aspects of teachers' work and their lives.

DETAILING STUDENT THINKING

Although in the previous research (Franke et al., in press) we focused on teachers' detailed knowledge of student thinking, its organization, and how teachers viewed it, we did not realize the extent to which understanding the details of students' mathematical thinking supported teachers' generative growth. Our current focus on communities of practice allowed us to examine teachers' detailed knowledge of student thinking as they interacted with each other inside and outside of their classrooms. We learned that in their interactions with each other, teachers did not just describe a student's strategy. Instead, teachers detailed the thinking of a number of students in relation to each other, they described the circumstances within which student mathematical thinking occurred, and they used the details of student thinking to support their conversations about the issues surrounding the teaching and learning of mathematics. We provide a few examples of how generative teachers described their students' work in the context of workgroup sessions.[7] In the session described, the teachers are discussing the monthly problem they had all posed to their students.

In the first example, Kathy talks about her second- and third-grade students' solutions to the word problem, "I have 67 baseball cards, how many more do I have to collect to have 105 baseball cards?" Kathy does not detail just one student's thinking when describing her students' thinking for the group. She describes a number of students' strategies in relation to one another. Along with detailing some of her students' thinking, she details the support she provides:

Kathy: We did that one [the problem] but with larger numbers. The strategies varied . . . Some of them made the first set. The 67.

Megan: So the numbers were 67, how many more to?

Kathy: 105. Which is a really good number to pick . . . I have probably had 4 or 5 kids who tried to do the subtraction. 105 minus 67. And some of them really get that. And some of them really don't. So they tried another strategy. Luis ended up doing it but counted by tens, 67, 77, 87, 97. And then he went 1, 2, 3, 4, 5, 6, 7, 8, like that. So he got 38. And then Kim also did it that way. She was another one who wrote it a different way. And I said, "Well what did you do when you counted." And she said, "67 to 77 was 10. And 10 more was 87." She did it the same way.

Kathy goes on to talk about student thinking and in doing so provides a sense that she adapts her problems and asks questions based on the student thinking.

Kathy: I gave some kids the 17 and then the 8. [referring to another set of numbers she used]. And then when they solved that, they could move on to the 101 and 62. And it was interesting. I had one who with the smaller numbers, she did counting. She went 9, 10, 11, 12, 13, 14, 15,

---

[7] We have detailed elsewhere how the teachers were characterized as generative. In each case data was drawn from workgroup sessions, classrooms, informal conversations and formal interviews throughout the first year of working together (see Kazemi, 1999).

16, 17. And then went back and counted how many were there. And then when she got into the higher numbers, she counted up by 10.

Megan: Ohh, how did she do that?

Kathy: She went from 62. Wait. [Looks at student work] . . . I started giving her really high numbers. She went to 520, 205. The first one was 75. She has 215 and then 75. So she went 75 plus 10 plus 10 plus 10 is 105 plus 100 is 205 plus 10 is 215 . . . And then she went back and added what she added on. How many tens she added on and the 100. So she had 140.

Megan: So she knew this [the 75 plus 3 tens] was a 105. Then she added 105 plus 100. And she got 205 plus 10 is 215. And then she went back and added these [pointing to what she had added on].

Kathy: And she continued to use that strategy. Then I gave her higher numbers. She used 500s.

We use Kathy's description to illustrate that teachers who we characterized as generative experimented with the problems we provided. Their adaptations were frequently woven into their detailed description of students' strategies.

In the next example, Alma, like Kathy, went beyond detailing a single strategy and elaborated how a student's strategy emerged. The problem was, "There are 231 children taking a computer class after school. If 20 students can work in each classroom, how many classrooms would we need?"

Alma: Most of them put out all of their tens. But I had one who did like the 200 blocks first, and then he did three bars of ten, and then he did his single unit. And then he circled, he connected two of the ten bars. He drew a line between two of them. And then I said, "Okay, what are you going to do next?" And he was stuck. He was completely stuck. And I said, "Well, how many students in a class?" And he said, "20." I said, "Okay, what can you do?" And I just stood there looking at him. And he said, he didn't know what to do. And I said, "Look at the 100s bars. What could you do with those?" And then he went, "Ohhhh." And so he totally erased everything, and he started doing everything in the 10 bars. So he broke down the 200 into 10 bars. He told me there are 10 tens in a 100. So he started grouping those [every two tens]. And then he circled them when he was done.

The teachers drew the connections they were making about the student strategies not only to their pedagogy but they also drew connections from the student thinking to the mathematical ideas. Lupe's description shows that mathematical ideas were central to the observations and descriptions that teachers made while interacting with their students' work. Lupe was concerned that the students were not thinking about multiplication and division as grouping. During the workgroup, she reflects on the students' solutions and details their thinking in relation to this mathematical idea. Her comments relate to two different problems, one involving dividing 231 by 20 (just described) and the other 31 by 4. ("There are 31 children in a class. If four children can sit at a table, how many tables would we need?")

Lupe: Like for example, one little girl. This was interesting. For the easier one . . . she added 4 plus 4 plus 4 plus. And she grouped them into little tables. But for the bigger number . . . she took 231 and she subtracted minus 20 minus 20 minus 20. And she went, okay, the first 20 is one classroom and the second 20 is the second classroom like that. But what I noticed is that everyone who got [the problem], they figured out how to group It . . . Another student grouped it by tens, but he clumped the two tens together to make them 20s. So it was the bigger number; it was 231 kids and you've got, you can only put 20 in a classroom. So what he did was he went 10 plus 10 plus 10 plus 10 plus. He grouped them into tens first and then he had 11 at the end. So it was 231. But then he went back and grouped two tens, that was one classroom. And he counted, that was one classroom. Two more tens, that's another classroom. But they were all able to group. And I think that's why they were all able to solve it.

The ways in which Kathy, Alma and Lupe discussed students' mathematical thinking made a relational way of thinking apparent; the strategies were considered in relation to one another and in relation to the mathematical ideas. The teachers contextualized the students' thinking and understanding within a given problem that was posed in a particular way under particular conditions and included particular ways of teacher support. The ways in which the teachers interacted with regard to their students' thinking pointed out how their detailed understanding of student thinking was becoming more complex.

There were many discussions that moved from the details of solving a particular problem to the issues that surrounded those details. The teachers used the detailed discussions of students' mathematical thinking to pursue discussions about broader issues about the teaching and learning of mathematics. For instance, throughout the workgroup meetings, the teachers challenged each other's long-standing ideas about the standard algorithm. The teachers pushed each other, listened, but looked hard at the student work for evidence to support their own [teacher's] positions. These conversations were often long and involved. Here we provide a small portion of one exchange to provide an illustration of the teachers' participation and use of student thinking to support their own [student's] arguments. Notice how some of the teachers focused the discussion on the public list of strategies the group generated from their students' solutions. (The teachers referred to these strategies by number, the number related to the strategies' position on the list.)

Megan: What do you think is the most sophisticated strategy that you saw?

Miguel: Probably using the algorithm.

Megan: The algorithm? Do you all agree about that?

Teachers: No.

Natalie: They don't know what they're doing [when they do the algorithm].

Kathy: And you don't have to think about the problem when you're doing it. Like you have to think about 40 as a unit in other strategies.

Natalie: I think that like on number 7 [on the list of strategies the teachers created during the meeting] for example, like Vincent, he solved it by doing the algorithm, but he explained, "Mrs. Mosby used [$7.05] to buy animal cookies. Each box cost 47 cents and she bought 15 boxes so I multiplied 15 and 47." So he was able to explain why he did it.

Miguel: One thing why I said the algorithm is important for me is that later on when you get—I don't know if this is on the off chance--but if you get into physics and chemistry, you start memorizing constants and stuff.

Patrick: I think [strategy] #3 and #4 are a pretty clear differentiation in place value, which is sort of the critical thing. So they [the students using these strategies] are understanding -- the person who added up rows of 4 and knew it was 10s. And added up rows of 7 and knew it was the units, that kind of blows me away.

Natalie: They were able to keep track of it.

Patrick: Also the people who knew how to do the lines and circles. [pointing out the direct modeling by tens strategy]. That shows that they've really got the concept of groups.

Not all of the teachers in the conversation agreed about the most sophisticated strategy nor did they all use specifics of student thinking to marshal their evidence. However, the details of student thinking allowed the teachers to engage in a discussion that was mathematical, detailed in students' strategy use and thorough in examining the issues involved in using the standard algorithm.

Summary

The ways teachers elaborated and contextualized the details of the students' mathematical thinking enabled them to understand the strategies, not simply identify them. The teachers could see how the context influenced student strategies, how the strategies related to the questions teachers ask, how the strategies change when particular materials are provided, and more generally, how to reason through and learn more about the details of student thinking and student meanings. The elaboration of the student strategies also provided an anchor to challenge existing notions about the teaching and learning of mathematics in ways that supported collaboration and learning.

IDENTITY

The sociocultural perspective has challenged our understanding of teachers' generativity with respect to issues of identity. In our previous conception, we saw that the teachers engaged in generative growth articulated that the knowledge they acquired about students' mathematical thinking was theirs to adapt and create. They saw themselves capable of acquiring more knowledge about student thinking and saw themselves as able to make sense of what they heard from their students. Taking a sociocultural perspective allows us to view teachers in terms of their developing identities as mathematics teachers. As we examine all aspects of teachers' work in our current project, we see that the generative teachers are developing identities as mathematics teachers that include attributes of seeing knowledge as their own.

The way Jazmin, a kindergarten teacher, participated in our project provides an example of identity development in a teacher engaged in generative growth. While we view identity as continually developing, here we provide a snapshot of Jazmin's development across several contexts. We emphasize that a critical component of Jazmin's developing identity as a generative mathematics teacher is her view of herself as always learning and changing. We also highlight the context in which her identity developed and the ways in which those interactions influenced or shaped her identity.

In the Workgroup Meetings

Jazmin came to the initial workgroup meeting because she was not comfortable with her teaching of mathematics. She was not sure she was "doing it right." During the first workgroup meeting, Jazmin had not posed the workgroup problem to her class, she did not speak, and told us she did not feel as though she had anything to share. However, by the March workgroup meeting, Jazmin not only posed the workgroup problem but also posed three variations of the workgroup problem. She brought work from each of her students, and she shared a variety of strategies. In addition, she asked questions of the other teachers about the strategies they had shared, continuously trying to make sense of the conversation. In particular, she wanted to make sense of the strategies and the mathematics in relation to her kindergartners. As the workgroups progressed, Jazmin gained confidence in her developing understanding of students' thinking and her teaching and this confidence influenced her participation in the group. Although she was always a presence in the group, by the end of the year, Jazmin often described what she felt were the amazing mathematical ideas her students had developed and how surprised she was at herself and her ability to support her students' learning. She challenged her colleagues by asking them questions about their students' mathematical thinking and how to foster its development. Jazmin had always seen herself as a good literacy teacher, but now she saw herself as someone who could provide mathematical opportunities for her students that she thought led to increased learning.

In Her Interactions With Her Students

As Jazmin began to experiment with the workgroup problems, she also began purposely listening to her student' explanations and asking questions to push their understanding. Through her listening and asking questions, Jazmin recognized that her students could be learning about tens. She tried a number of different tasks but was dissatisfied with how these tasks supported the development of the students' understanding of ten. She told us that she needed to engage the students in some tasks that would provide her more information about what the students understood about ten. Late in the year, one of her lessons began when Jazmin sat at a table with a group of six children and Tomas said, "I have 500 cents in my pocket." Jazmin replied, "Wow, that is a lot of money. Are you sure you want all of that in your pocket? Let's see what you have." Tomas pulled out three handfuls of nickels and then three dimes. Jazmin asked the other students if they could count the money. They started with the nickels and the group counted by fives. Jazmin provided counting support from 50 to 75. She then asked what they could do with the dimes. One girl said, " It would be 75, 85 then 95." Another child continued the sequence by saying, "And then 100." But another boy said, "No it would be 105." Tomas then said, "Oh yeah . . . it was 105 cents."

Jazmin continued the lesson by dumping over 500 colored teddy bear counters on the table and asking the children if they could figure out the total number of teddy bear counters. The children excitedly responded "yes." She asked the students how they were going to count them. The children responded that they would count them by fives or tens. She asked each child to show her a group of 5 or 10. All but one child decided to work with tens. She checked over their groups and asked if they could make more groups. As the children created more groups, Jazmin asked them how many counters they had and how many groups they had. For example, one child, Maricela, had made six groups of ten. She color-coded them by having each ten a different color; one group of ten was all blue bears, another red, and so on. Jazmin looked at her counters and asked her how many teddy bears she had so far. Maricela immediately began to count her bear counters by ones. She reported she had 63. Jazmin then asked, "How many groups of ten do you have?" Maricela counted, "1, 2, 3, 4, 5, 6" pointing once to each group. Jazmin moved away and two minutes later returned to Maricela and asked, "Now how many bear counters do you have?" Maricela counted, "10, 20, 30, 40, 50, 60, 61, 62, 63, 64, 65, 66, 67." "Okay and how many tens." Maricela replied without counting, "Six." As the students counted and recounted their groups, they found more and more sophisticated ways to count and keep track throughout the lesson.

Jazmin's learning began as she pursued Tomas' thinking and asked him about the money in his pocket. Her involvement in the group's counting of Tomas' nickels and dimes provided support for Jazmin's intended lesson. Following the lesson, Jazmin expressed how excited she was at how much she had learned about the children's ways of thinking about tens. Her excitement was not related to how well the lesson had gone but rather was focused on all that she had learned about her students' understanding of tens. She wanted to talk about how she could change the questions she asked to gain even more insight. Jazmin allowed her curiosity about her students' mathematical thinking and her mathematical goals (relationships between tens and ones) to guide her interactions.

In Her Informal Interactions

Often the development of Jazmin's identity was best captured in the stories that she would tell us in our informal interactions. Jazmin always had a story to share. Typically, she told stories about her students and their recent mathematical accomplishments, often something she viewed as amazing. One day as she sat with us at lunch, she said, "Guess what happened today. Gabriel was solving a multiplication problem (2 x 3), it was about a girl who had three dolls each 2 inches tall. He solved the problem by counting 1, 2, 3 – 4, 5, 6. He reversed it. Isn't it amazing what they can do." Her stories always told us something about how she was thinking about the mathematics, the students' thinking, and herself as a mathematics teacher.

On another occasion, Jazmin stopped us in the teachers' lounge. She was off track (not teaching), but she had been substitute teaching at other schools in the district. She had stories to share.

> I was substituting at [names another school] and I called my dad to check in with him at lunch time. He hasn't been feeling well. [We talked about her dad for a few minutes.] I told him that I just wanted to come home I was so bored. All they [the students in the class she was substituting in] were doing was drill, drill, drill and the kids were working with such low numbers, and they couldn't talk about what they were doing. . . . I realize now that I could not work anywhere else but here. Subbing at these other schools, I see that they are not doing what we are doing, and I couldn't do that.

What was most telling about Jazmin's informal interactions with us was how these interactions mirrored her shifting identity and the changes in her participation with us. In our initial encounters, Jazmin was seeking help. She was looking for direction. However, after a year, Jazmin sought us out because she saw us as sharing her passion; rarely did she look for specific advice and often she had already conceptualized a number of ways to work through her ideas before even speaking with us.

For example, after a year of working together, we stopped in to see Jazmin in her classroom. She immediately launched into a description of her students' success on the fair sharing problem she posed for the upcoming workgroup meeting. She then went on to describe how a few children had gotten stuck that morning on a partitive division problem of 43 divided by four. She detailed her problem posing, the materials available and the children's initial attempts at a solution. She felt that the students did not understand what the problem was asking. She mentioned how she and Monica, her team teacher, had already discussed their concerns following the lesson that morning. She outlined how they adapted their lesson for the afternoon group. They planned to focus the students by having them listen to the entire problem a couple of times, discuss it together and then have the children retell the story before beginning their solutions. Jazmin moved on to a new topic after her description, as if they had settled it for now but had wanted to let us know what was going on. The teachers then shifted to discussing how they noticed their students were not as familiar (as they were last year) with writing number sentences for the problems they were solving. Jazmin was not unhappy. Jazmin commented that she had been focusing so much more on the students' solutions and their articulation of their solutions that they had not been writing number sentences. Monica then pointed out that they were now going to build that into their current problems. The two teachers went on to tell a couple more stories about particular children and what they were doing in mathematics. This conversation lasted about 15 minutes.

Jazmin did not see that she needed us to solve her teaching dilemmas. She never explicitly stated this; rather she elaborated her concerns and detailed her options without ever looking to us for a response. She had taken over the responsibility of constructing with her teaching partner the reasons why students' mathematical thinking was progressing in the way it was and then creating ways to move that thinking forward. We were there as her "someone else" to talk with about their decisions.

Summary

Coming to know Jazmin across multiple settings provided us with a rich picture of her development as a mathematics teacher. Wenger (1998) described learning and identity in practice. He states,

> Because learning transforms who we are and what we can do, it is an experience of identity. It is not just an accumulation of skills and information, but a process of becoming. . . . Viewed as an experience of identity, learning entails both a process and a place. It entails a process of transforming knowledge as well as a context in which to define an identity of participation. As a consequence, to support learning is not only to support the process of acquiring knowledge, but also to offer a place where new ways of knowing can be realized in the form of such an identity. . . . The transformative practice of a learning community offers an ideal context for developing new understandings because the community sustains change as part of an identity of participation (p. 215).

Both the changes in the workgroup participation and the changes in Jazmin's participation with her students, her colleagues, and us, provide examples of how identity becomes developed within the community and how that community serves to sustain that change. Jazmin went from a teacher who would not speak in the first workgroup and thought the problem was too difficult to pose to her students, to a teacher who was willing to try almost any problem with her students. Jazmin became a teacher who liked to experiment in her classroom, who liked to try problems out and see what her students would do, who enjoyed asking questions and then "tweaking" the problems. Jazmin became a learner in her classroom. She was a learner in her informal interactions with us and in the workgroup meetings.   Her work with her team teacher, her comments about her participation in the workgroup, and her interactions with us highlight how Jazmin's interactions provided support for her continued learning. She was learning about herself, her students, her colleagues and mathematics. Jazmin saw herself as generative. She saw herself as needing to be in a place where her generativity was valued.

COMMUNITIES OF PRACTICE AND GENERATIVE CHANGE

Generative growth is more than what goes on in a teachers' mind or a reflection of what happens when teachers interact with their students. Generative growth occurs as teachers participate in communities of practice. Teachers engaged in generative growth develop identities within the communities of practice that highlight their learning. The teachers see themselves as learning the mathematics, learning about their students' mathematical thinking and learning how to learn in the context of their ongoing work. Generative growth is not about a set of characteristics the teacher possesses; it is about how the knowledge and skills the teacher develops in relation to the development of students' mathematical thinking supports the development of the teacher's identity as a mathematics teacher. Generative teachers all possess substantial knowledge about the development of students' mathematical thinking and, as we saw in our current work, the knowledge is detailed in a way that includes the context in which the strategy occurs, the mathematical ideas involved, and the teachers' beliefs and values about the teaching and learning of mathematics. This learning provided the support for teachers' developing identities.

We have seen that seeing one's knowledge as one's own goes beyond how the teachers see the knowledge of children's mathematics and more toward their identity as teachers and learners. We noticed in our previous work that the teachers engaged in generative growth saw their classrooms as places for experimentation and their learning. We see in this work that the way in which the teachers see themselves and their negotiation of that identity becomes critical to their generativity.

RESEARCHERS' LEARNING

Taking a sociocultural approach to understanding generativity changed the ways in which we interacted with the teachers and enriched our understanding of the characteristics of generative growth. Redesigning our work with teachers so that we focused on the communities of practice, the artifacts that supported their learning within the communities, and our developing relationships with the teachers enriched opportunities for the development of generative growth. We feel we have only begun to understand the ways a sociocultural perspective can shape our understanding of generative growth. Our use of this perspective has not only challenged how we describe our work and the ways we characterize generativity, but it has also challenged the way we think about our own learning and the approaches we take to that learning. Our current work suggests that rethinking how to use and understand the stories teachers tell, what constitutes teachers' practice, and the artifacts and tools that support teacher learning will move our understanding of and support of teachers' generative growth forward.

TEACHERS' STORIES

In our CGI work, we regularly noticed how teachers engaged in generative growth told stories about themselves and their students. Their stories documented their own learning, how they used mathematics in their interactions with their families and friends, and how they learned from their students. The teachers would tell us how they used particular strategies they learned from their students to balance their checkbooks, how they posed problems to their spouses to learn about their thinking, how they noticed a child use a strategy they had never seen before, and so on. The stories most typically served as supporting evidence and have not been seen as central to understanding teacher learning. In reading Lave's work and in hearing these same teacher stories repeated, we have come to find ways to understand how these stories contribute to our understanding of teacher learning. The teachers' stories can serve as a way of capturing their developing identities. The teachers communicate through their stories how they think about teaching mathematics, how they have made sense of the development of children's mathematical thinking, how they think about supporting student learning, and what they know about mathematics. Their stories provide a context for hearing how the teachers make the knowledge of children's thinking their own. The mathematics plays a central role in the stories the teachers tell. The mathematics their students are engaged in serves as a site for teachers' own learning, much as Cobb (1999) described. The teachers' stories communicate how they have created a way of being, an identity, as Lave describes, or a stance as Cochran-Smith and Lytle describe. The teachers' stories allow us to understand teachers' views of themselves as learners engaged in generative growth.

We are beginning to understand how teachers' identities developed. We are exploring the interrelationships that exist in teachers' identities in different communities of practice, the relationship between individual identities and the identities of the community of practice, and teachers' relationships with us within a community of practice. We have a great deal to learn in each of these areas. However, our current work provides support for continuing to investigate teacher learning and generativity through investigating shifts in practice. Not only are our ideas about generativity enriched, but we also are coming to a better understanding of teacher work and learning how to engage in this work with teachers.

TEACHERS' PRACTICE

As we reevaluated our work with teachers, we also came to expand our notion of teachers' practice. Traditionally, teachers' practice involves teachers' engagement with students in classrooms. However, focusing only on those interactions as teachers' practice limits our understanding of generative growth and constrains what we see as teachers' knowledge, skills, and identities. In our work, we now consider teachers' classrooms, the work in professional development meetings, and teachers' informal interactions with colleagues and staff as sites for their learning and practice.

Our previous professional development work has always been central to our understanding of teacher learning; however, the professional development was seen as a way to engage teachers with important ideas about the development of children's mathematical thinking. Although this is valid and important, it limited our developing understanding of teachers' learning. The professional development the teachers engage in is a part of their practice. Just like their classroom, in which we looked to see how teachers are learning and thinking, the professional development sessions serve as a site in which teachers and professional developers engage in learning together as a community. The professional development sessions are not separate from teachers' ongoing work but rather an integral part of it. Understanding this community of practice provides an opportunity to better understand teachers' learning and legitimizes the learning occurring within the professional development.

The informal interactions we observed and participated in also provided us insight into the teachers' forming identities about the teaching of mathematics, their knowledge and skill related to teaching mathematics, and the types of relationships they were developing with their colleagues. Often these interactions are seen as peripheral in understanding teachers and teaching. We have found them to be a significant aspect of teachers' work and a necessary part of our coming to understand generativity.

SUPPORTING ARTIFACTS

In considering teacher learning in the different communities of practice and the formation of teachers' identities, we have created conjectures about the ways artifacts and tools played a role in the stances teachers developed. We are examining the ways in which artifacts that exist in both the professional development setting and the classroom setting can provide support for teachers to reconstruct their identities and their classroom practices. Wenger (1998) pointed out that we can think of a tool or artifact as providing a focus for the negotiation of meaning. He also argues that this focus enables the community to organize the negotiation of meaning and create understanding.[8] Wenger's ideas provide a cohesive way of thinking about how the artifacts that we worked with focused teachers as they negotiated of meaning and supported the development of their understanding. The selection of common mathematics problems for students discussed in workgroups provided the tools for focusing the teachers' creation and negotiation of meaning. Because the artifacts themselves centered on the mathematics and the children's thinking, these ideas became the focus for the meaning developed, and other issues of pedagogy were woven into these understandings. Some of

---

[8] Wenger (1998) terms this process reification.

the artifacts, like the problem posed, existed within both the workgroup setting and the teachers' classroom settings. Thus, although the communities of practice included different participants and different histories, the artifact focused conversation in both settings. The artifacts supported the development of language and interaction that could be used to support the development of new relationships. As we continue to learn how the artifacts within the various communities of practice focused negotiation, we can use Wenger's ideas to provide a frame for analyzing the features of the artifacts that evolve and how those features support the development of teacher learning and identity.

CONCLUSION

Teaching mathematics is not just the pedagogical practice that teachers perform. Teaching mathematics involves communities of practice, communities that create and recreate goals and norms, communities that develop around a set of artifacts and structures of practice, communities where identities are co-constructed. Communities of practice exist inside and outside of classrooms and schools and take on different forms. Understanding teacher learning and generativity involves coming to understand all dimensions of teachers' mathematical practice.

ACKNOWLEDGMENTS

The work reported here is a product of the SSGC working group. The ideas shared here were developed within the working group and especially with our colleagues Stephanie Biagetti, Jeffrey Shih and Jo Ann Isken. The teachers and staff that we worked with also contributed in innumerable ways to the work shared here.

The research reported in this chapter was supported in part by a grant from the Department of Education Office of Educational Research and Improvement to the National Center for Improving Student Learning and Achievement in Mathematics and Science (R305A60007-98). The opinions expressed in this paper do not necessarily reflect the position, policy, or endorsement of the Department of Education, OERI or the National Center.

REFERENCES

Carpenter, T. P., Fennema, E., & Franke, M. L. (1996). Cognitively Guided Instruction: A knowledge base for reform in primary mathematics instruction. *Elementary School Journal, 97,* (1), 1-20.

Cochran-Smith, M., & Lytle, S. (1999). Relationships of knowledge and practice: Teacher learning in communities. In A. Iran-Nejad & D. Pearson (Eds.), *Review of Educational Research, 24,* 249-305

Cobb, P. (1999). Individual and collective mathematical development: The case of statistical data analysis. *Mathematical Thinking and Learning, 1,* 5-43.

Fennema, E., Carpenter, T., Franke, M., Levi, L, Jacobs, V., & Empson, S. (1996). A longitudinal study of learning to use children's thinking in mathematics instruction. *Journal for Research in Mathematics Education* 27(4), 403-434.

Franke, M. L., Carpenter, T. P., Levi, L., & Fennema, E. (in press). Capturing teachers' generative change: A follow-up study of professional development in mathematics. *American Educational Research Journal.*

Franke, M. L., Fennema, E., Carpenter, T. P. (1997). Changing teachers: Interactions between beliefs and classroom practice. In E. Fennema & B. Nelson (Eds.) *Mathematics teachers in transition.* Mahwah, NJ: Lawrence Erlbaum Associates.

Franke, M. L., Fennema, E., Carpenter, T., Ansell, E., & Behrend, J. (1998). Understanding teachers' self-sustaining change in the context of professional development. *Teaching and Teaching Education, 14,* 67-80.

Kazemi, E. (1999). *Teacher learning within communities of practice: Using students' mathematical thinking to guide teacher inquiry.* Unpublished doctoral dissertation, University of California, Los Angeles.

Lave, J. (1996). Teaching, as learning, in practice. *Mind, Culture, and Activity, 3,* 149-164.

Lave, J., & Wenger, E. (1991). *Situated learning: Legitimate peripheral participation.* Cambridge, MA: Cambridge University Press.

Rogoff, B. (1994). Developing understanding of the idea of communities of learners. *Mind, Culture, & Activity, 1,* 209-229.

Rogoff, B. (1997). Evaluating development in the process of participation: Theory, methods, and practice building on each other. In E. Amsel & A. Renninger (Eds.), *Change and development: Issues of theory, application, and method* (pp. 265-285). Mahwah, NJ: Lawrence Erlbaum Associates.

Saxe, G. (1991). *Culture and cognitive development: Studies in mathematical understanding.* Hillsdale, NJ: Lawrence Erlbaum Associates.

Stein, M. K., & Brown, C. A. (1997). Teacher learning in a social context: Integrating collaborative and institutional processes with the study of teacher change. In E. Fennema & B. S. Nelson (Eds.), *Mathematics teachers in transition* (pp. 155-191). Mahwah, NJ: Lawrence Erlbaum Associates.

Tharp, R .G., & Gallimore, R. (1988). *Rousing minds to life.* New York: Cambridge University Press.

Wenger, E. (1998). *Communities of practice: Learning, meaning, and identity.* Cambridge, MA: Cambridge University Press.

Wertsch, J. V. (1991). *Voices of the mind: A sociocultural approach to mediated action.* Cambridge, MA: Harvard University Press.

Wertsch, J.V. (1998). *Mind as action.* New York: Oxford University Press.

Developing a Professional Vision of Classroom Events

Miriam Gamoran Sherin
Northwestern University

Imagine that you are standing at the site of an archeological dig. On your left, you see a large rock with a dent in the middle. Next to it you see a pile of smaller stones. Aside from this, all you see is sand. An archeologist soon appears at the site. What looked like just a rock to you, he recognizes as the base of a column; the small stones, a set of architectural fragments. And where you saw only sand, he begins to visualize the structure that stood here years before.

What is this ability to see and interpret a landscape that distinguishes the archeologist from the layman? To answer this, anthropologist Charles Goodwin introduces the term *professional vision*. According to Goodwin (1994), professional vision involves "socially organized ways of seeing and understanding events that are answerable to the distinctive interests of a particular social group," (p. 606). The idea is that, as we become part of a professional discipline, we are trained to look at and see a certain set of phenomena in a particular way. In the example just cited, the archeologist has learned to notice variations in the color, texture, and consistency of sand and to see collections of stones as possible elements of a larger structure. This then is part of the archeologist's professional vision.

Just as we say that archeologists develop professional vision, I believe that it makes sense to say that teachers develop professional vision. As teachers move from novice to expert pedagogue, they form expertise in a number of areas. For example, experienced teachers are able to implement classroom routines fluidly, and they respond flexibly when something unexpected occurs in a lesson (Berliner, 1994; Leinhardt & Greeno, 1986). Here, I examine one area of teachers' expertise, the ways in which teachers learn to interpret classroom events. For unlike the archeologist who examines stones and sand, teachers look at classrooms. It is this professional vision concerning classrooms in action that is this focus of this chapter.

In addition to teachers, there are other groups that develop professional vision of classroom events. Educational researchers are one such group. In my own experience as a researcher, over time I have learned to look for and identify various aspects of the interactions that occur during mathematics classes. This perspective has been shaped primarily by observing in and watching videotapes of mathematics classrooms, and by studying the ways that teachers' understanding of mathematics affects their own actions in these classrooms. There are of course differences between the professional vision of teachers and researchers. Geologists, archeologists, and construction workers can all look at the same site, but see very different things. The same is true of teachers and researchers. My goal in this chapter is to examine some of the components of researchers' and teachers' professional vision. In addition, I explore the possibility that a shift in teachers' professional vision toward some aspects of what researchers attend to may help to support teachers' efforts to implement mathematics education reform.

To investigate the issues surrounding teachers' and researchers' professional vision, I present two personal stories. Both of these stories concern the development of professional vision specifically with respect to mathematics classrooms. I first explore the development of my own professional vision, and describe the key experiences that shaped how I have come to interpret classroom events. The second story is that of David Louis, a mathematics teacher with whom I have been collaborating for the past 4 years. In presenting David's story, I focus on the ways in which his interpretations of classroom events have changed during our collaboration. Before concluding, I identify three factors that contribute to the development of one's professional vision of classroom events that can further help to explain some of the distinctions between teachers' and researchers' professional vision.

HOW I LEARNED TO INTERPRET CLASSROOM PRACTICE

Analysis of video had always been an important feature of my graduate training at the University of California, Berkeley. However, a central experience for me came in 1992 when I joined the Video Portfolio Project (Frederiksen, Sipusic, Sherin, & Wolfe, 1998). The goal of the Video Portfolio Project was to design a performance assessment of mathematics teaching. A key component of the assessment was a "video portfolio" consisting of a set of videotapes along with background information and brief reflections. My role was to train those who would score the video portfolios.

The basis for the training was the idea that, when watching a videotape of a classroom, one first identified *callouts*, those episodes in the video that were noteworthy. Upon identifying a callout, one catalogued it according to the aspect of classroom practice about which it was noteworthy. After months of discussion and testing, we chose four areas that we hoped captured the essence of classroom practice: management, pedagogy, mathematical thinking, and climate. The idea then was to train scorers to catalogue each callout with respect to these four categories (Frederiksen, 1992).

I began, of course, by training myself. I had been a mathematics teacher prior to coming to graduate school, and I relied heavily on those experiences in order to understand the different activities that took place within a classroom. In addition, my previous experience analyzing video as a graduate student helped me to feel comfortable using a given analytic framework to view the classroom video. I found that it soon became relatively easy to identify callouts in a video and that, for the most part, my callouts and corresponding codings agreed with those of the other researchers involved. With time, I found that I could watch a videotape of a class period in its entirety, without stopping, and identify and catalogue the callouts. In a sense, identifying callouts can be thought of as a component of professional vision of classroom events. Given the length of a class period and the variety of activities and potential highlights, deciding where to focus attention is a critical step.

The following year, I began to focus on my dissertation research, which explored the role of teachers' content knowledge in the implementation of mathematics education reform (Sherin, 1996). I decided to use observations and videotapes of mathematics classrooms to study the ways in which teachers' content knowledge influenced their practices. To do this, I applied my video portfolio training with two key changes. First, I identified new criteria for the callouts. Rather than looking for callouts in the areas of management, pedagogy, mathematical thinking, and climate, I now focused on those areas where teachers' content knowledge was likely to come into play (Leinhardt, Putnam, Stein, & Baxter, 1991). This included looking at the ideas and methods that students raised in class and how the teacher responded, the explanations given by the teacher, their choice of representation, and the teachers' responses to students' questions. Second, I did not rely exclusively on videotapes in order to analyze the classroom practice. Instead, I began to make my assessments on-line, during live classroom observations. Analysis continued after the observation, and was greatly aided by the videotape data. However, I found that I was able to identify most of the callouts during the original classroom observation.

What I want to emphasize here is that, through this process, I developed a professional vision of classroom events. I attended to specific kinds of events that occurred in the mathematics classroom and, in my case, these were events that involved the discussion of mathematical ideas. Furthermore, my professional vision was tuned not only to notice and catalogue these events as noteworthy; in addition, my goal was to interpret what the teacher or student had said and to determine what this implied about his or her understanding of mathematics.

At the same time, I began to meet regularly in video club meetings with the teachers I was observing. In these meetings, we watched and discussed excerpts of videotapes from the teachers' classrooms. Although I had originally hoped that the teachers would select the excerpts for us to watch, they felt that they did not have the time, and we decided instead that I would prepare the video excerpts for us to view together. In choosing these excerpts, I selected from those moments that I had noted already as callouts. Thus, I had essentially done part of the work of "seeing" for the teachers. Nevertheless, through our discussions I found that what the teachers noticed in these excerpts was often very different from what I had noticed. It was as if the teachers were using a different lens to interpret classroom practice (Gamoran, 1994). As a postdoctoral fellow at Stanford University, I continued my work with video clubs and explored the relationship between teachers' interpretation of video and their classroom instruction. It is in this context that I met David Louis.

DAVID LOUIS' STORY: CHANGING PERCEPTIONS OF CLASSROOM PRACTICE

My collaboration with David Louis began in January of 1996. I had just received a grant from the McDonnell Foundation to study mathematics teachers' efforts to implement the pedagogical reform Community of Learners (Brown & Campione, 1996; Shulman & Shulman, 1994). David had been teaching mathematics for 5 years, and for the previous 1 ½ years, he had been working to design and implement curricular units that he thought supported the Community of Learners principles. As part of our work together, I observed and videotaped, along with my colleague Edith Prentice Mendez, in David's classroom on a regular basis. In addition, the three of us met weekly to watch excerpts of video from David's classroom and, once a month, we participated in a video club with other mathematics teachers at David's school.

David's initial reaction to watching excerpts of video from his classroom was to question the pedagogical strategies that he had used, or failed to use. David would ask, "What could I have done here?" "How should I have responded to that question?" "What else might I have wanted to do then?" David's professional vision of classroom events focused on pedagogy, and in particular, on considering alternate pedagogical strategies that he, as the teacher, might have used.

For example, in May of 1996, David selected two video excerpts from a recent class to share with Edie and me. In this lesson, the students were using Cuisenaire Rods to create figures of different sizes that were shaped like people (Fig. 5.1). Students were asked to devise a method to find the surface area of the figure they had created. In the first video excerpt, a student, Amy, demonstrates her solution strategy for David. Amy's method involved finding the surface area of the limbs, the head, and the body, and then subtracting two for each point on the figure where two rods meet. The second excerpt came from later in the same class period. Here, David asks Amy to share her method with the class. Amy gives a brief explanation of her strategy, asks for questions from the class, but receives none. David then calls on the next presenter.

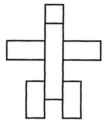

FIG. 5.1. The figure Amy had created out of Cuisenaire Rods.

In our meeting, David explained that he was frustrated because he believed that he had let a "teachable moment" slip away in not promoting discussion of Amy's method. He asked "What could I have done at that point to maybe start some discussion on what she did and why that was useful?" David suggested that perhaps he should have pointed out to the class that Amy's method of dealing with the contact points would work for any number of contact points. David also wondered how he might have used Amy's method as a way of moving the class from an arithmetic representation of surface area to one that was more algebraic. In addition, David was concerned because he felt that, as the teacher, he needed to provide guidance for those students who would be presenting their work in class. David wondered how he might do this more effectively.

A few weeks later, David chose this lesson as the topic for a narrative case that he was asked to write. In the case, he explains

> This situation created many questions for me. How could I have helped Amy better explain her method? What could I have done to assess and possibly enhance [the students'] understanding? I was excited earlier in the class because Amy's solution seemed as though it could develop into a "teachable moment." . . . It often depends on the teacher, though, to facilitate a discussion about the students' ideas and the mathematical content. (Louis, 1996a, p. 3)

This example illustrates the ways in which David's professional vision of classroom events emphasized the role that the teacher played in orchestrating classroom interactions. During instruction, David was constantly weighing a variety of options for the teacher, and he brought this perspective to viewing video of classrooms as well. In particular, when David looked at a video, he noticed what the teacher was or was not doing and considered what the teacher might have done. I found that this focus on pedagogy when watching video was not unique to David. The other teachers participating in the video club had similar tendencies and often offered suggestions concerning what the teacher in the video might have done.

A Shift in Professional Vision

This focus on alternate pedagogical strategies was quite different from the usual stance I took in looking at classroom video. I tended to focus on interpreting the mathematical ideas that arose in class, while David seemed more focused on considering what action he should have taken in the given situation. Part of this difference, I believe, came from our two different points of view; David, as a teacher, was naturally concerned with what the teacher should do, while I, as a researcher, had the luxury to concentrate (sometimes at great length) on interpretation rather than on action.

Yet, it seemed to me that a focus on interpretation might also be valuable for David. In implementing the Community of Learners pedagogy, David had begun to open up his classes to mathematical discourse, and in particular to discussion and comparison of the ideas that students raised (Sherin, Mendez, & Louis, 2000). One of David's primary roles then, was to interpret the students' ideas as they came up in class and to help the class as a whole understand and build on these ideas. I hypothesized that because David's attention when watching video was immediately drawn to pedagogical issues, he was unlikely to engage in a detailed examination of what had happened in the class and why this had happened. Therefore, I encouraged David to shift away from this focus on pedagogy and on *what might have happened* and move toward the goal of trying to make sense of *what did happen*. As a result, David began to analyze video in new ways, focusing on what were for him different aspects of classroom interaction. In particular, rather than focusing on the teaching that was evident, two other issues became central to David's analysis of video. He began to closely examine the student ideas that arose as well as to consider the mathematics that was discussed.

This new perspective can be seen in the following example from the September, 1996, video club. At this meeting, David and two other teachers from his school, Ron Martin and John Yee, watched an excerpt from Ron's classroom. Ron had recently joined the video club and was enthusiastic about sharing an excerpt from his classroom at the meeting. In the video, two students are talking with Ron about an assignment in which they are supposed to interpret the graph of a swim race. The graph represents the position of three swimmers with respect to the time elapsed (Fig. 5.2). The students are discussing the first question given in the assignment: "Who jumps out of the blocks the fastest?" "The slowest?" The two students quickly agree that swimmer B jumps out of the blocks the slowest. However, the students are unclear as to whether swimmer A or swimmer C jumps out the fastest and they discuss this with the teacher.

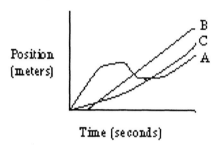

FIG. 5.2. The swim race: Who jumps out of the blocks the fastest? The slowest?

Jason: The slowest is C.

Barry: Yes C.

Jason: No, it's not. It's B. He jumps off after a couple of seconds.

Barry: Oh yeah.

Jason: I have a question.

Barry: The slowest is B.

Jason: Mr. Martin . . . his guy obviously jumps off the slowest because he is here (indicating swimmer B's position). These guys (pointing to swimmers A and C), don't they jump off basically at the same time?

Mr. Martin: Yes, when the race starts.

Jason: But why does it say the slowest and fastest? The slowest is this guy. But the fastest are both of them. Because even though this one is going faster . . .

Mr. Martin: I want, (pause) hold on.

Jason: But this one is going faster in the water. They both jump off at the same time.

Mr. Martin: Okay, so then say that.

No longer focused solely on pedagogy, David's initial response to the video concerns the content of Jason's comment. "That's a good point, that's a really good point. This (pointing to the graph) is their swim time." David is highlighting a contrast that he sees between the question asked in the assignment and the question that the students are trying to answer. David suggests that the assignment intends for the students to identify which swimmer has the fastest and which swimmer has the slowest initial speed. But, he claims that the students are trying to figure out which swimmer has the quickest reaction time. Furthermore, David argues that the swimmers' reaction time cannot be determined from the given graph. Ron and John disagree with David's claim. They point out that time elapsed is represented on the graph in seconds, therefore swimmer A can be considered as having the fastest reaction time.

After this initial discussion of mathematics and of the students' ideas, Ron turns the group's attention toward pedagogical issues and asks about his own interaction with the two students. Ron explains that he wanted the students to discuss the issue of initial speed among themselves. Ron knew that he did not want to answer their questions directly, yet at the same time, he was unsure of how to facilitate a discussion among the students. This was Ron's first video club meeting, and his comments are reminiscent of the types of questions and issues that David had raised in the past. In contrast, David's response to Ron at this point indicates a very different perspective. Rather than responding to Ron's pedagogical concerns, David continues to pursue a discussion of student ideas. Because the group had not yet come to consensus concerning the meaning of Jason's comment, David wished to investigate this further, and he asked the group to watch the video excerpt once again with this in mind.

David's response illustrates the depth to which he had begun to value understanding of what had happened during a small segment of classroom interaction that he watched on video. Much like a researcher, David tried to piece together comments from the video into a coherent story about what had occurred. Furthermore, David did this with a particular goal in mind, making sense of student ideas that appeared on video as well as the mathematics under discussion. Although it is possible that David was more interested in focusing on student thinking than on pedagogy because the excerpt came from Ron's classroom instead of David's own, additional data show that this is not the case. In looking across the video club data, it is clear that David's primary interest was no longer on pedagogy—whether or not he was the teacher being viewed. In its place, David had become comfortable looking closely at excerpts of video to try to understand what had occurred, to find the meaning in students' comments, and to understand the mathematics that had been discussed.

Over time, David himself became quite aware of this shift in his professional vision of classroom video. In the spring of 1998, he wrote a summary of our collaboration up to that point. On his own initiative, David discussed this change in perspective as a critical part of his experience.

> When I first started reviewing video, my perspective was "How could I have done that differently?" or "What could I do next time to make that a better lesson?" With this lens, I had difficulty understanding the mathematics, the interactions among the students and between me and the students. My colleagues taught me to view the tapes with a different lens. They taught me to separate myself as teacher from myself as viewer. They taught me to try to understand the mathematics and the interactions because that is what was interesting (Louis, 1998, p. 8).

I claim that this new stance on interpreting video of classroom events reflects an important element of a researcher's approach—an orientation toward viewing video as an observer rather than from the perspective of one who must act on what is seen. Furthermore, within this perspective, David was being analytic about specific issues that are of great importance today in mathematics education research. To be clear, I do not mean to imply that teachers' professional vision is any less professional or less analytic than researchers' professional vision. On the contrary, teachers' standard focus on pedagogy can be quite analytical—it is just that the categories of this analysis differ between researchers and teachers. Then why encourage David Louis to take on the perspective of a researcher when watching video? Why not let teachers be teachers and researchers be researchers, each analytic in their own way? In the next section, I try to answer these questions by showing that this shift in professional vision with respect to video influenced David's teaching practice in valuable ways.

Impact on David's Teaching

Thus far, I have illustrated a shift in David's professional vision of classroom events by describing new ways that David began to look at video. However, this shift in professional vision was not limited to David's reaction to watching videotapes of classrooms. David also began to look at classroom events somewhat differently during his own teaching. In particular, as he had done with video, David now began to look more closely at the mathematics and at the student ideas that arose during instruction. In doing so, David developed new teaching practices that aligned with a central goal of recent mathematics education reform efforts.

When asked how his experience in the video club had influenced his teaching, David offered two examples. First, David explained that in the video club, he began to focus in a detailed manner on the ideas and comments that students raised. Somewhat surprising to him, David found that this new focus on student thinking also permeated his classroom instruction. Specifically, David said that he spent more time during instruction trying to understand the flow of ideas in the classroom. For example, in some instances, David slowed down the pace of whole-class discussions so that he could follow the different ideas that came up and could decide how to proceed with the lesson. In addition, he implemented several new instructional strategies including asking probing questions, rephrasing students' ideas, and introducing graphical or pictorial representations in order to make sense of and elaborate on student thinking. This emphasis on understanding the ideas that students offer is one of the hallmarks of mathematics education reform. In David's case, he first learned to engage in such analysis via video, yet he soon came to apply this perspective in his teaching as well.

> Here's what [the video club has] done for me . . . it's enabled me to consciously, really listen and to try to understand what students are saying. Cause so often I find myself...almost saying something before a student's even done. I'm not even listening to what they're saying. And so it's helped me to slow down my own thinking and the classroom discussion, so I feel like the kids are actually listening to other kids, and I'm actually listening to what they're saying and responding to what they're saying, not to what I want to respond to . . . I think it's helped . . . to make me more aware of the specific things that are being said in discussions.

Second, David explained that he had developed a somewhat different technique for reflecting on his teaching. When watching video, David was often drawn to particular moments within the video that seemed to require analysis. He later found himself doing the same during instruction. For instance, while teaching, David would identify what was essentially a callout, a noteworthy moment of instruction that he planned to reflect on further after the lesson. David kept a journal in which he would write about these moments, and he found that doing so helped him to learn even more about his students' thinking.

For example, one day in November of 1996, David and his students were exploring the relationship between fractions and ratios. A student suggested that "you could build $\frac{2}{5}$ into $\frac{4}{10}$" because if you "divided $\frac{4}{10}$ by 2, it was the same as $\frac{2}{5}$." David understood that one actually needed to divide $\frac{4}{10}$ by 1, which could be represented as $\frac{2}{2}$, in order to reduce $\frac{4}{10}$ into the fraction $\frac{2}{5}$. Therefore, he asked the class, "Is this dividing by 2?" The students then engaged in a lively discussion of the relationship between the fractions $\frac{2}{5}$ and $\frac{4}{10}$. In writing about the discussion after class, David reflected on what the students understood about the mathematics involved. In addition, he considered why they held certain beliefs and how their experiences with mathematics thus far might have influenced their understanding of simplifying fractions.

> I don't think any of them had any idea that it was dividing the ratio by a form of one, $\frac{2}{2}$. Why should they? Their use of simplifying so far this year has been to reduce the ratio of a . . . geometric figure, [and to create a new geometric figure with the same shape but] a smaller size. Simplifying the ratio would actually [involve] dividing each of the two lengths by the same number . . . so they would see it as two division problems . . . Julie even commented that it doesn't make sense to divide the number by one. She said that if you divided it by one, then you would not actually be changing the value at all. The reason she said this, I'm hypothesizing, is that it seems like dividing by one, would not change the size of the [geometric figure]. (Louis, 1996b, p. 6)

This example illustrates how David had begun to use what he recognized during instruction as a callout as the basis for reflection and analysis after instruction. Furthermore, his reflection is again focused on understanding and interpreting the student ideas and the mathematics that were discussed during class.

In sum, although the shift in David's professional vision of classroom events began in the context of watching videotapes, David also developed a new way of "seeing" classroom practice during instruction. Rather than focusing exclusively on the teacher's role, David spent time during class trying to understand students' comments and ideas about the mathematics under discussion. In addition, an important part of reflecting on his teaching came to involve writing about critical moments of instruction, trying further to make sense of what had happened and why.

Over the last 10 years, those involved in mathematics education reform have come to recognize the critical role that teachers play in the implementation of reform and that, for many teachers, implementing reform involves making changes in their teaching practices. As a result, mathematics educators have been exploring a variety ways to help teachers make these changes and move toward mathematics teaching that is based on the goals of reform. I claim that for David Louis, the process described in this chapter provided that support. As David came to interpret classroom events in new ways, his teaching changed as well. In particular, David developed teaching practices designed to support a key aspect of mathematics education reform—a classroom in which student ideas are at the center.

ISSUES IN THE ANALYSIS OF PROFESSIONAL VISION

In the stories that I have presented, I contrast the professional vision of a researcher with that of a teacher. However, I believe that it would be a mistake to limit ourselves to such a simple characterization of the issues involved here. As a first step toward exploring this more deeply, I introduce three factors that contribute to the development of professional vision of classroom events: (1) our role in the classroom, (2) the medium through which we observe a class, and (3) the strategies we use to interpret the practice.

Interpreter's Role in the Classroom

One's role in the classroom clearly influences one's perspective on classroom practice. For example, as shown here and as documented by other research (Copeland, Birmingham, D'Emidio-Caston, & Natal, 1994), teachers tend to respond to instances of classroom interactions in terms of pedagogy. And this makes sense—a teacher's job is to make pedagogical decisions, hence the focus on pedagogy. Similarly, we would expect a curriculum designer working on revisions to have a particular focus and an administrator evaluating a teacher to have a different focus. Each of these people comes to the classroom with his or her own professional identity and related to this, his or her own understanding of the key features of classroom practice. My point here is that our professional vision is tuned to helping us perform the tasks that we do.

Medium Through Which Classroom is Interpreted

A second key influence on our professional vision is the medium through which a classroom is viewed. Clearly, observing a class live is different from watching it on video or reading a written transcript of the lesson. These media present the viewer with different kinds of information and therefore focus the viewer's attention in different ways. For instance, when observing a classroom live, one can decide where and how to pay attention to the variety of activities taking place. In contrast, a viewer cannot change what is presented on a video of a classroom—if a student's initial comment is of interest, but the student then moves "off camera," there is nothing the viewer can do but to look elsewhere on the video. Similarly, a transcript can provide the viewer with the comments of all participants, but other key contextual features of the interaction may not be available. It is interesting to note that, in some cases, a video of a classroom can provide access to conversations that would otherwise be inaccessible to an observer. Through of the use of a wireless microphone, a videotape can capture conversations that the teacher has with individual or groups of students even when they are not in earshot. And although there is no way to observe two groups simultaneously using multiple cameras, video can record the work of more than one group of students on the same activity.

Another important medium I want to consider is teaching. I claim that not only does a teacher have a specific job to do in the classroom (this has just been mentioned above in discussing the interpreter's role), but in addition the act of teaching provides its own set of cues for interpreting classroom practice. Thus, while both observing and teaching are live, I find that the information one receives as a teacher is very different from the information presented to a classroom observer. For example, in interpreting classroom events, a teacher takes into account a great deal of background information about the students, the lesson, and the school. An observer would simply be unaware of much of this. In sum, different media such as observing, teaching, and viewing video affect what one sees and hears and, as a result, where one focuses attention in the classroom.

Strategies for Interpretation

The third factor I want to introduce concerns the strategies we use to focus our interpretation. For example, consider the following two such strategies. We can begin by identifying callouts, and can then identify the aspect of classroom practice for which the callout is noteworthy. In this case, we may find that two people identify the same callout, but for different reasons. In contrast, a second strategy would be to first narrow the lens through which we plan to view the classroom practice. It is then through this lens that we would identify callouts. Thus, if your purpose is to catalog student conceptions, then that is precisely what you look for.

So how do these three factors help us to untangle the differences between the professional vision of teachers and researchers? First, consider the interpreter's role. A teacher's role in a classroom is very different from the role of a researcher and our professional vision will reflect this. In other words, because teachers and researchers have set out to do different jobs, they inevitably pay attention to different things in the classroom. Second, the medium of interpretation is an issue. Professional vision in relation to video is simply not the same as professional vision in relation to teaching. And in general, researchers' professional vision is for observing and for watching video, whereas teachers' professional vision is for teaching. Therefore, researchers' and teachers' professional vision are by their nature two very different perspectives.[1] With respect to the third factor, interpretation strategy, there are also distinctions worth noting. For example, researchers often choose a specific focus for their examination and then look for callouts within that area. In contrast, teachers tend to look at classroom practice on a broader scale, keeping track of multiple issues and decisions at the same time and assessing classroom practice as a whole.

Thus far, I have discussed each of these three factors individually. Yet I do not mean to imply that they are distinct influences on our

---

[1] There are a growing number of cases in which the teacher acts as both teacher and researcher (for example, see Ball, 1993; Heaton, 1994; and Lampert, 1989). It would be interesting to explore the ways such teacher researchers use different media to interpret classroom practice and how their interpretations differ in these varied contexts.

professional vision. Much the opposite, these three factors most likely interact throughout the development of one's professional vision. For example, it is partly because teachers interpret classroom practice through the medium of teaching that they tend to adopt a particular focus and strategy. Nevertheless, I have considered them separately up to this point in order to highlight some of their distinct contributions to one's professional vision.

Before concluding this section, I want to review the story of David Louis in light of the three factors that I have introduced here. I believe that doing so can provide further insight concerning why and how David's professional vision was transformed. In particular, I claim that the medium of interpretation played a significant role in the initial change that occurred in David's perspective. Watching video prompted David to both take on a new role for himself and to use a different kind of interpretation strategy.

When David began to view classroom practice via video, it was not only the medium of interpretation that changed. David also accepted a new role for himself in this context—the role of an observer. In a conversation with a fellow teacher, David explained that when he watched video of his own classroom, he felt much more like an observer than a teacher. He simply did not need to respond to the video in the ways that he was used to doing as teacher. In particular, when teaching, David needed to attend simultaneously to multiple aspects of classroom practice. In contrast, when watching video, David was able (and willing) to take a much narrower view of classroom interactions, and, for example, to disregard management issues. As an observer, David felt more in control of which issues he choose to explore.

In addition to adopting a different role for himself, David also developed a new interpretation strategy. Again, I claim that video was a key factor here. Video simply lends itself to a different kind of analysis than is possible during teaching. In David's case, he began to recognize moments of instruction that appeared on video that he did not fully understand.

In addition, he found that he could use the video as a resource in pursuing an investigation of what had happened. This shift in interpretation strategy went hand in hand with David's new focus on student thinking and mathematics. Being more of an observer and having video as a resource allowed David to explore new avenues for interpreting classroom practice.

What I find particularly interesting in David's story is that this shift in perspective affected not only the way in which David viewed video of classroom practice, but also affected his teaching. Thus, even when he returned to his standard medium for interpreting classroom practice—the classroom, he brought with him this new interpretation strategy. And in addition, he maintained part of the stance that he had acquired as an observer of classroom practice. David began to mold his instruction and his interactions within the classroom so that they supported this new professional vision. Examples include "slowing down discussion" and taking time to "understand students' ideas." David also brought the notion of callouts to his teaching; he began to notice, while teaching, moments of instruction that he found interesting and wanted to consider further after class.

CONCLUSIONS

In this chapter, I argued that both teachers and researchers develop professional vision of classroom events. In particular, we examined the case of one teacher, David Louis, who moved from an initial emphasis on pedagogy to a more critical stance toward student thinking. I claimed that in making this shift in perspective, David turned toward some aspects of what researchers typically attend to, and perhaps beyond the standard trajectory of most teachers' professional vision.[2]

I want to be clear, however, that I do not mean to dismiss teachers' focus on pedagogy as unimportant or not valuable. Thus, my point is not that David's initial focus on pedagogy was any less valid than his later focus on student thinking, nor am I suggesting that our goal should be to encourage teachers to stop thinking in terms of pedagogy.

Instead, I offer David's story as one possible trajectory in the development of teachers' professional vision of classroom events. Moreover, this was a trajectory that David believed contributed positively to his teaching and that aided his efforts to implement mathematics education reform. I claim that profitable changes can occur in teachers' practices when they see as their goal the

---

[2] It may also be the case that participating in video clubs with teachers influences the trajectory of researchers' professional vision of classroom events. In other work, I describe how the complementary character of the expertise brought by the teachers and the researcher in a video club influenced the ways that all participants learned to interpret classroom videos (Gamoran, 1994).

understanding of classroom practice as it unfolds. Furthermore, I find that reflecting on video can be a key catalyst in supporting the development of teachers' professional vision in this area.

Finally, I want to make one strong claim about video clubs: I believe that when teachers look at video, as in video clubs, it is essential that they learn to adopt a focus on interpretation before commenting on pedagogy. That is, before exploring pedagogical alternatives, teachers should examine what has happened, what student ideas arose, where the class is making progress, and what difficulties have come up. It is this shift in perspective then, in professional vision, that teachers carry back to their classrooms, and that affects the stance through which they interpret mathematics teaching and learning.

ACKNOWLEDGMENTS

The research reported in this paper was conducted under a grant from the Andrew W. Mellon Foundation to Stanford University and WestEd and by a postdoctoral fellowship from the James S. McDonnell Foundation. The author would like to thank Barbara Scott Nelson, Alan Schoenfeld, and Bruce Sherin for their thoughtful comments on this manuscript.

REFERENCES

Ball, D. L. (1993). With an eye on the mathematical horizon: Dilemmas of teaching elementary school mathematics. *Elementary School Journal, 93,* 373-397.

Berliner, D. C. (1994). Expertise: The wonder of exemplary performances. In J. M. Mangier & C. C. Block (Eds.), *Creating powerful thinking in teachers and students: Diverse perspectives* (pp. 161-186). Fort Worth, TX: Holt, Reinhart & Winston.

Brown, A. L., & Campione, J. C. (1996). Psychological learning theory and the design of innovative environments: On procedures, principles, and systems. In L. Schauble & R. Glaser (Eds.), *Contributions of instructional innovation to understanding learning.* Hillsdale, NJ: Lawrence Erlbaum Associates.

Copeland, W., Birmingham, L. D., D'Emidio-Caston, M., & Natal, D. (1994). Making meaning in classrooms: An investigation of cognitive processes in aspiring teachers and their peers. *American Educational Research Journal, 31,* 166-196.

Frederiksen, J. R. (1992, April). *Scoring video portfolios.* Paper presented at the annual meeting of the American Educational Research Association, San Francisco.

Frederiksen, J. R., Sipusic, M., Sherin, M. G., & Wolfe, E. (1998). Video portfolio assessment: Creating a framework for viewing the functions of teaching. *Educational Assessment, 5 (4),* 225-297.

Gamoran, M. (1994, April). *Informing researchers and teachers through video clubs.* Paper presented at the annual meeting of the American Educational Research Association, New Orleans, LA.

Goodwin, C. (1994). Professional vision. *American Anthropologist, 96,* 606-633.

Hammer, D. (1999). *Teacher inquiry.* Newton, MA: Center for the Development of Teaching, Education Development Center, Inc.

Heaton, R. M. (1994). *Creating and studying a practice of teaching: Elementary mathematics for understanding.* Unpublished doctoral dissertation, Michigan State University, Lansing.

Lampert, M. (1989). Choosing and using mathematical tools in classroom discourse. In J. Brophy (Ed.), *Advances in research on teaching* (pp. 223-264). Greenwich, CT: JAI Press.

Leinhardt, G., & Greeno, J. G. (1986). The cognitive skill of teaching. *Journal of Educational Psychology, 78,* 75-95.

Leinhardt, G., Putnam, R. T., Stein, M. K., & Baxter, J. (1991). Where subject knowledge matters. In J. Brophy (Ed.), *Advances in research on teaching: Vol. 2* (pp. 87-113). Greenwich, CT: JAI Press.

Louis, D. A. (1996a, July). *Amy's baby: A case study.* Paper presented at the FCTL Case Writing Conference, Stanford University.

Louis, D. A. (1996b). *Reflections on building a community of learners in a mathematics class: A teacher's journal.* Unpublished manuscript, Stanford University.

Louis, D. A. (1998). *Understanding communities of learners in a mathematics classroom: Summary report to the Spencer Foundation.* Unpublished manuscript.

Sherin, M. G. (1996). *The nature and dynamics of teachers' content knowledge.* Unpublished doctoral dissertation, University of California, Berkeley.

Sherin, M. G., Mendez, E. P., & Louis, D. A. (2000). Talking about math talk. In M. Burke (Ed.), *Learning mathematics for a new century, 2000 Yearbook of the NCTM* (pp.188-196). Reston, VA: National Council of Teachers of Mathematics.

Shulman, L. S., & Shulman, J. H. (1994). *Fostering a community of teachers: A proposal submitted to the Andrew W. Mellon Foundation.* Unpublished manuscript, Stanford University.

Commentary 1

Questions and Issues

Barbara Jaworski
University of Oxford

In response to the first set of papers at the conference at Purdue many questions and issues emerged. These questions were recorded for addressing as part of this book. It is my task to address these questions. There are four questions to be addressed in this section.

1. What is the relationship between teaching and learning? Can/should we separate the study of teaching from the study of learning?

In chapter 4, Miriam Sherin speaks of the shift made by the teacher, David Louis, from a focus on pedagogical issues to one on students' learning. She claims that this shift was highly significant in David's development of teaching. In chapters 3 and 4, Megan Franke and Elham Kazemi and Tom Carpenter, Ellen Ansell, and Linda Levi speak of teaching and learning within an extended Cognitively Guided Instruction (CGI) project. Here, teachers are encouraged to analyze students' learning and to reflect on their own understandings of learning in devising a teaching approach.

These, very brief, characterizations of the teaching–learning relationship, as I see it, from the chapters in Part I, carry with them a commonality in linking teaching and learning. Briefly, the relationship suggested is that effective teaching derives from a sustained and in-depth focus on the mathematical learning of students. However, as we delve more deeply into these constructs, we recognize a complexity that deserves unpacking.

In the CGI Project, teachers study and analyze learning episodes from classrooms at the same levels as those in which they themselves teach. These episodes are concerned with students' learning of mathematics at the relevant level. From such study *outside* the classroom, teachers go on to analyze episodes from their *own* classrooms where the teaching has been organized according to the CGI approach. In Chapters 3 and 4, we are given examples of students working on early arithmetic relationships involving operations of addition, subtraction, multiplication, and division. Teachers provide problems on which students will work together, but do not prescribe the methods by which the problems will be solved. Students are encouraged to devise their own problem-solving methods, using a variety of materials as they wish, and to discuss, challenge, and justify their methods. Teachers analyze videotapes arising from the children's work, and become skilled in recognizing elements of mathematical skill, learning, and understanding. Such recognition feeds back into teaching situations, allowing teachers to recognize learning as it occurs and to ask suitable guiding or probing questions. The process thus includes the following elements, not necessarily in linear progression, although roughly so:

1. Examples of students' dialogue;
2. study and analysis by teachers;
3. teachers' construction of learning situations;
4. students tackling problems (recorded and transcribed);
5. teacher facilitation of students' problem solving;
6. teacher study of student videotapes.

Activity in Stage 6 in this progression is similar to that in Stage 1 and 2, except that teachers now have considerably more experience of the processes and strategies that students are using, having experienced these first hand in their own classrooms. As Stage 6 feeds back to a new cycle at Stage 3, teachers develop awareness of their study of students' mathematical ideas and this guides their constructions of teaching. The process might now be seen as cyclic and dialectical:

 Teachers' study of episodes from
students' mathematical learning
Teachers construction of
classroom situations

It becomes dialectical when either of these states causes a flip into the other state, which is an ultimate aim of the process. Thus, in studying a student's response in the classroom the teacher's design of activity is challenged requiring instant modification, and further study of students' responses. This design of activities based on analysis and interpretation of students' ideas, is what Franke calls "generative" teaching, and it seems to be this learning cycle for teachers that forms the basis of generativity.

Although at a different level of mathematical learning for the students concerned, Sherin's description of David Louis's learning fits this same cycle. As Sherin describes, once the teacher was persuaded to focus on his students' ideas rather than immediately on his own teaching decisions, his own knowledge and awareness grew and his teaching developed. The *essence* of the model of teacher learning in these examples is that it is based on a study of students' ideas and attempting to understand their meaning. Whether we can or should separate the two is not an issue, given this basic premise. However, this is not to suggest there are not other models for studying teaching, or for developing teaching. These concerns will be taken up in later sections.

2. Unpacking--What we mean by "paying attention to children's learning."
What are we paying attention to? What is involved? Why pay attention?

These questions take us into the processes just discussed above at a finer level of detail. In both CGI classrooms and the classroom of David Louis, certain mathematics concepts and processes are under negotiation: those of basic arithmetic in the former, and interpretation of graphs in the latter. What we seem to be paying attention to is the dialogue of the students in tackling the problems posed by the teachers. So, for example, we read the dialogue between Jason, Barry and Mr. Martin (Sherin p. 82), which provides insights into Jason and Barry's perceptions of the graph and the mathematical concepts underlying their interpretation of the graph. In Carpenter, Ansell, and Levi's chapter, we read a dialogue between Kim, Peter, Ms. Keith, and other students. This provides insights into students' methods of subtracting 4 from 27.

So, one focus is the mathematics, and teachers have to "know" this mathematics sufficiently well to be able to interpret their students' perceptions of this mathematics and to judge appropriate teaching responses. Issues of mathematical knowledge will be addressed in the next section.

In reading the transcripts or analyzing videotapes, teachers have to recognize and analyze students' mathematical engagement in order to judge their understanding. In the Carpenter, Ansell, and Levi transcript, Kim describes how she used the cubes to find $27 - 4$. Ms. Keith's questions guide her explanation, but not her process. The articulation of her process allows insight into her structuring of the problem: first her composition of 27 through 2 tens and 7 units; her removal then of 4 units from the 7; her subsequent counting of 2 tens and 3 units. From this articulation, the teacher might judge Kim's capability of answering subtraction questions more generally, and also the sophistication and generaliztability of Kim's method. Such judgments inform the teacher to allow appropriate decisions to be made regarding what problems it might be valuable for Kim to tackle next. Thus, teachers' insights into the meanings students' hold, strategies, or structuring lead potentially to more effective teaching decisions — the cycle we just indicated.

In Sherin's example, the students' focus on reaction times rather than on the speed of reaction was informative for the teacher. It was clear here that the mathematical concepts involved were more complex than had been initially recognized; also that interpretation of the graph could lead to extremely valuable questioning of concepts and critical attention to the language used. Potentially, as a result of the discussion of the graph and the study of the transcript, the teacher could devise further questions to address the required concepts. The open nature of the situation, in which students were encouraged to offer their own perspectives and articulations of the problem proved informative at both mathematical and pedagogical levels.

3. Tensions between: educators knowledge of learning; wider societal expectations; curriculum driven classrooms; open problem-solving classrooms.

In the CGI classrooms, there is an overt development of norms for classroom interaction based on expectations of open problem solving and minimal teacher direction. Such norms do not develop overnight. They take time to establish in the classroom, and, moreover, considerable time to be established in the consciousness of teachers who have previously worked in more traditional ways. The CGI project encourages the developing awareness of teachers through its emphasis on a study of children's learning.

Here we see educators' knowledge being translated into activity for teachers through which teachers' learning is manifested. The CGI literature testifies to the success of the processes involved through its reporting on teachers' learning in the project. As teachers' awareness grows, so their ability to transform theoretical ideas into practical ways of working with students develops. In the Carpenter, Ansell, and Levi transcript, we see evidence of Ms. Keith's skills in developing classroom norms. For example, she says to the class "Are we going to just let her give the answer?" and "What are we going to say to her?" Such questions seem designed to develop approaches that require questions and explanations of students to and from students. Such questioning and explanation is part of the developed classroom norms for these classrooms. Later in the dialogue, Ms. Keith asks "How did you count?" and then, "You didn't use your tens?" We assume she knew that Kim had indeed used her tens, but her words indicated to Kim and others the level of detail required in articulation. Thus Ms. Keith developed norms of explanation and the degree of detail necessary to explain clearly.

Here we see norms being established for the implementation of researchers' theories for effective classroom teaching of mathematics. How does this fit with the requirements of curriculum-driven classrooms or with societal expectations of mathematical learning in classrooms? I am reminded here of the work of Cobb, Wood and Yackel (Wood, Cobb, Yackel, and Dillon, 1993) in which they developed classroom norms that seemed similar to those just mentioned, but were very different to those expected by parents and other members of the community in which the school was based. The project was seriously challenged by those external agencies and their criticisms had to be faced. What seems essential is to be able to convince the wider community that the methods valued by educators achieve societal goals and more. This means that students should be seen to have achieved basic skills and to do well in national and international tests. These issues will be addressed further after Section 3 papers.

Where such achievements are not evident, for whatever reason, it is likely that researchers' theories take the blame. In the United Kingdom, we saw a serious backlash in the 1980s against child-centered methods developed since the 1960s. The Plowden Report (1967) advocated a child-centered pedagogy based on Piagetian principles. This led to a movement of so-called "progressive" education, particularly in primary schools. Children were encouraged to participate in open activities, to be creative and to develop at their own rate, an educational model not well understood by the wider community, and certainly not gaining its approval. When, subsequently, a significant percentage of children were seen not to have achieved basic skills in literacy and numeracy, this was blamed on progressive teaching and a "back-to-basics" movement followed, led by the government of the day.

One problem with progressive teaching was that it was ill-defined. Teachers were encouraged to engage children in creative activity, but the goals of such activities were not always clear and it was far from evident how children would achieve understanding of curriculum concepts. Indeed, the curriculum was itself left to schools to define. History shows us that this position, well meaning though it was, was far from satisfactory, and that clearer curriculum objectives and ways of achieving them are necessary for schools and teachers. In the United Kingdom, this had led to statutory National Curricula, both for schools and for teacher education, with rigorous national testing. It means that educators' theories for effective teaching are now required to meet these statutory demands or be discredited.

What is perhaps necessary is that educators should see the statutory demands as minimum levels of achievement. If teaching is designed to achieve conceptual understanding of mathematical concepts, this should be demonstrated, at the very least, by children being able to do well in tests at all levels. The problem arises when curriculum and testing are too demanding, and teachers resort to teaching "to the test." Unfortunately, even for conscientious teachers, this is a serious danger, especially where the bureaucracy of curriculum and testing places severe constraints on teachers' time and energy.

Teachers, required by law (or society) to deliver a curriculum, must be convinced that the methods and processes they use will "deliver" the outcomes required. The teaching approaches discussed in this section of the book are time consuming, at least in their initial stages. They are also demanding of teachers' intellectual and physical energy. This means that they have to be super-convincing to the teachers who will use them.

4. What is teaching? Generative Teaching? Standards? How does teaching relate to visions of learning? Where and how do we learn about teaching?

Traditionally, teaching has often been seen as a form of "direct instruction" (Romberg & Carpenter, 1986). Direct instruction is teaching-led. It can be rooted firmly in curriculum and delivered to students by exposition and explanation. The responsibility of the teacher is to deliver well, and it is the responsibility of the student to learn. The teaching seen in the just cited examples is very different. It is the responsibility of the teacher to create an environment of opportunity for learning. This is not a *laissez-faire* approach, but a very rigorously designed methodology. The rigor lies in clear educational principles, associated, well-defined, methods, and clear goals. Students' conceptual understanding is the required outcome and teachers have to be able to recognize and foster such understanding.

The methodology needs to be consistent at all levels of learning. Thus, the ways educators work with teachers must be philosophically compatible with educators expectations for the classroom. The chapter written by Megan Franke and Elham Kazemi demonstrates how this might be achieved through what the CGI team calls generative teaching, requiring detailed knowledge, rich in structure and connections, and owned by the learners who create it, adapt it, or both.

For teachers, this knowledge is both mathematical and pedagogic. Although little is said in these papers about teachers' mathematical knowledge, it seems evident that the pedagogic principles cannot be successful without a satisfactory mathematical grounding. Teachers must be able to understand themselves the concepts on which they work with students, and, ideally, be able to fit these concepts into a wider mathematical framework. This will be taken further in the next section. The pedagogic principles are based in a requirement for teachers to explore their students' understanding through close observation and analysis of the students' responses to problem-solving tasks. Thus teachers are required to engage in research activity into the learning of the students they teach. Inquiry on the part of teachers has been shown to be a powerful force for the development of teaching (Jaworski, 1994, 1998), and we certainly see this in the teaching Franke describes. For example, Ms. Andrew "wanted to know more than just the surface features of whether the students got a correct answer, drew a picture, or did it in their heads" (p. 50). And Ms. Baker declares, "every time you interact with a child you're gaining knowledge of how to interact with other children" (p. 53). Such statements testify to these teachers' engagement in an inquiry process, and to the knowledge that they gain overtly from it.

For students, the detailed knowledge, rich in structure and connections, is mathematical knowledge. The pedagogic approach to students' learning requires students to explore for themselves the relationships in mathematical processes and objects deriving from problems provided by their teacher. The classroom approach, requiring mathematical activity, discussion, negotiation, and justification by students, is designed to create this mathematical knowledge. If indeed this is detailed, structured, and connected knowledge, rather than merely a superficial memorization or rote application of given algorithms, then the students should be able to apply this knowledge successfully in a variety of activities, including national tests. Students should achieve both the NCTM Standards, requiring rigorous conceptual understanding, and societal visions of learning based on basic skills.

However, lest the enterprise take on a simplistic clinical patina, let us recognize the complexity and challenge of the teaching task. We need only return to the referred to Sherin example to perceive this complexity. Here the mathematics to be understood involved not only an appreciation of how to interpret a graph such as the one given, but also an appreciation of relationships between speed, distance, and time, and their graphical representation. Mathematically speaking, these are sophisticated concepts. The graph problem seems designed to encourage students' exploration in the area of these concepts in order to develop ownership and, ultimately, understanding. In designing the task, I suggest the teacher had in mind particular images of these concepts that the problem was designed to address. Students' freedom of activity in exploring the problem and subsequent discussion led to a realization by the teacher of alternative images of the meaning of the graph. Students did not seem to reach the expected understandings, although the alternatives were valuable stepping stones toward their conceptual development. Perceiving the students' alternative images also enriched the teachers' understanding, both mathematically and pedagogically. Further problems would be required for students to reach towards firm connections and structures that would indicate a fuller conceptual understanding. At these levels of mathematical complexity, the pedagogical choices are considerably greater than in early arithmetic, although the principles of practice are much the same.

We remain with the question of where and how we learn about effective teaching relative to these issues. In the papers of Section I, teachers learn by being involved with educators in research projects where the nature of teaching is the subject of the research. Let us leave things at this stage with the following question:

> Do teachers have to be part of research projects with experienced educators for such teaching development to occur?

We shall return to this question in later sections.

REFERENCES

Jaworski, B. (1994). *Investigating mathematics teaching: A constructivist enquiry.* London: Falmer Press.

Jaworski, B. (1998). Mathematics teacher research: Process, practice and the development of teaching. *Journal of Mathematics Teacher Education, 1,* 3-31.

Plowden Report (1967). *Children and their primary schools.* London: Central Advisory Board Council for Education.

Romberg, T. A., & Carpenter, T. P. (1986). Research on teaching and learning mathematics: Two disciplines of scientific inquiry. In M.C. Wittrock (Ed.), *Handbook of research on teaching* (3rd ed., pp. 850-873). New York: Macmillan.

Wood, T., Cobb, P., Yackel, E., & Dillon, D. (Eds.). (1993). *Rethinking elementary school mathematics : Insights and issues.* (Journal for Research in Mathematics Education, Monograph No. 6.) Reston, VA: National Council of Teachers of Mathematics.

Part **III**

TEACHING VIEWED FROM THE DISCIPLINE OF MATHEMATICS

OVERVIEW

We have characterized the chapters in this section as viewing teaching from the perspective of the discipline of mathematics. Chapters in this section extend the contribution of the psychological view, but take mathematics as the starting point. These chapters make apparent the importance in teaching of attending to the mathematics in what students are saying and doing, attending to their mathematical logic and reasoning, and identifying the specific conceptual issues with which students are occupied. Specific actions by the teacher consist of posing questions that go beyond asking children to describe their solution strategies to requiring them to think more deeply about the mathematics underlying those strategies and to critically examine that thinking to determine whether it is mathematically valid.

Learning to See the Invisible

What Skills and Knowledge are Needed to Engage With Students' Mathematical Ideas?

Deborah Schifter
Education Development Center, Newton, MA

Growing concern that our country's students are not learning to reason mathematically—concern validated by a series of national assessments (Carpenter, Corbitt, Kepner, Lindquist, & Reys, 1981; Kouba et al., 1988), has converged with several decades of research into children's natural abilities for mathematical thought (cf. Grouws, 1992) to encourage the development of a pedagogy "aim[ing] to take seriously both mathematics as a discipline and children's mathematical ideas" (Ball, 1998, p. 7; see also Cobb, Wood, & Yackel, 1990; Fennema et al., 1996; Hiebert et al., 1996; Lampert, 1988). Outlined in the National Council of Teachers of Mathematics (NCTM) Standards (1989, 1991, 2000), embodied in new curricular materials (cf. Education Development Center, 1998, 2000; The University of Chicago School Mathematics Project, 1998; TERC, 1998), this pedagogy is being put into play in school systems around the United States.

However, early on, it became clear that elementary teachers, now expected to teach mathematics very differently from the way they themselves were taught, needed opportunities to encounter disciplinary content anew (Cohen et al., 1990), for their responsibilities would extend far beyond demonstrating the next algorithm to be committed to memory. Instead, by setting challenging, often open-ended problems, they were to elicit and build on their students' mathematical insights and conjectures. And to some mathematics educators, myself included, it became equally clear that, more important to the future of reform than encouraging the teachers we work with to sign up for advanced mathematics classes, was the provision of courses designed to allow them to explore in depth the mathematics they were actually responsible for teaching (Borko, et al., 1992; Conference Board of Mathematical Sciences, 2000; Post, Harel, Behr, & Lesh, 1991). Although it is routinely assumed that elementary level mathematics is so simple that any educated adult knows it well enough to teach it, this is just not the case (Ball, 1989, 1990; Ma, 1999; Simon, 1990; Simon & Blume, 1994). The mathematics is, in fact, conceptually complex but rarely taught in the United States in ways that acknowledge this complexity. What is needed, I and like-minded colleagues argue, are pre- and in-service opportunities to address such topics as the structure of the base-ten number system, the meaning of the basic operations, the logic of rational numbers, and the properties of geometric shapes. Furthermore, in exploring these topics, teachers must be given experiences that support the development of richly connected mathematical concepts, for it is precisely such connections among concepts and their contexts, and the ability to use them flexibly and creatively that are called on in the classroom (Ma, 1999). Exposure to deductive derivations—for example, of computation algorithms from field axioms—while aesthetically pleasing, is not, by itself, sufficient to confer that ability.

This conviction has formed the basis of my practice for the last decade (Schifter, 1993, 1998; Schifter & Fosnot, 1993), but I have lately been asking myself what additional skills and knowledge (I think of these, too, as mathematical) beyond what can be gotten from such explorations, is required of a practice in which teachers actively engage with their students' mathematical ideas. Preparation for so radically reconceived a pedagogy necessarily includes teachers' own mathematical explorations, but these are not, in themselves, sufficient. What else is needed, then, beyond deep knowledge of content?

For me, the answers to this question proceed from the premise that identifying such skills and knowledge can not be accomplished by studying effective teaching alone, because the most basic of these are likely so taken for granted as to be invisible. Instead, it is by listening to teachers who are in the process of change as they register new insights or recognize that an important piece is missing, that we can learn what needs to be taught.

To illustrate what it means to explore familiar content more deeply, I begin this chapter with reflections on some of my own experiences as a learner and teacher of mathematics, stressing how opportunities to develop new insights arising out of classroom interaction influence what I bring to teaching mathematics content to teachers. From there, I go on to consider what additional mathematical skills are required of a practitioner who engages with her students' mathematical thinking, presenting two scenes in which a teacher does just that. These vignettes then become touchstones in the section that follows, where I identify four critical skills teachers need to develop.

NEW CONCEPTS EMERGE FROM FAMILIAR CONTENT

I recall how my fifth-grade teacher introduced fraction division: beginning with a problem on the board (I'm not sure of the numbers; let's say 4 ÷ 3/5), then representing it as a compound fraction; next, multiplying by a carefully chosen form of 1, so that the denominator became 1, and so, on to the solution:

$$4 \div 3/5 = \frac{4}{3/5} = \frac{4}{3/5} \times \frac{5/3}{5/3} = \frac{4 \times 5/3}{1} = 20/3 = 6\ 2/3$$

Although I don't remember the numbers, I do remember my teacher standing at the board, taking us through the steps. Like so many of my experiences of school mathematics, this thrilling demonstration of how to divide with fractions gave me a sense of safety, pleasure, and beauty. I appreciated the orderliness, the way the numbers and operations fit together, and the assurance that one could figure out new things from what one already understood.

When, some years later, I began teaching, I wanted my students to see that order too, to appreciate the reasonableness of mathematics. After a typically trying first year, I seemed to be a pretty good teacher of high school, later sixth-grade, and then college mathematics. My students liked me, many said I made the math comprehensible, and almost all were at least moderately, if not highly, successful in their mathematics studies. So, in the mid-1980s, when I was assigned to teach my first "remedial" high school mathematics class, I was nervous. I didn't know how I was going to connect with failing students; I couldn't conceive that basic mathematical constructs — fractions, for example — could be difficult.

I soon realized, however, how unfounded were my concerns. Instead of the disconnection I feared, doors opened on new mathematical worlds. My students initiated me into unexpected ways of viewing the mathematical situations presented in class, and ideas and concepts that I had taken for granted so that they had become invisible to me, now emerged. The mathematical insights thus afforded me were both elegant and powerful.

For example, I remember sitting with Wanda (a pseudonym) while the class worked on division of fractions. The students had been given a list of "naked numbers," e.g. 3 ÷ 2/3, 1/2 ÷ 1/6, and they were asked to make up appropriate word problems, draw diagrams to match the arithmetic, and then solve. As Wanda set to work on 4 ÷ 3/5, in my head I mechanically inverted and multiplied — 20/3 or 6 2/3.

The class had already realized that any of these divisions could be about sharing food, and Wanda started by imagining that, one night, the girls in her dorm (this was a residential summer program) obtained 4 cakes, each girl to get 3/5 of one. (She did not care about making her problems realistic.) When I asked what question she was trying to answer, she replied, "How many portions?"

Wanda drew four circles, but had trouble dividing them into fifths, and so, at my suggestion, she drew four rectangular sheet cakes instead, dividing each one and shading 3/5 of each cake. Wanda explained that each cake was cut into five slices, three slices making up a portion. Then, to my surprise, she declared the answer to her question to be four. Here is her drawing.

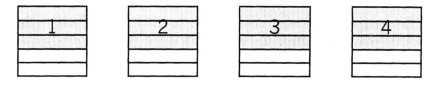

Wanda explained that you could get only one portion per cake; there was not enough for a second. This was the first time I saw a student look at such a problem that way — not collecting fractional amounts across the boundaries of single units, as I would have done — but I have seen it many times since then. Although I could not articulate it at the time, other students, including teachers, have helped me see the difference between viewing each cake as a physical object, the fraction representing just a part of that object, versus viewing each cake as a unit of measure with the fraction designating a quantity in relation to that unit.

Taken aback, I elaborated the story: The four girls had already helped themselves to their portions before Wanda entered the room. Was there now a portion for her? "Oh, yeah," she said, and after working some more on her diagram, now decided her answer was 6.

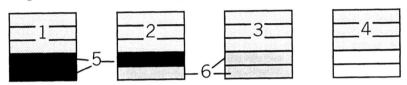

Her reasoning was easy to see: 6 designated the number of whole portions. "Okay," I said. "Now six girls have taken their portions. What if one more comes in?" Wanda understood that though there was not enough left for another whole portion, this newcomer could have *some* — so, she said, that made a total of 6 2/5.

Checking her diagram again, I saw that, yes, of course, it *could* look like 6 2/5, but the answer was still 6 2/3. So the relevant question was, 2/5 of which thing, 2/3 of which other thing? Why do we say it's 6 2/3 when it's so easy to see that 2/5? Questions that I had never thought of before, and answers to them, were suddenly coming up for me. When we perform the division for this problem, we are finding how many portions there are. The units we start with are cakes — there are four cakes; but the answer is about portions — there are six and two-thirds portions. As I thought some more about Wanda's diagram, I also understood how the story problem could be transformed into whole-number division (20 slices grouped into 3s) or a multiplication problem (four cakes, each yielding 5/3 portions).

I do not, in fact, remember how Wanda sorted out those ideas; I do not expect that she worked through her confusions in that one sitting. But, I do remember my pleasure over my own mathematical insight, my awareness of the slipperiness of the units, and my realization that by keeping track of those units, one can see, within the context of these cakes, the equivalence of a fraction division problem, a whole-number division problem, and a fraction multiplication problem. Why, I had new and satisfying ways of thinking about the invert-and-multiply algorithm! I also appreciated the numbers in this particular problem — 2, 3, 4, 5, 6, 20, 2/5, 3/5, 2/3, and 5/3 — each associated with just one unit (cakes or slices or portions), and each small enough so that I could at once hold all the parts of the problem together, yet keep them separate.

MATHEMATICS CONTENT FOR TEACHERS

Since that day, I have spent more than 10 years working with teachers, and "Wanda's Cakes" has been a staple of our investigations into fractions. Sitting down with Wanda led me to many new insights and now I work to frame that same problem, as well as others I have come across in similar fashion, so that teachers, too, can confront such core conceptual issues as: How do we sort out units when dividing fractions? How does attention to units help us understand computational procedures for dividing fractions?

For many teachers and students, the consistency and order of our number system that I had so appreciated as a child do not come together in that immensely satisfying "click" of understanding. What I have come to see (and research has verified; see Carpenter, Fennema, Peterson, Chiang, & Loef, 1989; Fuson, in press) is that grounding the concepts in such familiar situations as sharing slices of cake does support insight into mathematical connections. Yet, it must be emphasized that solving problems about sharing cake is not the point of these lessons. Instead, the context provides a starting point from which we can move to questions of a more general nature: What does division mean when we are working with fractions? Why does it make sense to invert the second number and multiply? Our fraction division sessions always generate a great deal of pleasurable excitement. And teachers frequently use Wanda's problem to work on these same issues with their own students (Schifter, 1998; Schifter, Bastable, & Russell, 1999a).

Wanda's Cakes is an example of the kind of mathematical exploration for teachers that enriches classroom work. Although most can correctly apply an algorithm for dividing fractions, they usually lack a sense of why the algorithm works, how it's related to what they already do understand about division, or what size number to expect as an outcome (Ma, 1999). For example, if teachers remember that dividing with a fraction sometimes results in an answer larger than the dividend, this fact is often relegated to their "incomprehensibles" bin, along with many other observations inconsistent with notions (now overgeneralizations) developed back when mathematics still made sense. Through working on problems in context, they can sort out what is happening to the numbers through the operation of division and come to see why (in the realm of positive numbers) a divisor between 0 and 1 results in a quotient larger than the dividend.

Many other such problems have come to me in similar ways through my work with teachers. For example, one day, before I entered Mary Ryan's (a pseudonym) fifth-grade classroom, she showed me a problem she had written to introduce addition of fractions to her students: *One fifth of the boys in the class are absent; two fifths of the girls are absent. What fraction of the class is absent?* Although this problem *looks* like addition (after all, if one boy and two girls are absent, 1 + 2 equals 3 absent children), the total number of students absent does not make up 3/5 of the class. As we stood talking in the hall, the role of the units in addition was suddenly highlighted for me. This was an issue that I had never articulated for myself, but I recognized it as soon as I saw Ryan's problem. Another submerged idea had suddenly become visible.

After I pointed out her error, Ryan rewrote the problem—*One fifth of the girls in the class are wearing long sleeved sweaters; two fifths are wearing short sleeved sweaters. What fraction of the girls is wearing sweaters?* — and it led to a successful lesson. Ryan's original problem became part of my repertoire.

When I consider my work with Wanda or Mary Ryan, I recognize how many mathematical insights came, and still do come, to me in analogous ways and how they contribute to my own growth as a teacher. However, unless teachers come to see mathematics as active discovery and assume ownership of their powers of mathematical thought, their own lessons will not yield them comparable insights. They must learn how to learn on their feet.

Opportunities to explore mathematical problems like these allow teachers to build the deep conceptual connections necessary for effective teaching. However, teachers' mathematical needs go beyond exploring mathematical content for themselves, and beyond learning how to conduct such explorations. If newly learned mathematical concepts often do translate directly to practice (for example, when teachers give Wanda's Cakes to their class), they are prepared to help their students confront the same conceptual questions they themselves have just worked through; these are nonetheless frequently insufficient to meet the mathematical challenges of the classroom. But what more it takes is not obvious. If we promote a pedagogy in which teachers proceed from and keep returning to their students' mathematical ideas, in which students' mathematical questions, insights, and conjectures are foregrounded, and in which teachers work with those questions, insights, and conjectures to support their students' learning, what must teachers come to know that they themselves are unlikely to learn as students in a well-taught mathematics lesson?

BEYOND MATHEMATICS CONTENT, WHAT MORE DO TEACHERS NEED TO LEARN?

For the last 10 years, I have been working with teachers anxious to develop a practice grounded in a deep understanding of the mathematics they teach and an appreciation of their students' mathematical thinking. To this end, I have offered a variety of activities in the context of summer institutes, school-year courses, and short-term workshops. These consist of mathematical explorations, discussions based on videotaped and written cases in which students talk about mathematics, analyses of students' written work, reflective journal writing, and case writing. In addition, I have visited teachers in their classrooms and met with them afterwards to discuss the mathematics of their lesson and their students' mathematical thinking.

In this work, I must constantly try to assess what teachers understand and what they still need to learn in order to improve their mathematics teaching. And in this context, I have come to see that teachers have mathematical needs beyond those that their own mathematical explorations can address. It has not been primarily through reflecting on my own teaching, or by observing *fluent* teaching in action, that I have come to recognize much of what teachers still need to learn. When I study teachers who have the mathematics in place, I cannot *see* the basic knowledge and skills brought to bear as they react to their students' mathematical ideas. In their taken-for-granted nature, these are invisible to me. In the same way that Wanda could reveal to me new mathematical concepts precisely because she didn't have them, it is when I become aware that something is missing for teachers that I know where to look for what is absent. When teachers exclaim over their new insights, or share their exasperation over what they cannot do, they help to make visible the invisible.

Once the knowledge and skills become visible by their absence, then I can turn back to illustrations of effective teaching to see them in place. The two classroom scenes now presented offer such illustration. They will be used as touchstones in the section that follows in which I identify and describe four skills put into play by this fifth-grade teacher.

TWO SCENES FROM A FIFTH-GRADE CLASSROOM[1]

Scene One, from Liz Sweeney's Fifth-Grade Classroom

The class has been asked to solve 29 x 12, first working individually, and then sharing methods with partners and small groups. Jemea has solved 29 x 12 and explains her solution method to her partner:

> Jemea: I did—since 29 was closer to 30, I added 30 twelve times because it was closer. I just rounded it to the nearest 10. So that was 30. I added that, I got 360. I had to take away 12 because I had put 1 more to 29 to get to 30, so I had to take 12 away and took that away and I got 348.

After a break in the tape, Jemea is now working with a group of four students. Liz Sweeney, her teacher, approaches and looks at Jemea's page. She then addresses the group:

> Ms. Sweeney: I saw, I was confused when I came over here because the problem said 29 x 12. When I came over here I didn't see that Jemea had done anything with 29. I didn't see any 29 here, okay? I saw all these 30s and didn't see any 30 in the problem. Where did this all come from?

Jose, a member of Jemea's group, explains:

> Jose : She rounded it to the nearest 10. So when she was done with the problem she took away 12. Twelve because she, um [pause]. Twenty-nine, she rounded it to the *next 10*, so it was 30. She added them up 12 times, so when she got her answer she minused 12—'cause she, because there were twelve 30s and there probably was 29 and when she minused it she got her answer 348.

> Ms. Sweeney: (turning to Jemea) Why did you choose to work with 30?

> Jemea: Nines I think are very hard to work with and zeros are easy to work with because it will just end up to be zero.

---

[1] The classroom scenes are taken from videotape (Russell, Smith, Storeygard, & Murray, 1999).

Afterwards, Liz Sweeney was asked by an interviewer to reflect on Jemea's work:

> Ms. Sweeney: I thought what Jemea did with the problem, 29 x 12, was really exciting. I could picture kids getting stuck if they tried to do this by the traditional algorithm, using 29. It's kind—is, she even said, an awkward number, nines are awkward to use. But to just make it so neat to go to 30 and say, okay, I had 30 twelve times. And then how clearly she knew she had to take away, that she had put 1 extra in, each of the 12 times, so that she had to take away 1 twelve times—was really exciting to me. I felt like it was really neat and I felt like it was exciting and I felt like it showed such flexibility of thinking to know that nines are hard to work with, zeros are easier to work with, 29 is one away from 30 and I did that 12 times. So that at the end, I have to go back and take that away. And I felt like when Jose was explaining it, I felt like he had a clear sense of what she had done also.

Scene Two, From Liz Sweeney's Fifth-Grade Classroom

Thomas is standing at the board where he had put up an (incorrect) method for solving 36 x 17:

$$36 + 4 = 40 \qquad\qquad 40$$
$$17 + 3 = 20 \qquad\qquad \underline{\times 20}$$
$$\qquad\qquad\qquad\qquad\qquad 800$$
$$\qquad\qquad\qquad\qquad\qquad \underline{-\ 4}$$
$$\qquad\qquad\qquad\qquad\qquad 796$$
$$\qquad\qquad\qquad\qquad\qquad \underline{-\ 3}$$
$$\qquad\qquad\qquad\qquad\qquad 793$$

Thomas addresses the entire class:

> Thomas: What I did was, I wanted to make it easier to—I wanted to—make 36 x 17 easier to times. So I added 4 to 36 to make it 40 to make it easier, and I added 3 to 17 to get to 20. So I timesed 40 x 20 to get up to 80. [Thomas says 80, although he is pointing to 800 written on the board.] And—I got 80, but I knew it wasn't the answer so I minused 4 because I added 4 to get up to 40 to

make it easier and that brought me to sum of 96 [pointing to 796]. And I minused 3 because I had to add 3 to get to 20 and I got the answer — 793.

Ms. Sweeney: [explaining to the class what happened when she had seen Thomas present this method to his small group] So I liked this, I was feeling all comfortable with it and I liked it and it looked like a good strategy and it was neat. And then Dima was all antsy in his seat because he's saying, "That's not what I did and my answer is really different," and that "I disagree with Thomas."

Okay, and then Thomas explained it again, and I *still* liked it, and then Dima was still getting antsy in his seat and O'Brian was having a problem in his seat, too, because I wasn't getting where the mistake was — or where the thinking was.

So, tonight for your homework, I want you to copy down this model that Thomas did — in your homework books, and I want you to figure out: What was Thomas thinking, and using his strategy, how would you come up with a different answer?

WHAT MATHEMATICAL SKILLS DO TEACHERS NEED?

In this section, I describe four skills I have identified by recognizing their absence in teachers' practice: (1) attending to the mathematics in what one's students are saying and doing, (2) assessing the mathematical validity of students' ideas, (3) listening for the sense in students' mathematical thinking even when something is amiss, and (4) identifying the conceptual issues the students are working on.[2] Once these skills are made visible, I turn back to particular classroom events — scenes from Liz Sweeney's fifth-grade classroom, for example — to see how they are employed.

---

[2] Some of these skills are analogous to those required of professional mathematicians, for example, following the logic of an argument and determining its mathematical validity. Others — e.g., identifying the conceptual issue a child is working on — are particular to the classroom context and, thus, would fall into Shulman's category, "pedagogical content knowledge" (Shulman, 1986).

Skill 1: Attending to the Mathematics in What One's Students are Saying and Doing

Which teacher will deny that she pays careful attention to her students? The bald injunction that teachers learn to do so means almost nothing. And yet, as teachers begin to change their practice, they testify that the quality of their attention changes.

What this might mean was brought to light for me when I gave a group of teachers an assignment to transcribe a conversation from their own classrooms about a particular piece of mathematics and then to incorporate it into a narrative account of the lesson. The purpose of the assignment was to produce the sorts of vivid images that could help other teachers envision new possibilities for their own classrooms. I was surprised when, the following week, my students reported that this was the most powerful professional development exercise they had ever been given.

Teachers found different ways to approach the assignment—audio taping, note taking during class, or writing from recollection as soon after the lesson as possible. But no matter which strategy they employed, the teachers agreed that having been asked to write down what their students were saying and doing forced them to attend to the children in new ways.

Since the day in 1991 when I gave that assignment, I have paid particular attention to shifts in the way teachers attend to student thinking. Indeed, it is not that the teachers were not already paying close attention to their students. They were! And most do! In any classroom moment, teachers attend to a myriad of different facets of what their students do and say. When a child stands at the board, say, to show the class his solution to a problem, the teacher is likely to notice the clarity of his speech, his emotional tone, and his classmates' responses. She or he might notice how the student writes numerals, perhaps the color of the chalk chosen, and the student's gestures. The list goes on. However, as the teacher attends, she often does *not* realize that the child is expressing mathematical ideas worth noticing—"I'm usually listening for whether what the child is saying matches up with my assessment instrument." "When a student is talking, I'm thinking about what I'm going to say next."

Writing down the children's words in a mathematics discussion filters out such issues as the child's penmanship or a classmate's inattention; instead, the task focuses in on the mathematics in what the child is saying and doing. And now having his or her own written record, the teacher can consider the mathematical ideas the child is expressing. Through such regular writing assignments, teachers develop the habit of listening with a new ear, particularly when the assignments are coupled with opportunities to discuss with colleagues what they hear in their students' mathematical talk. They begin to listen to their students with sharpened curiosity and interest.

In recent years, I have tried various strategies to promote such shifts. In addition to asking teachers to write narratives from their own classrooms, my colleagues and I now use case discussions to foster this kind of attentiveness to the mathematics in what students actually say and do. But even with the cases at hand, teachers initially tend to look past the children's mathematical thinking. Without the firm guidance of a facilitator, discussion is more likely to be about, say, the task the teacher set and how it should have been done differently, or how to structure things to ensure that students will get correct answers. Especially when working with a new group of teachers, the facilitator needs to continually draw teachers' attention back to the mathematics in what the children are saying and doing. For example, when studying children's invented procedures for computing with multidigit numbers, we present a case in which a child solves a particular problem and then ask teachers to use the child's method on a different set of numbers.

In her own professional development work, Liz Sweeney engaged in all of these activities. She wrote narrative accounts of mathematics conversation in her classroom and studied print and video cases to track what the children were saying and doing. By her own account, her teaching changed as a result. Indeed, interviewed about Jemea's work, she could play back what Jemea had done: "[Since] nines are awkward to use . . . [she could] make it so neat to go to 30 and say, okay, I had 30 twelve times, and then how clearly she knew she had to take away."

This video clip also attests to a second important consequence of the teacher's careful listening: the children listen to one another, too. When Liz Sweeney comes to Jemea's group and asks about her method, it is Jose who explains exactly what Jemea had done.

Skill 2: Assessing Mathematical Validity of Students' Ideas

Imagine a professional development setting in which a group of teachers is involved in the activity just described. They watch videotapes of second graders demonstrating ways to decompose and recombine two-digit numbers to solve addition and subtraction problems. For example, one child solves 34 + 28 by adding 30 + 20 to get 50, then 4 + 8 to get 12, and finally 50 + 12 to get 62. Another child adds 34 + 20 to get 54 and then brings in the 8: 54 + 8 = 62. A third child explains that she takes 6 from the 28 and adds it to 34 — 40 — and then adds in the 22 left from 28 — 62. The teachers' task is to apply these same procedures to different sets of numbers. To do so, they must listen carefully to what the children are saying, observe what they are doing. The group is successful at this task, but toward the end of this activity, one of the teachers blurts out, "I can apply each step exactly as the children did, but it's just another meaningless algorithm to me. I don't know why it works." She is joined by a chorus of "Yeahs."

Scenes like this one highlight how much help many teachers need in order to develop the skills necessary to assess the validity of a mathematical argument or method of solution. They have gone through school, sometimes very successfully, memorizing facts and procedures, yet have no sense of a mathematical logic. Sometimes, it seems, they do not know that there is anything to appraise except whether an answer is correct or a particular method has been faithfully applied. Even teachers like those described who know what mathematical logic is (or at least that it exists), stopped thinking mathematically so long ago that evaluating the soundness of something so basic as a child's procedure for adding two-digit numbers is a mathematical challenge.

The task now for these teachers is to think through and reconnect with the basic mathematical principles students' employ to perform their computations. For example, teachers need to think through the fact that, in addition, the addends can be broken into component parts that can be recombined in any order. Or they need to see why, if the minuend and subtrahend in a subtraction problem are increased or decreased by the same amount, the difference remains constant. Or, again, in multiplication, if one factor is rounded up, they need to know how to compensate, and why.

In Liz Sweeney's class, the thinking does not stop once Jemea produces the correct answer to 29 x 12. Instead, Jemea, her classmates, and the teacher think through why Jemea's procedure works. In her interview, Liz Sweeney goes through the logic again: "29 is . . . an awkward number . . . so go to 30, and say, okay, I had 30 twelve times and . . . she had put 1 extra in, each of the 12 times, so that she had to take away 1 twelve times." Liz Sweeney's justification of Jemea's method is based in her own understanding of what multiplication is.

In this case, Liz Sweeney is in a position to affirm as sound the thinking of a child who has correctly calculated the answer to 29 x 12. Jemea, Jose, and their classmates have opportunities to apply and analyze what makes sense to them and are encouraged to stay connected to their own powers of mathematical thought. But what happens if something is amiss?

Eleanor Norris's (a pseudonym) combination third and fourth grade class[3] is also working on multiplication. When Jen (a pseudonym), a third grader, is challenged to solve 27 x 4, she writes

First way — 2 x 27 = 54   2 + 2 = 4
            4 x 27 = 108   54 + 54 = 108
I found out that 2 x 27 = 54 and then I added 54 + 54.

Second way — 20 x 4 = 80
             7 x 4 = 28
I did 80 + 28; 20 x 4 and 7 x 4 and then added them together.

Jen has applied two valid strategies for solving the problem: (1) doubling 27 twice and (2) decomposing 27 into 20 and 7, multiplying each part by 4, and adding the two products.

A few days later, Eleanor Norris gives her students a story problem about 14 people buying 16 things each; how many items were bought all together? In her math log, Jen interprets the problem as 14 x 16, and writes

2 = 28, 3 = 42, 6 = 84, 7 = 103, 14 = 206, 16 = 234.

Jen seems to be using a variation of her first strategy, now applied to larger numbers: She adds 14s, sometimes doubling her sum, and keeps track of the number of 14s she has included. Although she is using the conventional symbol "=" incorrectly, and although she gets the wrong answer, her strategy is valid. And in spite of her faulty notation and addition mistake (going from 6 to 7 groups of 14, Jen should have gotten 98 as the result of 84 + 14), her teacher recognizes the validity of the strategy. According to Eleanor Norris, "I wonder if she wasn't working with such new material and ideas that they left her juggling too much. Had she found what 8 fourteens were, she might have doubled that and gotten her answer." Having analyzed

---

[3] This example was taken from a case in Schifter, Bastable, and Russell (1999b), pp. 72-75.

the mathematical validity of her student's approach, Eleanor Norris can affirm Jen's logic and encourage her to perfect this strategy, one that makes such sense to her, before moving on. Indeed, a few days later, when the class is given a problem that can be solved by 12 x 63, Jen writes:

2 x 63 = 126
4 x 63 = 252
8 x 63 = 504
12 x 63 = 756

Ms. Norris comments:

> Jen shows great progress in the past two weeks . . . she is now using notation for multiplication in a way that states her ideas more powerfully; the notation is becoming standard form for her. By adding the last two steps together (4 x 63 and 8 x 63) to find 12 x 63, Jen indicates a solid grasp of the idea that she can partition and regroup the 12.

With her ability to think through her students' mathematical reasoning, Eleanor Norris can support them as they learn to exercise their own logic.

Next, consider Maureen Gardner (a pseudonym) who has asked her second graders to create their own word problems and then demonstrate different methods of solution. Karl (a pseudonym) writes, "I saw 12 people. Then I saw 26 more. How many did I see?" On the first day he works on the problem, Karl presents two methods:

$$
\begin{array}{c}
12 \\
\underline{+26} \\
3^{t}\ 8 = 38
\end{array}
\qquad
\begin{array}{c}
12 + 26 \\
\diagdown\!\!\times\!\!\diagup \\
30 + 8 = \\
\diagdown\!\diagup \\
38
\end{array}
$$

This seems fine. In each case, the child presents the same correct answer, 38, for the word problem that can be solved by 12 + 26. In his first method, Karl uses the traditional algorithm with a slight variation in notation. He adds the numerals in each place, indicates with a small "t" that the 3 stands for tens, and includes a separate step, adding the 3 tens and 8, 38. In the second method, the notation is different but the logic is the same: he adds the 10 from 12 and the

20 from 26 to get 30, then adds the ones to get 8, and finally finds 30 + 8, 38.

The next day, however, when her students return to the same problems, Maureen Gardner is disturbed to find the following on Karl's page:

$$12 + 26$$

$$10 + 10 + 10 + 8 = 38$$

Karl ends up with the same, correct, answer. But this time, though Karl finds four addends that sum to 38, it is not at all clear how he derives those addends from 12 and 26. He uses the same form of notation as he has before—lines drawn from 12 and 26 to his next row of numbers—but 12 does not decompose to 10 + 10, nor 26 to 10 + 8. Ms. Gardner is troubled by this third method and so questions whether Karl understands the mathematical reasoning behind the earlier procedures. "Karl worked on his combining problem the day before . . . . He arrived at the answer 38 for 12 + 26. Now as he tries a new [method], he shows confusion."

Ms. Gardner recognizes that her job as a mathematics teacher involves not only checking to see whether her students get the correct answer, but also requires her to assess the validity of their solution strategies. Unable to see the logic in one of Karl's methods, she questions whether he understands the basic principles that underlie the methods he employs. His correct answer notwithstanding, Karl's reasoning does not appear to be grounded in mathematical principles.

Teachers Sweeney, Norris, and Gardner are working to develop a pedagogy that focuses on children's mathematical reasoning and takes seriously the integrity of the mathematics they are teaching. Critical to their practice is the ability to listen as their students offer mathematical arguments and to assess the validity of those arguments. The three examples just presented are instructive. In the first, a child argues validly and produces a correct answer. In the second, a student employs a valid method but makes a slip in her addition; despite her mistake, she is encouraged to follow her own line of reasoning. In the third, a child has the correct answer, but in spite of this, his teacher cannot see the logic in his method and suspects confusion. Because of the care with which Liz Sweeney, Eleanor Norris, and Maureen Gardner attend to the soundness of their students' reasoning, these children have opportunities to develop their own powers of mathematical thought.

The facility with which these three teachers assess the mathematical soundness of their students' thinking cannot be taken for granted. Most teachers, indeed, most of us, never had similarly attentive teachers. Unable as students to recognize the logic behind the procedures they were being taught, many never registered the existence of such a logic, or if they did, believed it was inaccessible to them. Cultivating the ability to discern that logic must be a principle goal of teacher development efforts.

Skill 3: Listening for the Sense in Students' Mathematical Ideas—Even When Something is Amiss

A group of teachers watches the videotape of Thomas explaining his procedure for multiplying 36 x 17: Add 4 to 36 and add 3 to 17 and you get 40 x 20, which is 800. Subtract the 4 and the 3 you added on, and you get 793.

Having watched videos on which other students solve the same problem (Russell, Smith, Storeygard, & Murray, 1999), and having multiplied the numbers out for themselves, the teachers know that 793 is incorrect and that Thomas's strategy is mathematically invalid. They comment on his lack of number sense—it's obvious that the product should be less than 20 x 36, which is 720—and are ready to move on.

However, after determining that a student's strategy is mathematically unsound, teachers working toward a practice built on children's mathematical thinking must learn to ask themselves: Where did that strategy come from? For example, is there any sense in what Thomas is doing? But in order to think this way, one must be prepared to look beyond the boundaries of the traditional textbook chapter. To one who has explored the basic operations in depth, Thomas's solution method is familiar, appropriate to an addition problem. To solve 36 + 17, one can round up to 40 and 20, add them to get 60, and then subtract the 4 and 3 to get 53 (Russell, 1999).

Thomas's mistake, applying an addition strategy to a multiplication problem, is quite common. When faced with multidigit multiplication, both children and adults frequently try (10 x 10)+ (2 x 8) for 12 x 18 (after all, to add 12 and 18, one could operate on the tens, operate on the ones, and then add the total) or 14 x 20 for 16 x 18 (after all, to add 16 and 18, one could take 2 from the 16 and add it to the 18 to get 14 + 20). Instead of dismissing Thomas, one could instead identify a mathematical strength. When faced with a problem that he didn't know how to solve, he thought he saw an analogy to something he did know and so he tried it.

The lesson here is that teachers must learn to range across traditionally defined topic areas; they must begin to see how basic mathematical concepts and ideas are used in contexts that have been treated as conceptually discrete. For example, they might learn to ask questions like: How is the base-10 structure of number exploited in multidigit computation for all the operations? What is conserved from operation to operation and what is different?

Liz Sweeney wasn't interviewed about her decision making here. We do not know how she analyzed Thomas's method. However, given her remarks to the class, we do know that she recognized there was sense in what Thomas presented, and she invited the class to consider it. She knew that here was a learning opportunity.

Some further examples: A class of kindergartners, keeping track of the number of days they have been in school, have come to the 59th + 1 day. "What number should we record on our days-in-school chart today?" the teacher asks, and Andrew answers, "Fifty-ten." Looking across the row of numbers the class has been considering all week—fifty-one, fifty-two, fifty-three—Andrew has extended the pattern.[4]

Sarah, a third grader, trying to act out the conventional addition algorithm with unifix cubes (black cubes are ones; yellow, tens) is mystified when her manipulations yield 174 as the sum of 45 + 39. She joins the 14 black cubes, breaks off 10, moves them to the next "column," and then combines those ten with the yellow cubes for a stack of 17. She reads these as 17 tens and 4 ones.[5]

A fifth-grade class has been given a problem that involves a jeweler who has three small amounts of gold: 1.14 g, .089 g, and .3 g. The class debates whether the total amount of gold is 1.529 g or 2.06 g. Those defending 2.06 apply a rule they generalized from adding whole numbers—line up the numbers at the right—and once they find a sum, choose the best place to put the decimal point.[6]

In these examples, the children's mathematics is incorrect. However, each of them exhibits elements of thought important to acknowledge and cultivate. In fact, it is that very capacity to reason that can be leveraged to help the children work through their illogic.

---

[4] Schifter, Bastable, and Russell (1999b).
[5] Schifter, Bastable, and Russell (1999b).
[6] Schifter, Bastable, and Russell (1999b).

Finally, let us return to Karl. He has made up a word problem, presented two methods of solution that his teacher, Maureen Gardner, can interpret as mathematically sound, but a third that appears invalid. Compounding her concern is his fourth method:

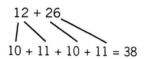

$$10 + 11 + 10 + 11 = 38$$

Why has Karl produced this set of pages? Maureen Gardner wonders. Where did Karl's strategy come from? She hypothesizes, "He has watched children in the room break numbers apart and combine tens and ones to find a total. I think because of his previous answer, he is trying to manipulate the numbers to arrive at the answer 38." Might we identify in Karl a mathematical strength, as well? Perhaps, having found the correct answer, he now works backwards to try to figure out another solution method.

However, we must also consider the possibility that he is working without mathematical direction. Is he, at this moment, in the position described by so many teachers who, early in their schooling, were separated from their own powers of mathematical thought? Is Karl, trying his best in math class, imitating methods demonstrated by classmates and teacher, picking up the notation but not the core concepts that are employed? Is Karl learning that getting through math class involves meaningless manipulation?

In each of these examples, the teacher appreciates her students' sense-making ability and looks for it even when their logic has gone awry. In order for students to sort out conceptual confusions, they must feel grounded in their capacity for mathematical reasoning. And in order for teachers to help, they must find the firm ground in their students' logic on which to build new ideas.

It may happen, at times, that the search for sense in a students' work is fruitless. Or the logic might be restricted to, "This is what I think I need to do in order to get by in class." Still, in seeking the child's mathematical logic, the teacher discovers the work that needs doing.

Skill 4: Identifying the Conceptual Issues the Students are Working on

Let us return to Thomas's method for solving 36 x 17. Seeing (or hypothesizing) where his idea for a solution comes from allows us next to identify the idea he's working on and where his method has gone awry. He has learned that multidigit computation is made easier by rounding to tens, and that when one does so, one must compensate at the end. Now he must consider how addition and multiplication differ. What is the meaning of the action of multiplication? When a factor is changed, how does that affect the product?

Retracing Thomas's thinking would allow his teacher to engage Thomas and his classmates around an important idea. Advancing their mathematical development is not merely a matter of showing Thomas that he is wrong and having his classmates demonstrate strategies that work. Instead, Thomas's error has uncovered a deep mathematical question for the class to consider and discuss. How does multiplication differ from addition, and how and why does that change the computation strategies one can employ?

Note that the question: What is the issue with which Thomas is occupied? is not the same as: What is the mathematics that is missing? An answer to the latter question might be that Thomas does not apply the distributive property. That claim is certainly true, but it does not necessarily position his teacher to help Thomas move forward. In order to understand the distributive property, Thomas still needs to go back to a prior question, one that engages him in the very meanings of multiplication and addition.

Having identified the idea that needs work, the teacher can now draw in Thomas's classmates. For example, Jemea correctly used a round-up strategy to solve 29 x 12: "Twelve 30s is 360; take away 12 and it's 348." Liz Sweeney can now introduce Jemea's ideas into a discussion of Thomas's approach, setting up an explorartion of the principles underlying multidigit multiplication.

Returning to the other examples in the last section, Andrew and his classmates describe the different patterns they see in the numeration system; at the beginning, one of the kindergartners suggests they count aloud from 1 and come to agree that 60 follows 59. Third grader Sarah and her teacher talk through her unifix-cube procedure to add 45 + 39 until she discovers her mistake, clarifying for herself how the 1 to 10 relationship between places is utilized in the conventional additional algorithm. And the fifth graders turn to physical representations of decimal addition to reconsider their rules, concluding that "You need to add tenths to tenths and hundredths to hundredths or you wouldn't get the right answer."

As for Karl's difficulties, Maureen Gardner, too, must wrestle with the question: What is the idea this child needs to work on? In her correspondence with her in-service instructor, she writes,

> He has watched children in the room break numbers apart and combine tens and ones to find a total. I think because of his previous answer, he is trying to manipulate the numbers to arrive at the answer 38. He knows that there are some tens, but it seems he is not sure how to break the numbers apart to show the tens and ones. I don't think he is making the connection between the numbers [in the original problem] and the tens and ones they contain. Which numbers show the tens and which numbers show ones and where are they located?

Gardner's instructor, in her written response, also ponders Karl's work.

> I'm mostly curious what he thinks the long drawn lines mean. When we see most kids use them, we see them as either "record keepers" — as in, this number is broken into these two numbers — or as paths of a sort — as in, I'll put this part of the number down this path and this part of the number down this path. The lines are part of a drawing of what's happening in the transformation of the problem. In Karl's [methods], I don't have that sense at all. Do you have different ideas about what he's up to?

The hypotheses and questions these two educators pose in their correspondence point toward two different issues that might be troubling Karl: the base-ten composition of two-digit numbers (how many tens and how many ones) and the meaning of the notation he is using. But underlying their considerations is concern whether Karl is engaged in mathematical reasoning at all. Maureen Gardner can return to class and, testing out these hypotheses, continue to help Karl develop his capacity to reason.

The teachers I work with have helped me see how I employ these skills. As Wanda worked to solve her division of fractions problem, I could discern the mathematics in what she said and did, and follow the reasoning behind her mathematical moves. Where she made false steps, I could see the logic in what she did and then identify the general mathematical concept with which she was having difficulty. Having identified that concept, I could then reframe the problem or pose a question to help her see the situation in a new way; later, in other contexts, I could bring her back to that concept, perhaps talk about it explicitly. Finally, the knowledge I acquired through my interactions with Wanda would inform my teaching of the same content with other students.

CONCLUSION

In order to improve mathematics education in the United States, teachers must enter the classroom with stronger mathematics backgrounds. But just what should such a background include? It seems inarguable that teachers need to understand deeply the content of their own curriculum, and to this end, that elementary teachers be given opportunities to explore basic principles of arithmetic, geometry, early algebra, and statistics.

However, there are additional mathematical skills that teachers need to call on in order to respond to their students' thinking, skills unlikely to be cultivated in such explorations of mathematical content: attending to the mathematics in what one's students are saying and doing, assessing the mathematical validity of their ideas, listening for the sense in children's mathematical thinking even when something is amiss, and identifying the conceptual issues on which they are working.

These latter skills, though they rarely rise to conscious articulation in the classroom, are mathematically fundamental, and if they are not made explicit in discussions of the mathematics teachers need to learn, they are likely to remain undeveloped. But, if cultivation of these skills is woven into investigations of mathematics content, each aspect of study will enrich the other.

ACKNOWLEDGMENTS

This work is supported by the National Science Foundation under grant number ESI9731064. Any opinions, findings, conclusions, or recommendations are those of the author and do not necessarily reflect the views of the National Science Foundation.

Acknowledgment is owed to Alan Schiffmann, Cathy Miles Grant, Amy Morse, Annette Sassi, Sophia Cohen, Barbara Scott Nelson, Janet Warfield, Terry Wood, and Alan Schoenfeld for their helpful comments on earlier versions of this chapter.

REFERENCES

Ball, D. (1989). Research on teaching mathematics: Making subject matter knowledge part of the equation. In J. Brophy (Ed.), *Advances in research on teaching: Vol. 2. Teacher's subject matter knowledge and classroom instruction* (pp. 1-48). Greenwich, CT: JAI Press.

Ball, D. (1990). Teaching mathematics for understanding: What do teachers need to know about subject matter? In M. Kennedy (Ed.), *Teaching academic subjects to diverse learners* (pp. 63-83). New York: Teachers College Press.

Borko, H., Eisenhart, M., Brown, C. A., Underhill, R. G., Jones, D., & Agard, P. C. (1992). Learning to teach hard mathematics: Do novice teachers and their instructors give up too easily? *Journal for Research in Mathematics Education, 23,* 194-222.

Carpenter, T. P., Corbitt, M. K., Kepner, H. S., Lindquist, M. M., & Reys, R. E. (1981). *Results from the second mathematics assessment of the National Assessment of Educational Progress.* Reston, VA: National Council of Teachers of Mathematics.

Carpenter, T. P., Fennema, E., Peterson, P. L., Chiang, C. P., & Loef, M. (1989). Using knowledge of children's mathematics thinking in classroom teaching: An experimental study. *American Educational Research Journal, 26,* 499–531.

Cobb, P., Wood, T., & Yackel, E. (1990). Classrooms as learning environments for teachers and researchers. In R. Davis, C. Maher, & N. Noddings (Eds.), *Constructivist views on the teaching and learning of mathematics* (pp. 125-146). (Journal for Research in Mathematics Education, Monograph no 4). Reston, VA: National Council of Teachers of Mathematics.

Cohen, D. K., Peterson, P. L., Wilson, S., Ball, D., Putnam, R., Prawat, R., Heaton, R., Remillard, J., & Wiemers, N. (1990). *Effects of state-level reform of elementary school mathematics curriculum on classroom practice* (Research Rep. 90-14). East Lansing, MI: The National Center for Research on Teacher Education, College of Education, Michigan State University.

Conference Board of Mathematical Sciences (in press). *Mathematics education of teachers.* Washington, D.C.: author.

Education Development Center (1998). *Math scape.* Mountain View, CA: Creative Publications.

Education Development Center (2000). *Connected geometry.* Chicago, IL: Everyday Learning Corporation.

Fennema, E., Carpenter, T. P., Franke, M. L., Levi, L., Jacobs, V., & Empson, S. (1996). A longitudinal study of learning to use children's mathematical thinking in mathematics instruction. *Journal for Research in Mathematics Education, 27,* 403-434.

Fuson, K. (in press). Developing mathematical power in whole number operations. In J. Kilpatrick, W. G. Martin, & D. Schifter (Eds.), *Research Companion to the Principles and Standards of School Mathematics.* Reston, VA: National Council of Teachers of Mathematics.

Grouws, D. (Ed.) (1992). *Handbook of research on mathematics teaching and learning.* New York: Macmillan.

Hiebert, J., Carpenter, T. P., Fennema, E., Fuson, K., Human, P., Murray, H., Olivier, A., & Wearne, D. (1997). *Making sense: Teaching and learning mathematics with understanding.* Portsmouth, NH: Heinemann.

Kouba, V. L., Brown, C. A., Carpenter, T. P., Lindquist, M. M., Silver, E. A., & Swafford, J. O. (1988). Results of the fourth NAEP assessment of mathematics: Number, operations, and word problems. *Arithmetic Teacher 35*, 14–19.

Lampert, M. (1988). The teacher's role in reinventing the meaning of mathematics knowing in the classroom. In M. J. Behr, C. B. Lacampagne, & M. M. Wheeler (Eds.), *Proceedings of the Tenth Annual Meeting of the North American Chapter of the International Group for the Psychology of Mathematics Education* (pp. 433-480). DeKalb, IL: Northern Illinois University.

Ma, L. (1999) *Knowing and teaching elementary mathematics: Teachers' understanding of fundamental mathematics in China and the United States.* Mahwah, NJ: Lawrence Erlbaum Associates.

National Council of Teachers of Mathematics (1989). *Curriculum and evaluation standards for school mathematics.* Reston, VA: Author.

National Council of Teachers of Mathematics (1991). *Professional standards for teaching mathematics.* Reston, VA: Author.

National Council of Teachers of Mathematics (2000). *Principles and standards of school mathematics.* Reston, VA: Author.

Post, T. R., Harel, G., Behr, M., & Lesh, R. (1991). Intermediate teachers' knowledge of rational number concepts. In E. Fennema, T. P. Carpenter, & S. J. Lamon (Eds.), *Integrating research on teaching and learning mathematics* (pp. 177-198). Ithaca, NY: SUNY Press.

Russell, S. J. (1999). Mathematical reasoning in the elementary grades. In L. Stiff & F. Curio (Eds.), *Developing mathematical reasoning in grades K--12.* Reston, VA: National Council of Teachers of Mathematics.

Russell, S. J., Smith, D. A., Storeygard, J., & Murray, M. (1999). *Relearning to teach arithmetic .* Parsippany, NJ: Dale Seymour Publications.

Schifter, D. (1993). Mathematics process as mathematics content: A course for teachers, *The Journal of Mathematical Behavior, 12(3)*, 271-283.

Schifter, D. (1998). Learning mathematics for teaching: From the teachers' seminar to the classroom. *Journal for Mathematics Teacher Education, 1*, 55-87.

Schifter, D., Bastable, V., & Russell, S. J. (with Lester, J., Davenport, L., Yaffee, L., & Cohen, S.) (1999a). *Making meaning for operations, facilitator's guide. Developing mathematical ideas.* Parsippany, NJ: Dale Seymour Publications.

Schifter, D., Bastable, V., & Russell, S. J. (with Cohen, S., Lester, J., & Yaffee, L.) (1999b.) *Building a system of tens casebook. Developing mathematical ideas.* Parsippany, NJ: Dale Seymour Publications.

Schifter, D., & Fosnot, C.T. (1993). *Reconstructing mathematics education: Stories of teachers meeting the challenge of reform.* New York: Teachers College Press.

Shulman, L. S. (1986). Those who understand: Knowledge growth in teaching. *Educational Researcher, 15(2)*, 4-14.

Simon, M. A. (1990). Prospective elementary teachers' knowledge of division. In G. Booker, P. Cobb, & T. de Mendicuti (Eds.), *Proceedings of the Fourteenth Psychology of Mathematics Education Conference* (Vol. 3, pp. 313-320). Mexico: Psychology of Mathematics Education.

Simon, M. A., & Blume, G. (1994). Building and understanding multiplicative relationships: A study of prospective elementary teachers. *Journal for Research in Mathematics Education, 25*, 472–494.

TERC (1998). *Investigations in number, data, and space.* Parsippany, NJ: Dale Seymour Publications.

The University of Chicago School Mathematics Project (1998). *Everyday mathematics.* Chicago, IL: Everyday Learning Corporation.

Where Mathematics Content Knowledge Matters

Learning About and Building on Children's Mathematical Thinking

Janet Warfield
Purdue University

The importance of teachers' knowledge of content is currently a prominent issue in calls for education reform in the United States. Although there is widespread belief in the importance of teachers' content knowledge, it is not clear how such knowledge plays out in instruction. This lack of clarity is due, in part, to the complexity of teaching and, in part, to the complexity of teachers' cognition in general and their specific knowledge. It is, for example, impossible to separate teachers' knowledge from their beliefs (Fennema & Franke, 1992; Thompson, 1992). Further, "Common sense suggests that teacher knowledge is not monolithic. It is a large, integrated, functioning system with each part difficult to isolate" (Fennema & Franke, 1992, p. 149). This makes it difficult to know how specific types of knowledge influence teaching.

Ball (1998) spoke about the need for further research on the impact of teachers' mathematics content knowledge and suggested that we need to know more about the sites in teachers' practice where their mathematical knowledge matters. In this chapter, I argue that teachers' mathematical content knowledge matters as they attend to the mathematical thinking of children in their classes.

There is wide agreement about the value of teachers' attending to the mathematical thinking of children in their classes (Carpenter,

Fennema, Peterson, & Carey, 1988; Cobb, Wood, Yackel, & Wheatley, 1993; Schifter & Fosnot, 1993; Warfield, 1996). This view, which is inherent in much of the recent reform literature in mathematics education, is based on the Piagetian notion that learning occurs when connections are formed between new information and existing knowledge structures or when new information leads to cognitive conflict and, therefore, to reorganization of existing structures in order to resolve that conflict (Hiebert & Carpenter, 1992). Implication of this view of learning suggests that teachers can best facilitate the construction of knowledge by children in their classes if they base instruction on research-based information about children's mathematical thinking (Battista, 1999) and, more specifically, on the mathematical thinking of the children in their classes (Carpenter, et al., 1988; Cobb, et al., 1993).

Franke, Fennema, Carpenter, Ansell, and Behrend (1995) said that the research-based information on children's thinking shared in Cognitively Guided Instruction (CGI) workshops provides a focus that enables teachers to recognize opportunities for practical inquiry into the mathematical thinking of the children in their classes. That information is organized into a framework with two main components. First, there are several types of word problems that young children are able to solve without explicit instruction on how to do so. These problems are categorized based on the action or relationship in the problem as well as the location of the unknown. Consider, for example, the following problem: *Craig had 6 marbles. Jae-Meen gave him some more marbles, and now he has 13. How many marbles did Jae-Meen give him?* The action in this problem is a joining action; Craig got more marbles to join with the ones he already had. The unknown in the problem is the number by which the number of Craig's marbles will change. Therefore, the problem is classified as a join (change unknown) problem. The entire categorization scheme consists of 11 types of addition and subtraction problems and 3 types of multiplication and division problems.

Second, there are different strategies that children use to solve these problems. These strategies fall into three main categories: direct modeling strategies, counting strategies, and fact strategies. *Direct modeling* involves using counters (cubes, fingers, tally marks, etc.) to represent all of the objects in the problem and acting out the action or relationship in the problem. For the problem just mentioned, this entails counting out 6 counters, counting out more counters until there are 13 altogether and counting the second set to get the answer of 7. *Counting strategies* also involve following the order of the action in the problem. However, a child using a counting strategy does not represent all of the objects in the problem. For this problem, a child would say "six" and then count on from 7 to 13, extending one finger on each count until 13 was reached. The answer would be the number of fingers extended. *Fact strategies* are of two types. For this problem, a child using a *derived fact* might say, "The answer is 7, because 6 and 6 are 12, so 6 and 7 are 13." A *recalled fact strategy* entails knowing the fact called for in the problem; for this problem, this means knowing that 6 plus 7 equals 13.

At CGI workshops, teachers are shown videotapes of individual children solving word problems and engaging in discussions about the problems and the strategies used by children to solve them. Following the discussions, teachers are provided with written materials describing analyses of children's thinking and they are encouraged to assess the validity of the analyses in their own classrooms with their own children. A more complete description of CGI workshops can be found in Fennema et al. (1996).

I argue here that, although this research-based information on children's thinking can provide a focus for teachers to learn about the mathematics thinking of specific children, deep understanding of the mathematics they teach, what Ma (1999) called profound understanding of fundamental mathematics (PUFM), in conjunction with the research-based information on children's thinking can extend what teachers learn about the mathematical thinking of their children and the ways in which they use what they learn to inform their practice. This occurs in several ways. Teachers with such knowledge are able to: (a) pose questions that go beyond asking children to describe their solution strategies to asking them to think more deeply about the mathematics underlying those strategies; (b) understand students' mathematical thinking that differs from what might be expected based on the research-based information on children's thinking; (c) critically examine that thinking to determine whether it is mathematically valid; and (d) use what they learn about their students' thinking to create tasks that enable students to extend their understanding.

In order to place my argument in a context, I draw examples from the class of Carrie Valentine, a CGI teacher whom I observed teaching a group of fifth-graders at an elementary school in Madison, Wisconsin. Although the intent of this chapter is to address how teachers' mathematical knowledge in conjunction with their knowledge of research-based information on children's mathematical thinking plays out in their practice, rather than to address the origins of such knowledge, some of the sources of Ms. Valentine's knowledge are apparent in the following description of her background.

MS. VALENTINE

Ms. Valentine had been a secondary science teacher. She taught high school science for 5 years and then returned to college to take the courses required for elementary certification. I observed her during her fifth year as an elementary teacher. During her first year teaching elementary students, Ms. Valentine attended a CGI workshop.

Although the information shared at the CGI workshop focused on children's thinking, much of that information was inherently mathematical. Teachers in the workshop had opportunities to learn about distinctions among types of word problems that are important in understanding how children solve the problems and why they use specific strategies. For example, teachers learned about the different ways in which children typically model partitive and quotitive division problems. *Partitive division problems* involve situations in which a given number of items is to be distributed equally into a given number of sets; the answer is the number of items in each set. The partitive division problem *Mrs. White has 24 cookies that she wants to share equally among 6 children. How many cookies will each child get?* would be modeled by separating 24 objects into 6 equal sets. The number in one set would be counted to get the answer to the problem. On the other hand, *quotitive division problems* involve situations in which a given number of items is distributed into sets of a fixed size; the answer is the number of sets of the given size that can be made. The quotitive division problem *Mrs. White has 24 cookies. She wants to put 6 cookies on each plate. How many plates does she need?* would be modeled by putting 6 objects in a pile, putting 6 more objects in another pile, and so on until 24 objects had been used. The answer would be the number of piles. Through learning about the ways in which children model these problems, the teachers also learn about the mathematical differences in the problems.

It should be noted that the differences between partitive and quotitive division, while they may be familiar to many teachers, are not likely to have been addressed in mathematics classes taken by teachers. They are, however, important distinctions as teachers strive to learn about the mathematical understanding of their students. Knowing about the two types of division problems, for example, helps a teacher understand why a student who solves the stated partitive division problem does not then automatically know the answer to the quotitive division problem, which he may see as a quite different problem. In a discussion of PUFM, Ma (1999) gives examples of concepts important for teachers to understand that may not be as important for mathematicians who deal primarily in abstractions. The distinction between partitive and quotitive division is another such example.

During the year in which the examples given here occurred, Ms. Valentine was working with a group of CGI researchers and other experienced third, fourth, and fifth grade CGI teachers to develop information on children's thinking about multidigit multiplication and division and about fractions, topics that had not been discussed in the CGI workshops they had attended. This group met approximately once a month to talk about what they were learning about children's thinking on these topics. They shared children's work, discussed strategies that had been observed in their classrooms, and talked about what previous research had shown about children's thinking related to the topics. Teachers left the meetings with problems that they were to pose to their children before the next meeting. In addition, each teacher was paired with a researcher who observed in his or her classroom. I was the researcher paired with Ms. Valentine and observed her teaching 24 mathematics lessons over a 4-month period. Detailed field notes were taken during the observations. In addition, discussions with Ms. Valentine and, occasionally, with some of her colleagues were held after the observations. Notes were also made on these discussions.

THE CLASS

Ms. Valentine taught a combination fourth-fifth grade class; there were 13 fourth graders and 12 fifth graders in the class. Most of the fifth graders were in her class for the third consecutive year, first in a self-contained third grade class, then as fourth graders in a combination fourth-fifth grade class, and now as fifth graders in a combination class. Thus, Ms. Valentine had had extensive, and somewhat unusual, opportunities to learn about the mathematical thinking of the children in her class. In addition, the children were aware of and comfortable with the ways in which Ms. Valentine organized her mathematics instruction. Ms. Valentine chose to teach mathematics to her fourth and fifth grade students separately. The lessons described here involved only her fifth grade students.

The ways in which Ms. Valentine structured her classroom included elements that have been found in many CGI classrooms. Problem solving was the focus of the curriculum, children decided how to solve the problems and shared their strategies among themselves and with Ms. Valentine, and Ms. Valentine used what she learned about her own children's problem-solving strategies in conjunction with research-based information on children's mathematical thinking to plan instruction. She also, however, engaged her children in discussions of mathematics that extended beyond their strategies for solving particular problems to the mathematics underlying the problems and strategies.

Three sets of lessons, all involving division, are described. These particular lessons have been selected from among those observed for two reasons. First, they all deal with division, so themes in children's thinking and in the mathematics can be traced across the sets of lessons. Second, the role of Ms. Valentine's content knowledge is particularly apparent in these lessons. The first set of lessons deals with multidigit division with no remainder. The second set deals with equal-sharing situations in which there is a remainder that must also be shared. The third set involves division by 1/4.

MULTIDIGIT DIVISION

As was explained earlier, Ms. Valentine had learned about young children's strategies for solving partititve and quotitive division problems with small numbers, and she was exploring the strategies her children used for both types of problems with multidigit numbers. Ms. Valentine, like many CGI teachers, asked her children to explain how they solved word problems and to compare and contrast the strategies that were shared. Ms. Valentine, however, expected her children to go beyond sharing and comparing strategies. Drawing on her understanding of the mathematics involved and her understanding of how children solve word problems, she asked her children first to categorize their strategies for solving division word problems and then to differentiate between the operations used in those strategies and the structure of the problems that made them either partitive or quotitive division problems. This occurred over a series of lessons.

As Ms. Valentine's fifth-graders solved division word problems and discussed their strategies, they came up with names for types of strategies that were frequently used. A list of these strategies, with the names given them by the children, follows.

Strategies for Division

- Guess and Check
  Michael used this strategy to divide 91 by 7. He guessed that the answer was 12. He then found that 12 x 7 was 84 and added another 7 to get 91. He concluded that the answer to the original problem was 13.

- Take Numbers Apart
  John explained how to divide 424 by 4 using this strategy. He said he would divide 400 by 4 to get 100, 20 by 4 to get 5, and 4 by 4 to get 1, so the answer was 100 + 5 + 1 or 106.

- Counting Back
  Rachel demonstrated counting back to find 96 divided by 4. She counted "96, 92, 88, . . . 8, 4," using her fingers to keep track of the number of counts.

- Adding Groups
  Sarah wrote how she divided 96 by 4 as follows:
  $4 \times 4 \rightarrow 16 + 16 \rightarrow 32 + 32 \rightarrow 64 + 32 \rightarrow 96$
  4   4   8   8   16   8   24
  Each number in the lower row shows the number of fours in the number directly above.

- Division Form
  This method was the standard long-division algorithm. Although Ms. Valentine did not show her children standard algorithms, they did learn them from others and bring them to share in class. This strategy had been introduced by Jake, a child who had moved from Colorado to Wisconsin the previous summer and had learned the algorithm in school in Colorado. In fact, the children sometimes referred to the algorithm as "Jake's Way" or "the Colorado Way." Ms. Valentine discouraged the use of these names, however, preferring that the names used for strategies reflect what was actually done as the strategy was used.

- Division by Subtraction
  Division by subtraction was analogous to division by adding
  groups; it entailed subtracting groups of the divisor from the
  dividend and keeping track of the number of groups subtracted.

This list of strategies was not a list that Ms. Valentine had learned
about in a workshop. Rather, it was a list generated in her classroom
as her children solved problems and described and compared their
solution strategies. In Ms. Valentine's words:

> I was trying to get away from using the children's names as in "Jake's
> Way" and see whether the children could identify and later recognize
> features of the strategies (some of which came out in the names the
> students gave each strategy). We often look at the efficiency, what's alike
> and what's different between strategies. I think that naming is a way to
> make the talk a little easier (Carrie Valentine, personal communication,
> September 14, 1999).

The use of these labels helped the children analyze their strategies
and think about the operations they were using as well as the
problems they were solving. This played out in the discussion of a
homework problem.

Defining Division

The children had solved three division problems for homework and
had shared their strategies for the first of the three. They then turned
to the second problem: *Laura collected 7 Indian head pennies from one
year. If the collective age of the coins was 13,279 years, what year were the
coins made?* Rather than asking for the answer to the problem or how
the children had solved the problem, Ms. Valentine asked a quite
different question; she asked what kind of problem it was. The
following discussion ensued. (When discussions of mathematics
occurred in Ms. Valentine's class, they were truly discussions, in that
the children talked among themselves rather than being formally
recognized by the teacher before speaking.)

Annie: It's division.

Rachel: It's division, but I used subtraction to solve it.

Sarah: It's division, but it's also subtraction, if you use division by subtraction.

Leah: It's division. I agree that you might use subtraction to solve it, but that's more of a strategy.

Michael: It could be any kind.

Jake: I agree with Michael. It could be any kind.

Leah: If you said, "Write the problem," you would write 13,297 divided by 7. You wouldn't write about subtraction.

At this point, Ms. Valentine shifted the discussion from a particular problem to a more general discussion of division. She was aware that there was a distinction between the operation used to solve a problem and the operation inherent in the structure of the problem itself. Therefore, she choose to ask questions to ascertain whether the children were aware of that distinction. That is, her mathematical understanding contributed to her being able to learn about her children's thinking in ways that extended beyond the strategies they used to solve this problem.

She interjected, "What makes a division problem a division problem? Rajeev?" Rajeev didn't reply, and Ms. Valentine went on. "We have to come to a decision by the end of the year." When she was later asked about her intent in having the children focus on the definition of division, she elaborated:

> They had been solving these problems without much attention to the name "division" and had discovered many ways to solve them. I was hoping they could put those strategies under the big umbrella of acceptable strategies for division problems. Should anyone ask them whether they could solve division problems they could answer yes (Carrie Valentine, personal communication, September 14, 1999).

The discussion continued.

John: It gives you the numbers to divide it by. It's like taking a number and timesing it, but you don't know what you times it by. (He said 13,279 equals 7 times 1897 and Ms. Valentine wrote $13,279 = 7 \times 1897$.)

Ms. Valentine: What does the 13,279 correspond to?

Class: The total age.

Ms. Valentine: What does the 7 correspond to?

Class: How many pennies.

Ms. Valentine again attempted to shift the focus of the discussion to a more general discussion of division.

> Ms. Valentine: What if we change the words for what they correspond to in order to make it more generic? Seven corresponds to the number of groups; we're trying to find out how many in a group.

> Megan: It's division, because that's the main method people would use to solve it.

> Sarah: It depends on the numbers you're given. If you knew 7 x 1897, it would be multiplication.

> Ms. Valentine: Do you agree with Sarah? Many people did not use division to solve it.

The answer for her question was left for the children to reflect on. Ms. Valentine wanted the children to think about division more abstractly, apart from the context of a specific word problem. They were told that for homework they were to respond to the following: (a) Write an explanation of why you think or do not think the three problems you solved are division; (b) What makes a problem a division problem? The answer has to apply to all division problems. Two days later the children shared their responses to the second question. Those responses were:

> John: You have a large number and a smaller number that you divide into the large number.

> Peter: Mine was the same as David's.

> Michael: You have a total and are trying to find out how many parts there are or how big the parts are.

Brandon: The numbers and signs are different.   (He went on to explain that you use ÷ rather than +, −, or ×.)

Jake: When you're splitting portions, like a pie into equal parts. You have a big group and you are breaking it into little groups.

Derek: You have to divide two numbers to get your answer.

Rita: You have a big number and a little number and want equal groups.

Rachel: One number has to be bigger than the other number.

Megan: One number has to be the same or bigger than the other. You have to divide something into groups.

Sarah: It's a problem with one number bigger than the other that you can divide without a remainder.

Leah: You're trying to find out how many times a number goes into another number equally.

Jenny: You have a number and you're trying to find out how many times it goes into the other number.

As the children gave their descriptions of what made a problem a division problem, Ms. Valentine wrote them on the board, grouping similar ones together. She commented that they would need to talk more about the idea that seemed to be implicit in some of the definitions, that when you divide you are always dividing something into parts of a fixed size and finding the number of parts. In addition, she said they needed to address the notion included in several of the definitions that division required dividing a large number by a smaller one.

When all of the definitions had been collected, Ms. Valentine asked the children to compare and contrast them. Ideas brought up by the children included that all of their definitions said something about parts or groups, that all of the groups had to be of equal size, and that the number in a group is important. Ms. Valentine directed them to Michael's definition in which he said that you could be finding the number of parts there are or you could be finding how big the parts are. She referred to the two situations as "find the number of groups" problems and "find the number in a group" problems. She asked for an example of each kind of problem. After discussion, the children agreed on the following two problems.

Find the number in a group problem: *Dad caught 15 fish. There are 5 people. How many fish does each person get?*

Find the number of groups problem: *Dad caught 15 fish. Each person can eat 3 fish. How many people can eat?*

For homework, the children were told to write one problem of each type. The discussions of the two types of problems continued during the next three mathematics lessons.

Ms. Valentine's deep mathematical content knowledge is apparent in the descriptions of her instruction and in the personal communication I had with her at a later date. That knowledge strongly influenced what happened in her class and the ways in which she was able to reflect on her teaching and make appropriate instructional decisions given what she learned about her children's thinking. Ms. Valentine's knowledge of the contrast between partitive and quotitive division was evident in her noting that they would need to talk more about the idea that seemed to be implicit in some of the definitions, that when you divide you are always dividing something into parts of a fixed size and finding the number of parts. In addition, she demonstrated an understanding of division that extended beyond what she had the opportunity to learn at CGI workshops. She commented to the students that they needed to address the notion included in several of the definitions that division required dividing a large number by a smaller one. It was because of her mathematical understanding that she was able to verify whether the definitions the children proposed were mathematically valid and to identify Michael's definition as one that could be used to help extend the thinking of the other children.

DIVISION WITH REMAINDERS

In this section, I briefly describe one lesson in which children solved an equal-sharing or partitive division problem with a remainder that also was to be shared. This problem and others like it were used based on suggestions of the group of researchers and teachers with whom Ms. Valentine was working. Although it is not clear that Ms. Valentine would have used such problems without those suggestions, it is not my intent in this chapter to focus on the sources of her knowledge. Suffice it to say that she did learn from the research group, and one thing she learned was that these problems provided a framework for supporting children's learning about fractions.

The children had solved the following problem: *Ms. Valentine had 13 bars of clay to share among 8 children. How much clay could each child have?* It was in solving such problems that the children's former idea about always needing to divide a large number by a smaller one arose again, although it was not explicitly addressed. In the problem given, for example, most of the children distributed the bars of clay so that each child had one bar and then proceeded to divide the remaining five bars among the eight children. Some divided each of the five bars into eight parts and gave each of the eight children one part from each bar for a total of 5/8 of a bar of clay. Others divided 4 of the 5 bars into halves and gave each child one of the halves. They then divided the remaining bar into eighths and gave each child one of the eighths for a total of 1/2 and 1/8. Most of the children in the class could explain why this was equal to the answer of 5/8 arrived at by the others.

Division by One-Fourth

In March, another idea that many of the children had about division surfaced; they believed that the quotient will always be smaller than the dividend. That they believed this became apparent as the result of solving and discussing a long, somewhat complex word problem requiring several calculations, the purpose of which was to allow the children to practice multidigit computation. The problem was about a leprechaun who was observing their class and awarding points whenever he heard kind words or subtracting points when he heard negative remarks. At one point in the story, the leprechaun had accumulated 368 points. The next sentence said, "He noticed that a few students said some unkind words as they walked into their classroom, so he took 1/4 of the total away."

The children worked on this problem as a homework problem, and the class then discussed their answers and the strategies they had used to arrive at those answers. Derek explained how he had solved the problem and, as he did so, wrote his calculations on a sheet of newsprint. When he arrived at the point in the problem where the leprechaun takes away 1/4 of 368 points, Derek wrote 368 ÷ 1/4. Ms. Valentine asked whether he was dividing by 4 or by 1/4. Derek seemed confused by what she was asking and didn't answer. She then suggested that he wanted to put the points into four equal groups, and he altered what he had written to say 368 ÷ 4. Once again Ms. Valentine's mathematical knowledge played a role in her response to a child. It was clear that Ms. Valentine had recognized the difference between 368 ÷ 1/4 and 368 ÷ 4. It was also apparent than Ms. Valentine was aware that Derek's understanding of division by a fraction or of the notation used for such division was not complete. What was not clear was why she had chosen not to discuss the difference with the class. When asked, she replied that the children were involved in the details of the leprechaun problem and that the distinction between the two expressions was important enough that it should not be discussed as an incidental part of another problem; that she would bring it up again later.

Ms. Valentine's deep knowledge of the mathematics involved (division of rational numbers), of the importance of that mathematics, and of her students' mathematical understanding led her to make a deliberate instructional decision to postpone discussion by a positive number less than one at that time. She did, however, address it in her next mathematics lesson. Instead of demonstrating a procedure for division of fractions, as a teacher without her understanding of the mathematics involved and the thinking of her students might, she asked a question. She wrote 12 ÷ 4 and 12 ÷ 1/4 on newsprint and asked, "Can you compare or discuss these two problems?"

Although many of the problems solved in her class are word problems, in this lesson Ms. Valentine wanted to focus on the meaning of division and deliberately chose not to contextualize the problems. She could have used a word problem for 12 ÷ 1/4. For example, she could have said: *I have 12 yards of ribbon to make bows. It takes 1/4 yard for each bow. How many bows can I make?* In fact, later in the lesson, she did generate such a problem. However, she made a conscious choice not to begin the lesson that way. She recognized that her children would be likely to solve such a word problem by multiplying 12 by 4, rather than focusing on division by 1/4 as she wanted them to. Therefore, she began the lesson with what she called a "naked number" problem. The ability to make this decision, in fact, the ability to analyze the mathematics to be discussed in conjunction with her students' understanding of that mathematics and recognize that it was possible to make such a decision, demonstrate the sophistication of Ms. Valentine's thinking about mathematics and about her students' understanding.

Leah was the first one to answer Ms. Valentine's question. Her response was that the problems were the same and that they were both equal to three. It was obvious to her, she said, that $12 \div 4$ was three and $12 \div 1/4$ meant $1/4$ of 12, so that was also three.

John at first agreed that they had the same answer. He said that they were "opposite problems." He compared them to 3×4 and 4×3, which he said were opposite problems that have the same answer. He went on, however, to add that $12 \div 1/4$ could be 3 or it could be 48. It depended, he said, on what the $1/4$ meant—whether it was $1/4$ of 12 or $1/4$ of 1. If it meant $1/4$ of 12, the answer was 3; if it meant $1/4$ of 1, the answer was 48. The other children didn't understand John's comments. Sarah was particularly vocal in expressing her confusion; she asked, "What does 48 have to do with it anyway?"

Leah contributed a revision to her earlier response that both problems were equal to 3. She built on what John had said, asserting that $12 \div 1/4$ could be 4. If the $1/4$ meant $1/4$ of 12, then the $1/4$ meant 3 (which is $1/4$ of 12), so the problem said $12 \div 3$ which is equal to 4. Rajeev said he agreed with Laura.

Ms. Valentine wrote on the newsprint, $12 \div 1/4 = 3$ (?) or 48 (?) or 4 (?). Although Ms. Valentine wrote Leah's answer of 4 on the newsprint, she did not single it out for further attention. Instead she focused on John's answer of 48, asking if there was a way he could use paper to help the others understand why he said that $12 \div 1/4$ might be 48. While he worked on that, she asked the others if they remembered their earlier discussions about the two kinds of division problems. She said that those discussions might help them decide what the answer to $12 \div 1/4$ should be. The children remembered the discussions and searched through their notebooks for examples of the two kinds of problems. Before they found examples, John interrupted to say that he had a picture that showed why the answer could be 48. He had drawn 12 rectangles, each divided into fourths.

John described the drawing by saying that he had drawn 12 windows and divided them each into 4 pieces. He shaded in $1/4$ of a window and said there were 48 of those. The drawing did not clarify what John was saying for all of the children, although it did for some of them. Leah, for example, said that she was completely lost. Rachel, on the other hand, said that she understood. "If you divide 12 into $1/4$s, you get 48 of them." Interestingly, John had not convinced himself. He still thought that the answer could be 3 or it could be 48.

Ms. Valentine asked John what would help him decide. He answered that they could vote. Laughter erupted, but they did take a vote. Two children voted for 48, John didn't vote, and the other children voted for 3. John said that the reason he didn't vote was that you couldn't decide which one was correct without a story. At this point, Ms. Valentine did offer a word problem: *I have 12 sticks of butter. The recipe I want to make takes 1/4 stick of butter. How many recipes can I make?* The children solved the problem correctly. Rachel, for example, explained drawing 12 sticks of butter, dividing each one into 4 equal pieces, and counting the pieces. Ms. Valentine then told them that the number sentence that went with that problem was $12 \div 1/4 = 48$. In response, Rajeev said, "It makes sense to me, but I still don't get it, because how could you divide and get a bigger number?"

The children were next asked what $48 \times 1/4$ was equal to. Some were sure it was 192 (explanations for this were not given) and others believed it was 12. Among those who were convinced the answer was 12 was Michael, who commented, "This is really weird! It's going down for multiplication and up for division!" Other children made similar comments. Obviously, the children did not completely understand multiplication and division by numbers less than one at the end of the lesson. However, they had begun to explore the operations in ways that could lead to understanding.

After class, Ms. Valentine expressed her surprise that the children believed you should get a larger number when you multiply and a smaller one when you divide, since she knew she had certainly not told them that was the case. She later explained her surprise:

> I guess I was surprised that the kids had made the generalization without ever having it made it explicit in the classroom. In retrospect that was a silly assumption on my part. I probably hoped that I had given them enough counter examples so that they wouldn't have done that. Obviously, I hadn't (Carrie Valentine, personal communication, September 15, 1999).

That Ms. Valentine chose to teach this lesson in the way she did illustrates her understanding of the mathematics underlying the lesson. In addition, it illustrates her knowledge of her children and the trust she had in their thinking; she was confident that they could begin to make sense of multiplication and division by 1/4 through their own reasoning. Further, it illustrates that she was confident that she could work with whatever responses came up from her children.

MS. VALENTINE'S KNOWLEDGE

Throughout the examples drawn from Ms. Valentine's class, one can find evidence for the ways in which her mathematical knowledge increased her ability to learn about her children's mathematical thinking and informed her instructional decisions. In discussing how this occurred in Ms. Valentine's class, I return to the points made earlier about how teachers' knowledge of mathematics contributes to their learning about and building on the mathematical thinking of their children. Teachers with knowledge of both research-based information on children's thinking and the mathematics they teach are able to: (a) pose questions that go beyond asking children to describe their solution strategies; (b) understand children's mathematical thinking that differs from what might be expected based on the research-based information on children's thinking; (c) critically examine children's thinking to determine if it is mathematically valid; and (d) use what they learn about their children's thinking to create tasks that enable children to extend their thinking.

First, Ms. Valentine, like many CGI teachers, asked her children to explain how they solved division problems and understood the strategies the children described. Also like many CGI teachers, Ms. Valentine asked her children to compare strategies. Ms. Valentine's questioning, however, went beyond asking children to share and compare strategies. She posed questions that required them to think more deeply about the mathematics underlying both the strategies they were using and the problems they were solving. These questions included asking children to name and classify their strategies for solving division problems and asking them to explain what made a problem a division problem.

Second, Ms. Valentine understood her students' mathematical thinking in ways that extended beyond what she had learned at CGI workshops. Through the discussions she initiated about what makes a problem a division problem, she learned a great deal about the children's thinking that was not tied specifically to their strategies for solving problems. In the discussion about dividing by 1/4, she learned that the children believed that multiplication always results in a larger number and division in a smaller one.

Third, Ms. Valentine was able to critically examine students' ideas to determine if they were mathematically valid. She was able, for example, to listen to the students' definitions of division and respond to them based on the mathematical ideas behind them. She also was aware that when Derek wrote 368 ÷ 1/4, his understanding of division by a fraction or of the notation used for such division was not complete. And, when the children expressed their thoughts about multiplication making larger and division making smaller, she recognized that these were ideas that needed further attention.

Fourth, Ms. Valentine was able, like many CGI teachers, to use what she learned about her children's thinking to select appropriate problems for them to solve. However, Ms. Valentine was also able to use what she learned about her children's thinking to create, rather than select, tasks that enabled the students to extend their mathematical thinking.

CONCLUSIONS

The mathematics education literature contains numerous examples of the limited mathematical understanding of many elementary and middle-school teachers in the United States (cf. Ball, 1990; Fennema, & Franke, 1992; Ma, 1999; Post, Harel, Behr, & Lesh, 1991). Given the traditional view of mathematics teaching, one in which the teacher transmits a specified body of information to students who absorb it, the type of knowledge the teacher needs and the role of that knowledge in teaching is obvious. Teachers need to know the concepts and skills taught at the grade level they are teaching in ways that they can explain or show them to students. New views of how mathematics is learned and how mathematics should be taught, however, shift the focus from the teachers' knowledge of mathematics content as a body of information that can be directly transmitted to students.

In discussing the importance of teachers' knowledge of mathematics content, Fennema and Franke (1992) claimed that it is not sufficient to examine that knowledge apart from the teachers' practice or apart from other knowledge. Ball's (1998) call for investigating the sites in teachers' practice where teachers' mathematics knowledge matters reiterates Fennema and Franke's claim that teachers' knowledge must be examined in the context of their practice. This notion implies that there are differences between knowledge needed for teaching mathematics and knowledge that is sufficient for those who do not teach.

Ma (1999) described the knowledge of teachers with PUFM and the connections that those teachers make between their understanding of elementary school mathematics and mathematics teaching and learning. Ma does not, however, provide examples of how the differences actually play out in classrooms. The description given here of Carrie Valentine's teaching illustrates the role of PUFM in teaching and in learning about and building on the mathematical thinking of students. In the examples drawn from her class, it is apparent that the discussions of mathematics that occurred were possible because her knowledge of mathematics and of her children allowed her to make very sophisticated pedagogical decisions both during mathematics lessons and in planning future lessons.

As was said earlier, there is wide agreement about the value of teachers' attending to the mathematical thinking of their children and basing their instructional decisions on that thinking. I have suggested in this chapter that teachers' knowledge of mathematics can make a difference as they attend to the mathematical thinking of the children in their classes. Carrie Valentine's knowledge of mathematics influenced how and what she learned about her children's thinking and how she was able to use their thinking in making decisions for instruction. The case of Ms. Valentine illustrates the importance of teachers having deep understanding of the mathematics content they teach and linking that understanding to their knowledge of their children's mathematical thinking.

Additional research needs to be done on the role of teachers' content knowledge in teaching mathematics in ways consistent with the reform movement. One route researchers could take is to do as I have done in this chapter and focus on teachers who are successfully implementing the new vision of mathematics teaching in order to learn the role played by their mathematical knowledge. Another route researchers could follow is to investigate teachers who are in the process of changing their practice in order to understand the ways in which mathematical knowledge influences or lack of mathematical knowledge hinders teachers' abilities to transform their practice. Still another line of research could focus on the ways in which teachers' content knowledge changes in the context of their practice as they interact with children and as they reflect on the children's learning and their own teaching. And still another line of research could investigate the ways in which mathematics teacher educators can help teachers learn mathematics in ways that will be useful as they teach in ways in line with the calls for reform.

ACKNOWLEDGMENTS

The research reported in this paper was supported in part by a grant from the National Science Foundation (MDR-8954697). The opinions expressed in this paper do not necessarily reflect the position, policy, or endorsement of the National Science Foundation.

REFERENCES

Ball, D. L. (1990). The mathematical understandings that prospective teachers bring to teacher education. *Elementary School Journal, 90*, 450-466.

Ball, D. L. (1998, April). *Cattell lecture.* Paper presented at the annual meeting of the American Educational Research Association. San Diego, CA.

Battista, M. T. (1999). The mathematical miseducation of America's youth. *Phi Delta Kappan, 80*, 425-433.

Carpenter, T. P., Fennema, E., Peterson, P. L., & Carey, D. A. (1988). Teachers' pedagogical content knowledge of students' problem solving in elementary arithmetic. *Journal for Research in Mathematics Education, 19*, 385-401.

Cobb, P., Wood, T., Yackel, E., & Wheatley, G. (1993). Introduction: Background of the research. (in T. Wood, P. Cobb, E. Yackel, & D. Dillon (Eds.), *Rethinking elementary school mathematics: Insights and issues.,* (Journal of Research in Mathematics Education Monograph No. 6, pp. 1-4). Reston, VA: National Council of Teachers of Mathematics.

Fennema, E., Carpenter, T. P., Franke, M. L., Levi, L., Jacobs, V. R., & Empson, S. B. (1996). A longitudinal study of learning to use children's thinking in mathematics instruction. *Journal for Research in Mathematics Education, 27*, 403-434.

Fennema, E., & Franke, M. L. (1992). Teachers' knowledge and its impact. In D. A. Grouws (Ed.), *Handbook of research on mathematics teaching and learning* (pp. 147-164). New York: Macmillan.

Franke, M. L., Fennema, E., Carpenter, T. P., Ansell, E., & Behrend, J. (1995, April). *Changing teachers: Interactions between beliefs and classroom practice in the context of elementary school mathematics.* Paper presented at the annual meeting of the American Educational Research Association, San Francisco, CA.

Hiebert, J., & Carpenter, T. P. (1992). Learning and teaching with understanding. In D. A. Grouws (Ed.), *Handbook of research on mathematics teaching and learning* (pp. 65-97). New York: Macmillan.

Ma, L. (1999). *Knowing and teaching elementary mathematics: Teachers' understanding of fundamental mathematics in China and the United States.* Mahwah, NJ: Lawrence Erlbaum Associates.

Post, T. R., Harel, G., Behr, M. J., & Lesh, R. (1991). Intermediate teachers' knowledge of rational number concepts. In E. Fennema, T. P. Carpenter, & S. J. Lamon (Eds.), *Integrating research on teaching and learning mathematics* (pp. 177-198). Albany, NY: SUNY Press.

Schifter, D., & Fosnot, C. T. (1993). *Reconstructing mathematics education: Stories of teachers meeting the challenge of reform.* New York: Teachers College Press.

Thompson, A. (1992). Teachers' beliefs and conceptions. In D. A. Grouws (Ed.), *Handbook of research on mathematics teaching and learning* (pp. 127-146). New York: Macmillan.

Warfield, J. (1996). *Kindergarten teachers' knowledge of their children's mathematical thinking: Two case studies.* Unpublished doctoral dissertation, University of Wisconsin-Madison.

Two Intertwined Bodies of Work

Conducting Research on Mathematics Teacher Development and Elaborating Theory of Mathematics Teaching/Learning

Martin A. Simon
Penn State University

In this chapter, I describe how two lines of study, one empirical and one theoretical, can exist in a creative interdependence. Philosophers of science and many practicing scientists have described a dialectical relationship between theory and empirical research (cf., Kuhn, 1962; Cobb, 1995). The common application of this idea would result in considering the relationship between research on teacher development and theory of teacher development. However, my purpose in this chapter is to discuss the less obvious relationship between research on teacher development and theory of mathematics teaching/learning. (Note that I refer to teaching/learning to suggest an integrated theory as opposed to two separate ones.)

In an earlier article (Simon, 1997), I argued that for a research team studying mathematics teacher development, an essential part of its conceptual framework is its conception of mathematics teaching/learning, and that a lack of useful, articulated conceptions of mathematics teaching is hampering research on teacher development. I summarize this argument and then go beyond it to describe how the empirical study of teacher development fuels an active program of theoretical work on teaching/learning.

A research team's understandings of mathematics teaching/learning structure its investigation of teachers' teaching and the conceptions that underlie that teaching. The researchers use their understanding of teaching/learning (ideally identified explicitly) to determine what is important, interesting, or puzzling. These ideas determine to what the researchers pay attention. Often noticing occurs as a result of contrast between what the researchers observe in the other and the researchers' own cognitive structures.

This brings up a paradox that is fundamental in our[1] research. On one hand what we notice and take as significant is structured by how we conceive of mathematics teaching/learning; on the other hand, we must "set aside" our conceptions in order to make sense of the ideas and actions of the teachers that we study. (Henceforth, we will talk about teachers' pedagogical actions and conceptions related to mathematics, learning, and teaching as teachers' practices.) In other words, our conceptions of teaching/learning structure the nature of our inquiry and also serve as a basis for a contrast with the teachers in the study. When we note a contrast, we must attempt to understand how the teachers are making sense of the situation in ways that are distinct from our own.

The second part of the discussion is that our empirical study on teacher development has required us, from our perspective, to undertake an additional research program, the elaboration of theory of teaching/learning and how it contributes to that theory development. To contextualize this aspect of the discussion, I describe the goals of our empirical research and the methodology we employ.

GOALS AND METHODOLOGY FOR RESEARCH ON MATHEMATICS TEACHER DEVELOPMENT

The purpose of our research is to understand the process by which teachers can develop their practices to be more in line with current reform principles. In particular, we use our understanding of teaching/learning (summarized in the next section) to specify what we mean by "reform principles." Toward this end, we attempt to understand the practice of teachers at different points in time in the context of an ongoing teacher development program that we conduct. (Note that teachers refers to both inservice and preservice teachers unless otherwise specified.)

---

[1] The first person plural refers to the Mathematics Teacher Development (MTD) Project research team composed of Ron Tzur, Peg Smith, Karen Heinz, Margaret Kinzel, and myself.

Our overarching methodology, we refer to as the "teacher development" experiment (Simon, 2000), which combines teaching experiments conducted in courses for teachers with case studies of individual teachers. The teaching experiments include our ongoing attempts to understand the conceptions and practices of the teachers (as a group) as they participate in experiences designed to foster their development. The case studies, with selected members of the group, are used to generate accounts of the teachers' practices (Simon & Tzur, 1999) and ultimately to characterize changes in practices that occur in the context of participating in the courses and associated coaching. These accounts are based on our assumption that each teacher has a coherent practice and that it is our job as researchers to understand the perspectives from which that coherence derives.

Thus, in all aspects of the teacher development experiment, we endeavor to understand the mathematical and pedagogical conceptions and activity of the teacher. Our analyses result in the postulating of new constructs in order to characterize key components of the teachers' practice.

To summarize, our conceptual framework with respect to mathematics teaching/learning structures our noticing of aspects of the teacher's practice. However, the initial framework cannot account for the full set of observations. This leads us to postulate new constructs to account for the teachers' practices. These new constructs in turn provide a contrast on the basis of which we can look back at our original conceptualization of teaching/learning and further elaborate the ideas and perspectives involved. This evolution of our conceptualization of teaching/learning may involve making explicit some aspects that had previously remained implicit, identifying critical components that merit greater emphasis, and developing, or modifying current ideas. The modification of our theory of teaching/learning leads to a next cycle in which the modified framework structures the data collection and analysis which in turn leads to further modifications in the theory of teaching/learning. This cycle of influence is represented schematically in Fig. 8.1.

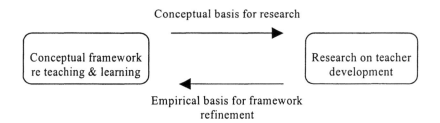

FIG. 8.1. Bi-directional influence between frameworks and research.

The key point is that we consider the study of mathematics teacher development to involve the making of distinctions about teaching. Any distinction requires a comparison between at least two states. Because the goal of mathematics teacher education reform is an evolving target, efforts to make important distinctions about teaching require that work on the goal (specified by a theory of teaching/learning) be commensurate with work on characterizing the practices of teachers in transition. Further, these two endeavors can each contribute to the growth of the other. (Note that teachers in transition refers to teachers who are participating in the current reform and who have begun to employ alternatives to direct teaching (telling and showing).) In the next section, I provide an example of this cyclical process from a recent research project.

AN EXAMPLE FROM THE MATHEMATICS TEACHER DEVELOPMENT PROJECT

The theoretical and empirical work described in this section was conducted as part of the Mathematics Teacher Development (MTD) Project, a 4 1/2-year research project designed to promote and study elementary mathematics teacher development. The research project used a teacher development experiment methodology and attempted to promote teacher development through five courses for a combined group of practicing and prospective teachers. Development was also supported by placing the prospective teachers in the practicing teachers' classes and providing classroom coaching for each pair. The purpose of this structure was to maximize the development of the teachers involved to allow us to study the nature of that development and the process by which it occurred. The development under study can be thought of generally as evolution from more traditional practices toward practices more consistent with current mathematics education reforms. Specifically, our notions of development were defined by our conceptualization of mathematics teaching/learning.

Conceptual Framework on Mathematics Teaching/Learning

Our conceptual framework builds on an emergent perspective (Cobb & Yackel, 1996; Cobb, Yackel, & Wood, 1993), a social constructivist perspective on mathematics learning that involves the coordination of a radical constructivist cognitive perspective with a social perspective (Cobb & Bauersfeld, 1995). Common to both the cognitive and the social perspectives is a view of mathematics as a product of human activity, not a reality independent of human activity.

For the example that follows, it is the cognitive perspective that is in the foreground. Consistent with this perspective, we see mathematics teaching as a process in which the teacher fosters the development of powerful mathematics (labeled reinvention by Freudenthal, 1991) among a group of students. What students can learn is afforded and constrained by their extant conceptions (Piaget's, 1985, notion of assimilation), individually and collectively. Thus, current knowledge influences how mathematical situations are understood (interpreted) and the potential transformations that the students' knowledge might undergo in the process of dealing with those situations.

The teacher's responsibility in these situations is to promote students' development of powerful mathematical concepts and effective ways of acting that might not occur in the absence of teaching or that would develop over a far greater period of time. According to our conceptual framework (see Simon, 1995 for a more detailed discussion), such teaching can be characterized by a cycle of interaction and reflection that encompasses the following:

Interaction Phase: (in the classroom)
- Ongoing assessment of the students' relevant mathematical understandings.
- Presentation of mathematical situations; facilitation of mathematical activity, communication, and student reflection; and negotiation (with students) of meanings, norms, and practices.

<u>Reflection Phase</u>: (Short periods of reflection that occur during teaching sessions and longer periods of reflection that occur between sessions).

- Interpretation of students' mathematical activity resulting in modification of teacher's understanding of individual and collective knowledge and the current state of classroom norms and practices.
- Development of hypothetical learning trajectories consisting of the goals for student learning, the plan for mathematical situations (problems, tasks to promote learning), and hypotheses by which the process of learning might proceed in the context of those mathematical situations.

To summarize, two prominent features of our perspective on mathematics teaching are the teacher's development of useful understandings of the students' mathematics and the teacher's generation of hypothetical (continually revisable) learning trajectories that guide her/his decision making and interactions with students.

Understanding the Perspectives of Teachers in Transition

One of the results of the MTD analyses of a large corpus of data is our postulation of a *perception-based perspective* on student learning that we believe characterizes many teachers in transition. The research that led us to postulate this construct is presented in Simon, Tzur, Heinz, Kinzel, and Smith (in press, 1998). I describe this perspective briefly and then contrast it with a traditional perspective and with the conception-based perspective held by the researchers.

Perception-Based Perspective on Learning

Characterizing a teacher's perspective as perception based indicates that she or he has moved beyond a traditional perspective on teaching and learning; that is, we consider teaching based on a perception-based perspective to generally afford greater opportunity for student conceptual learning. Such a characterization is the researchers' claim as to the organization underlying a teacher's practice, and is not a claim as to how he or she would represent that perspective.

A *perception-based perspective* is based on the assumption that coming to know mathematics is a matter of perceiving (noticing) mathematical objects and relationships that exist and are accessible independent of human activity. Cobb, Yackel, and Wood (1992) referred to this implicit assumption as a "representational view of mind" (p. 1). The assumption that people perceive mathematics "as it is" leads to an assumption that there is no variation in what is perceived by different perceivers.

From a perception-based perspective, mathematics is considered to be an interconnected set of relationships. These connections can be apprehended by the mathematics learner, revealing the inherent reasonableness and logical consistency of mathematics. From this perspective, mathematics is learned by perceiving mathematical objects and principles and the interconnections (relationships) among them. This is thought to be best achieved by students examining for themselves mathematical situations in which the relevant mathe-matics can be seen, that is, they learn best through first-hand experience with the mathematics. The teacher's role is to guide and afford students' direct apprehension of mathematics.

For example, in Simon et al. (in press), we describe Ivy's lesson with her sixth-grade class in which she endeavors to promote their understanding of the canonical long division algorithm by having the students do division problems with base-ten blocks while she points out the corresponding steps of the algorithm. Her immediate goal was for the students to understand the algorithm, that is, to "see the relationship between the blocks and the algorithm." Ivy expected that her students would see the connection between the blocks solution and the paper-and-pencil algorithm because she was orienting their perception toward the connection by juxtaposing the students blocks solutions with the steps of the algorithm.

A perception-based perspective differs from a traditional perspective on learning in its focus on the importance of learners' first-hand experience perceiving mathematical relationships. A traditional teaching perspective can be characterized as providing students with the conceptions of the teacher or those presented in the textbook. In our example, Ivy did not just present the algorithm or explain the meaning of each step. Rather, she had the students explore solutions using base-ten blocks in order for them to "see" long division in a meaningful context.

From our (researchers') perspective, which we refer to as conception-based, we emphasize that Ivy was able to see the relationship between the blocks solutions and the algorithm, because she has particular abstracted knowledge of division. Lacking that knowledge, the students could not see what was represented by the steps of the algorithm. We use the term *conception-based perspective* to refer to an array of perspectives that share the following assumptions:

1. Mathematics is a product of human activity. Humans have no access to a mathematics that is independent of their ways of knowing.
2. What individuals see, understand, and learn are afforded and constrained their current conceptions.
3. Mathematics learning is a process of transformation of learners' knowing and ways of acting.

Radical constructivism and the emergent perspective, discussed earlier, are examples of conception-based perspectives.

As mentioned earlier, from a perception-based perspective, learning is the result of seeing aspects of mathematics as it exists. Because it is assumed that everyone is looking at the same mathematics, what is seen is assumed to be unvarying from person to person. The teacher's concern is whether students "see" the mathematics in question. In contrast, from a conception-based perspective, perception, including seeing, is constrained and afforded by one's current conceptions and by the culture in which one participates. Therefore, in a particular situation, there is no assumption that what is seen matches what others see.

Resulting Modifications in Our Conceptualization of Mathematics Teaching/Learning

In this section, I demonstrate refinements in our conceptual framework that resulted from our analysis of mathematics teachers in transition. As a result of considering the contrast between a perception-based perspective and a conception-based perspective, the following issues were brought into focus or more fully articulated. When a teacher's practice is based on a perception-based perspective, the most common failing is that she poses a task to students that requires the conception to be developed in order to complete the task successfully. This aspect of our analysis of empirical data led to two modifications in our conceptualization of teaching and learning. The description follows.

Assuming That the Students Think Like the Teacher

As a result of the contrast between a perception-based perspective and a conception-based perspective, we began to focus more explicitly on whether the teacher assumed that students would interpret or perceive the situation in question as she herself would. That is, to what extent did the task require that knowledge be available of the type to be learned. One effect of this explicit focus is that we began to notice in our own teaching of both mathematics students and teachers how often we plan for instruction and interact with students in ways that look as if they derived from a perception-based perspective. That is, through retrospective analysis, we realized that we anticipated that the students would interpret the learning situations as we do and see the relationships that we see. At first, this seemed surprising, given our conception-based perspectives. Analyses of many of these teaching situations has led us to conclude that this phenomenon is an inherent aspect of teaching, even for teaching based on a conception-based perspective, and thus modifies our understanding of teaching. Let us consider this point in greater detail.

Steffe (1995) distinguished between first- and second-order models to contrast an individual's models of the world (or mathematics) from that individual's models of others' models of the world. A *second-order model* is the observer's (teacher or researcher in this case) attempt to organize his/her experience of another (a learner). So a teacher would have a *first-order model* (her own understanding) of the mathematics and a second order model of the students' mathematics. Although this distinction is important and the pursuit of second-order models is essential to teaching based on a conception-based perspective, our recent work suggests that the notion of second-order model needs to be modified or elaborated further.

Using Steffe's distinction, we rephrase our first observation and add a second. When we reflect back on our lessons that failed to promote the intended learning, we often observe that our hypothetical learning trajectory seemed to have been based, to some significant degree, on our first-order models (how we see the mathematics) rather than on our second-order models (how we understand the students' mathematics). A second observation is that a teacher's or researcher's second-order model of a learner tends to have less predictive value when the planned context differs from the contexts in which the learner was observed previously. Note that what constitutes a different context must be considered from the perspective of the learner and therefore often cannot be anticipated.

We have come to explain these observations in the following way. A second-order model is in all cases incomplete. That is, it is a way of explaining and organizing one's observations to that point. Reasonable conjectures can be made based on this model, and models can become more useful as they incorporate a greater range of observations.   However, it is always the case that there are characteristics (conceptions, motivations, affect, competencies, etc.) that can only be attributed to the learner as additional experiences are retrospectively analyzed.   (I would assume that to this point the discussion is consistent with Steffe's (1995) conception of a second-order model.)

The refinement in our thinking spawned by our work with conception-based and perception-based perspectives on learning is that the incompleteness of one's model of others is filled in by projections that others are like us. Generally we are not aware of these projections.   Rather, a platonic perspective, that we all experience the same independent reality, is the default perspective. For example, in most cases, we do not question when we use a word or phrase that others understand it the way we do, and that when we point to something, others see what we see. In the vast majority of human interactions, such assumptions are useful and unproblematic. Thus, we assume, to some extent, a shared reality and proceed to differentiate it, as we perceive that our experience of the other derives from a different reality. As we become aware of this differentiation, we develop a conscious albeit incomplete model of the other. What remains undifferentiated also generally remains unconscious.

This discussion explains a modification in our understanding and thus an additional specification in our conceptual framework of teaching. That is mathematics teaching (at any level) is a constant process of differentiating between the teacher's own mathematical reality and that of the students. An implication of this understanding is that it is often not possible for the teacher to anticipate where additional differentiation will be necessary.

Promoting Students' Development of New Mathematics Concepts

We now describe a second area of impact of the perception-based, conception-based distinction on our theory of teaching/learning. We experienced the need to do the theoretical work described in this section in two related ways. First, in focusing on the distinction, we were challenged to articulate how instructional tasks can be designed to foster new conceptions. Second, as discussed in the last section, the distinction contributed to our understanding of some of the failures in our own teaching, specifically the teaching of prospective and practicing teachers. We needed to have a more elaborated theory of teaching/learning that would guide how we conceived mathematical and pedagogical lessons. In particular, we needed to unpack the processes that I had identified earlier (Simon, 1995) as the hypothetical learning trajectory (HLT).

In defining this theoretical problem, we realized that it was the problem that Pascual-Leone (1976) called the "learning paradox." How can we explain how learners "get from a conceptually impoverished to a conceptually richer system by anything like a process of learning" (Fodor, 1980, p. 149, cited in Bereiter, 1985). This is referred to as a paradox for the following reason: Piaget's (1985) idea of assimilation, a core idea of constructivism, suggests that one needs to have a particular concept in order to use that concept to organize one's experience. (i.e., to see evidence of that concept). Thus, it would seem impossible for one's experience to result in a more advanced concept, because that concept would need to be already available. We undertook the challenge of finding a theoretical explanation for how humans construct more powerful concepts out of less powerful ones that could serve as a basis for articulating a role for pedagogy in promoting such learning processes.

Through the resulting theoretical developments, we have begun to specify a pedagogy that uses tasks to promote the students' use of activities already available to them in order to create contexts in which they can abstract relationships between their activity and its differential effects. It is these abstracted activity—effect relationships that evolve to produce the new conception. Simon, Tzur, Heinz, Smith, & Kinzel, (1999) and Tzur & Simon (1999) provide initial reports of this body of work.

THE CYCLE CONTINUES

The evolving aspects of out theoretical framework of teaching/learning that I have alluded to in turn affect our empirical study of teacher development. For example, our conceptualization of conceptual learning as abstracting activity—effect relationships has led us to focus on how teachers in the study use and conceptualize the use of activity in conceptual learning. It has also refined our goals for promoting teacher development in the context of our teacher development experiment.

FINAL COMMENTS

I described how researchers can use research on mathematics teacher development and development of conceptualizations of mathematics teaching/learning to build on each other in a cyclical fashion, that is, how the results of one can influence subsequent work in the other. In earlier work (Simon, 1997), I argued the critical importance of useful, articulated conceptual frameworks on mathematics teaching/learning for research on mathematics teacher development. In this chapter, I attempted to demonstrate that theoretically based research on mathematics teacher development can provide researchers with contexts for making empirically based distinctions about teaching/learning, distinctions that serve to promote discourse and advance understanding in the field of mathematics education and to enhance the frameworks available for research on teacher development. We as researchers find that it is impossible to conduct productive research on mathematics teacher development without ongoing, explicit modification of our conceptual frameworks with respect to mathematics teaching and learning.

ACKNOWLEDGMENTS

This research is supported by the National Science Foundation under grant RED-9600023. The opinions expressed do not necessarily reflect the views of the Foundation.

REFERENCES

Bereiter, C. (1985). Toward a solution to the learning paradox. *Review of Educational Research, 55*, 201-226.

Cobb, P. (1995). The relevance of practice: A response to Orton. *Journal for Research in Mathematics Education, 26*, 230-253.

Cobb, P., & Bauersfeld, H. (Eds.). (1995). *Emergence of mathematical meaning: Interaction in classroom cultures.* Hillsdale, NJ: Lawrence Erlbaum Associates.

Cobb, P., & Yackel, E. (1996). Constructivist, emergent, and sociocultural perspectives in the context of developmental research. *Journal of Educational Psychology, 31*, 175-190.

Cobb, P., Yackel, E., & Wood, T. (1992). A constructivist alternative to the representational view of mind in mathematics education. *Journal for Research in Mathematics Education, 23*, 2-33.

Cobb, P., Yackel, E., & Wood, T. (1993). Learning mathematics: Multiple perspectives, theoretical orientation. In T. Wood, P. Cobb, E. Yackel, & D. Dillon, (Eds.),

Rethinking elementary school mathematics: Insights and issues, (pp. 21-32). (Journal for Research in Mathematics Education Monograph Series, Number 6). Reston, VA: National Council of Teachers of Mathematics.

Freudenthal. H. (1991). *Revisiting mathematics education: China lectures.* Dordrecht, The Netherlands: Kluwer.

Kuhn, T. S. (1962). *The structure of scientific revolutions.* Chicago: University of Chicago Press.

Pascual-Leone, J. (1976). A view of cognition from a formalist's perspective. In K. F. Riegel & J. A. Meacham (Eds.), *The developing individual in a changing world: Vol. 1 historical and cultural issues,* (pp. 89-110). The Hague, The Netherlands: Mouton.

Piaget, J. (1985). *The equilibration of cognitive structures: The central problem of intellectual development.* (T. Brown & K.J. Thampy, Trans.) Chicago: University of Chicago Press.

Simon, M. (1995). Reconstructing mathematics pedagogy from a constructivist perspective. *Journal for Research in Mathematics Education, 26,* 114-145.

Simon, M. (1997). Developing new models of mathematics teaching: An imperative for research on mathematics teacher development. In E. Fennema & B. Nelson. (Eds.), *Mathematics teachers in transition* (pp. 55-86.) Hillsdale, NJ: Lawrence Erlbaum Associates.

Simon, M. A. (2000). Research on mathematics teacher development: The teacher development experiment. In A. Kelly & R. Lesh (Eds.), *Handbook of research design in mathematics and science education,* (pp. 335-359). Hillsdale, NJ: Lawrence Erlbaum Associates.

Simon, M., & Tzur, R. (1999). Explicating the teacher's perspective from the researchers' perspective: Generating accounts of mathematics teachers' practice. *Journal for Research in Mathematics Education, 30,* 252-264.

Simon, M., Tzur, R., Heinz, K., Kinzel, M., & Smith, M. (1998). Characterizing a perspective on mathematics learning of teachers in transition. In S. Berenson, K. Dawkins, M. Blanton, W. Coulombe, J. Kolb, K. Norwood, & L. Stiff (Eds.), *Proceedings of the Twentieth Annual Meeting of the of the North American Chapter of the International Group for the Psychology of Mathematics Education, Vol. 2,* Columbus, OH: ERIC, pp. 768-774.

Simon, M., Tzur, R., Heinz, K., Kinzel, M., & Smith, M. (2000). Characterizing a perspective underlying the practice of mathematics teachers in transition. *Journal for Research in Mathematics Education, 31,* 579-601.

Simon, M., Tzur, R., Heinz, K., Smith, M., & Kinzel, M. (1999). On formulating the teacher's role in promoting mathematics learning. In O. Zaslavsky (Ed.), *Proceedings of the 23rd Conference of the International Group for the Psychology of Mathematics Education, Vol. 4* (pp. 201-208).

Steffe, L. (1995). Alternative epistemologies: An educator's perspective. In L. Steffe, & J. Gale (Eds.), *Constructivism in education.* Hillsdale, NJ: Lawrence Erlbaum Associates.

Tzur, R., & Simon, M. (1999). Postulating relationships between levels of knowing and types of tasks in mathematics teaching: A constructivist perspective. In F. Hitt & M. Santos (Eds.), *Proceedings of the Twentieth-First Annual Meeting North American Chapter of the International Group for the Psychology of Mathematics Education, Vol. 2* (pp. 805-810). Cuernavaca, Mexico. Columbis, OH: ERIC.

Commentary 2

Questions and Issues

Barbara Jaworski
University of Oxford

The chapters in this section take a more overtly mathematical focus, addressing questions relating to teachers' mathematical knowledge and its relationship to students' development of conceptual understanding.

1. Do we need to establish the mathematical knowledge before we deal with situations in which that knowledge would be applied?

These chapters make a number of factors clear concerning mathematical knowledge and its importance to teaching:

(a) Many teachers have limited mathematical knowledge relating to the concepts they are teaching children.

(b) A focus by teachers on children's thinking strategies for solving mathematical problems enables teachers to be more aware of the mathematical processes with which they are dealing, and to be more sensitive to children's mathematical learning needs.

(c) Teachers' development of mathematical knowledge is complex and problematic, and it is far from obvious how educators might most effectively aid, or facilitate, this development.

I deal with each of these in turn.

(a) <u>Teachers' Limited Mathematical Knowledge.</u> Experienced mathematics educators throughout the world are aware of the limitations of mathematical knowledge of teachers in elementary schools (e.g., Jaworski, 1999). Here, for example, we see Mary Ryan, in Deborah Schifter's chapter, adding fractions inappropriately to solve the absence problem. Schifter acknowledges that certain mathematical knowledge might be instrumental rather than relational; that is, teachers have learned procedures and algorithms but have not appreciated the underlying structures (for example, as in division by a fraction being performed by inverting the fraction and multiplying).

One consequence of teachers' lack of conceptual understanding of the mathematics they are teaching is that a teacher, in Schifter's words, "often does not realize that the child is expressing mathematical ideas worth noticing." This might suggest a need for teachers to establish their mathematical knowledge before that knowledge could be applied.

(b) A Focus by Teachers on Children's Thinking Strategies. We saw from discussion of the chapters in Part I, that teachers' study of episodes from students' mathematical learning leads to teachers' ability to construct more effective learning situations for their students. Janet Warfield's chapter emphasizes the importance of teachers' own mathematical knowledge to interpret children's mathematical thinking effectively. According to Schifter, most teachers do attend to their students, for example to their clarity of speech, their gestures, how they write numerals, and so forth. However, what they attend to is often not the mathematical concepts underlying children's words or actions. If this is the case, a question to be addressed is *how teachers come to focus on mathematical conceptual understanding, and moreover, how they become able to address it.* Schifter offers a methodology through which teachers "develop the habit of listening with a new ear" with "sharpened curiosity and interest." Such shifts toward attentiveness to the mathematics in what students say and do have been promoted through assignments in which teachers record dialogues from their classrooms, analyze children's mathematical strategies, write classroom narratives, and discuss cases. However, even when teachers engage in these activities, there are still problems: in one teacher's words, "I can apply each step exactly as the children did, but its just another meaningless algorithm to me."

Schifter emphasizes how much help teachers need "in order to develop the skills necessary to assess the validity of a mathematical argument or method of solution." She observes that the guidance of a teacher is often required to keep the focus firmly on the mathematics of the situations being considered. This might suggest that teachers' focus on children's mathematical strategies is not by itself sufficient to ensure a deep engagement with the mathematics in question. As in the Cognitively Guided Instruction (CGI) project, discussed in chapters 3 and 4, Schifter's work with teachers provides the facilitative guidance through which attention to the mathematics can be at an appropriate depth. Research shows that, with guidance, teachers do become more able to make mathematical judgments and to enable students' mathematical learning more appropriately. A resulting question seems to be: *What is this inquiry process that educators provide for teachers, and that teachers consequently provide for their students?* Research shows that it is not unproblematic.

(c) Educators Facilitating Teachers' Development of Mathematical Knowledge Leading to Teachers Facilitating Children's Mathematical Understanding. In his chapter, Martin Simon talks about three perspectives on learning that influence ways in which educators and teachers act in learning situations: traditional, perception-based, and conception-based perspectives. Briefly traditionalists see the teaching/learning process as providing students with teachers' or textbook knowledge; perception-based teachers encourage exploration to enable students to achieve the understandings the teachers themselves hold, and conception-based teachers encourage students' ownership of knowledge through their own constructions related to experience of both a physical and social nature. Simon's chapter suggests that the most effective instructive process is one which operates from a conception-based perspective. To some extent this is born out in Warfield's chapter as we see Ms. Valentine's fifth graders identifying and naming the strategies they have used to solve problems. So, here was one teaching strategy that seemed to have some success. As Warfield indicates, Ms. Valentine's confidence in her own mathematical knowledge — "that she could work with whatever responses came up from children" — contributed to her ability to encourage students' own constructions. She was able to "verify whether the definitions the children proposed were mathematically valid," and find some way to challenge them if the definitions were not valid (e.g., through counter examples). It is not far-fetched to suggest, from the evidence of these chapters, that a conception-based perspective might depend on a teacher's confidence rooted in her own mathematical knowledge, as in Ms. Valentine's case. It certainly seems true that a number of teachers mentioned in Schifter's chapter do not exhibit this confidence, and their lack of efficacy is related to their limitations of mathematical knowledge.

However, we should not be too eager to conclude that the reverse is the case, (i.e., that a good mathematical conceptual grounding leads to effective interactive teaching). Simon is very honest in his chapter, in recognizing that even in his own team, where mathematical understandings are of a conceptually high quality and espoused perspectives are conception-based, they nevertheless find themselves operating in a perception-based fashion. Thus, teaching by good mathematicians operating from conception-based principles is far from straightforward, and creates tensions for teaching. I return to this issue shortly. It seems clear from the aforementioned discussion that mathematical knowledge is a seriously important factor for creation of effective learning situations, but by itself it is not sufficient to ensure such creation.

2. Is it okay if the teacher doesn't know everything the students know? What is the impact on their classrooms? In such situations, what "stance" might the teacher take?

I do not believe any of the chapters in Parts I and II suggest that it is all right if the teacher does not know everything the students know. Vignettes in Schifter's chapter suggest that it is seriously disadvantageous if the teacher is not able to judge effectively the mathematical implications of students' perceptions. A consequence, which has been demonstrated, is that the teaching becomes reductionist; either reducing to a focus on procedures and algorithms, or reducing to congenial discussions of students' ideas, but without the critical challenging element that is needed to help students develop their own mathematical judgments. In Warfield's chapter, we see the possibilities that open up when the teacher has confidence based on sound mathematical knowledge. When teachers do not have this confidence, it is most likely they are not able to open up situations effectively. However, having said all of this, even the best mathematicians are aware that they can learn from their students. It is not so much that the students know more than the teachers, but that access to students' alternative ways of seeing mathematical situations and concepts can lead to a teacher's own enhanced understanding. I know from considerable personal experience the value of opening up mathematical situations for the quality discussion of which Warfield speaks. I recognize however, the mathematical confidence that this requires of the teacher. When I have been teaching at the limits of my own understanding, I have been less confident at opening things up, lest I should be unable to deal with students' inquiries. This is a potential pointer toward the stance a teacher might take. Opening things up will result in students' exploration of areas of mathematics with which the teacher, possibly, is not confident. The teacher's response might be to admit ignorance (not usually of value to either student or teacher) or to close down the situation, so that the problematic elements are excluded and which restricts students' opportunity to learn. Alternatively the teacher might be willing to explore with the students using a wide range of resources (local educators might be one). In the projects quoted in various chapters so far, relationships between teachers and their educator colleagues have proved a source of support and encouragement to opening up learning situations. The generative teaching proposed in Franke's chapter in Part I relies fundamentally on teachers' confidence built through engagement in the CGI project. However, unless teachers have levels of support on which they can draw, they are unlikely to sustain activities that encourage students' exploration of mathematical ideas in open learning situations.

3. (a) What do we mean by and what is involved in a teacher understanding a child's thinking? (b) Where is the place for mathematical formalism?

(a) There are many examples in these chapters of teachers engaging with children's mathematical thinking, and learning from this thinking. In Warfield's chapter, we see Ms. Valentine engaging with partitive and quotitive aspects of division, and inviting her students to engage with these concepts through selected problems designed, in a sophisticated way, to elicit students' perceptions and understandings. She was surprised by some of their conceptions that emerged, for example, "that you should get a larger number when you multiply and a smaller when you divide." In Schifter's chapter, Liz Sweeney sees an unexpected line of reasoning in Jemea's solution and through her open questions is able to elicit a reasoned explanation from another student, Jose. We do not know if Sweeney understood Jemea's approach before Jose's explanation, but whether she did or not, her willingness to question the students led to a very effective interchange revealing the students' thinking. In order to understand students' thinking, opportunity has to be provided for students to reveal their thoughts, and such opportunity is demonstrated in these examples. Whether the teacher understands the thinking that is revealed is another matter. Schifter shows that teachers exposed to examples of students' dialogue, for their consideration, had difficulty in understanding its conceptual roots, because their own mathematics was inadequate for this. Simon's chapter highlights a significant paradox, "On the one hand what we notice and take as significant is structured by how we conceive of mathematics teaching and learning; on the other hand, we must 'set aside' our conceptions in order to make sense of the ideas and actions of the teachers we study." If this quotation is also applied to teachers and their students, we gain some insight into our substantive question. Teachers' conceptions of mathematics teaching and learning are very likely to depend on their own mathematical understandings, and ways in which they themselves have learned mathematics in the past. For many of these teachers, setting aside these conceptions is virtually impossible, because they have no experiences of alternatives to put in their place. Projects such as those described by Warfield and Schifter "just start" to offer teachers the alternative conceptions that allow them to just start putting aside those that limit their understanding of children's thinking.

(b) The place of formalism is a seriously difficult issue. Formalism means much more than algorithmic approaches to a mathematical process, for example, that of inverting a fraction and multiplying in order to divide by it. Such processes reduce mathematical formalism to mathematical mantras, memorized but meaningless. Another perception of formalism is that it involves the use of abstract symbolization without recourse to real world situations. Warfield talks of Ms. Valentine working with "naked number" problems, in other words, deciding overtly not to use a familiar context in which to make numbers and concepts more understandable to students. The result involves her students working directly with numeric representations, such as $(12 \div 1/4)$ without the familiar reassurance of word problems involving "buying yards of ribbon," for example, in which to situate the ideas. So, to some extent, this involves mathematical formalism, insofar as formal symbols are being used in their own right, and manipulated mathematically. However, true formalism involves expression of mathematical concepts in conventional symbolic forms, which carry with them generality and abstraction. Conceptual understanding of mathematics might be recognized by students' being able to move from a particular case of a mathematical idea, or a real world problem or example, to a symbolic expression, which carries with it the essence of the idea expressed in general terms. Formalism involves the shift to abstraction in terms that carry with them all the meaning of the situation being generalized. I see elements of this in Ms. Valentine's work, some in

Liz Sweeney's work, but little in some of the other examples quoted, as I think Deborah Schifter would acknowledge. For elementary teachers with little formal mathematical experience themselves and even less mathematical confidence, genuine mathematical formalism is probably beyond comprehension. This then is a serious problem for educators working with such teachers.

4. What are the consequences of making public the mathematics that teachers need to work on?

Schifter suggests that elementary teachers need to work on mathematics related to their students' mathematical thinking. An implication is that teachers do not need to study higher mathematics, as is often required in teacher education preservice courses at some universities. However, as we might expect, the matter is not so simple, and it is a question of what mathematics could be made "public" without over simplification. The chapters so far in this book, and in this section particularly, show that for many teachers, early number work is a priority. Their students have to be able to conceptualize numbers, that is, recognize ordinality and cardinality, count, name, and represent in conventional forms such as hundreds tens and units. They have to be able to perform operations of addition, subtraction, multiplication, and division. Superficially, this might seem to involve a small knowledge set, which might be expressed minimally in terms of counting and calculating, with appropriate algorithms to be learned. However, as soon as we perceive the need to consider concepts such as *commutativity, associativity,* and *distributivity* (the latter is particularly emphasized by Schifter), we recognize elements of mathematical structure that seem fundamental to an appreciation of learning at this level. In addition, to nurture students' ability to see generality, not just to work with particular numbers, teachers themselves need to work at general levels that include abstraction in a variety of forms. An appreciation of generic examples might be sufficient, but a basic algebraic awareness would provide greater security of perception and understanding. An example arising from Schifter's chapter will illustrate this: 16 x 18 is the same as 32 x 9 (a), but *not* the same as 14 x 20 (b). We might write each of these products (a and b) in terms of 16 and 18:

(a) $32 \times 9 = (16 \times 2) \times (18 \div 2)$ (b) $14 \times 20 = (16 - 2) \times (18 + 2)$

$$= \frac{(16 \times 2) \times 18}{2}$$ $= (16 \times 18) + (-2 \times 18) + (16 \times 2) + (-2 \times 2)$

$$= \frac{16 \times (2 \times 18)}{2}$$ $= (16 \times 18) - 36 + 32 - 4$

$$= \frac{(16 \times 18) \times 2}{2}$$ $= (16 \times 18) - 8$

$$= 16 \times 18$$ $\neq (16 \times 18)$

The demonstration of (a) involves commutativity and associativity, and of (b) involves distributivity. These are particular examples that use these mathematical properties. In order to perceive the properties more generally, teachers would be helped by knowing that for any numbers a, b, and c, the following relationships hold: $a \times b = b \times a$ (commutativity); $a \, (b \times c) = (a \times b) \times c$ (associativity); $a \, (b + c) = (a \times b) + (a \times c)$ (distributivity). These generalities are expressed here economically in algebraic terms. To be familiar with these meanings, therefore, teachers have to have some facility with algebra. Schifter suggests that in order to appreciate their students' logic, teachers need to explore various representations with blocks and with paper and pencil in order to develop a grounded sense of distributivity and so forth. I would certainly agree, but would feel also that some appreciation of formal structures would also be a helpful basis for a confident appreciation of children's logic.

In Warfield's chapter, we see Ms. Valentine confident of the differences between partitive and quotitive division, so that she can not only judge well her students' logic, but nurture their own perceptions of the difference between the two kinds of division problems. Warfield does not indicate the nature and source of Ms. Valentine's mathematical knowledge, but, from the examples given, we might suspect it had formal groundings. I am not suggesting necessarily that teachers should be taught formal processes of abstract algebra (groups etc.), but there needs to be some agreement as to what a course in mathematical structure might appropriately include and how far mathematically it would go. These are not simple issues, and it would be hard to share them with a general "public."

I have gone into somewhat excessive detail here to emphasize the complexity involved and the difficulties of communicating such complexity in the public domain. From these chapters, it is evident that teachers who want to teach their students through methods involving discussion, negotiation, and of meaning inquiry have difficulties both mathematically and pedagogically. The mathematical difficulties have been emphasized in this discussion, and the pedagogical difficulties raised in the previous commentary are often inseparable from the mathematical ones. Shulman's (1987) concept of the missing paradigm has become a guiding force for many educators in addressing these difficulties (see, e.g., Markovitz & Even, 1999). Shulman's concept of pedagogical content knowledge — in this case, pedagogic mathematical knowledge — is central to the difficulties we are addressing. Schifter's view that teachers need to be taught not solely the formal mathematics, but the necessary mathematics in a pedagogical context that relates directly to teaching for students' understanding, might be seen as an interpretation of Shulman's concept. However, it is more complicated than this. As McNeal's chapter shows us in the next section, even when teachers have the required mathematical knowledge, engendering an understanding in students is far from straightforward. Because McNeal's chapter speaks so strongly to these issues, I shall delay further consideration of these questions until my comments on Part III.

REFERENCES

Jaworski, B. (1999). The plurality of knowledge growth in mathematics teaching. In B. Jaworski, T. Wood, & A. J. Dawson (Eds.), *Mathematics teacher education: Critical international perspectives* (pp. 180-209). London: Falmer Press.

Markovitz, Z., & Even, R. (1999). Mathematics classroom situations: An inservice course for elementary school teachers. In B. Jaworski, T. Wood, & A. J. Dawson (Eds.), *Mathematics teacher education: Critical international perspectives* (pp. 59-68). London: Falmer Press.

Shulman, L. S. (1987) Knowledge and teaching: Foundations of the new reform. *Harvard Educational Review, 57,* 1-22.

Part IV

TEACHING VIEWED FROM A SOCIAL AND CULTURAL PERSPECTIVE

OVERVIEW

Extending the contribution of the psychological and mathematical perspectives, the sociological point of view makes apparent the importance in teaching of attending to children's participation in the process of sharing and negotiating mathematical meaning as well as to their mathematics and the logic and reasoning of their thinking. The nature of teaching is seen to consist of creating interactive situations for student participation that are related to opportunities for student thinking and discourse. Chapters in this section also discuss the several, overlapping contexts that create dilemmas for teachers to resolve that Ball addressed previously.

Extending the Conception of Mathematics Teaching

Terry Wood
Tammy Turner-Vorbeck
Purdue University

It is well known that the predominant practice of teaching mathematics has been to "show the children what to do and then give them practice in it" (Meserve & Suydam, 1992, p. 16). It is also recognized that these long-standing teaching procedures are considered most appropriate in learning that consists of the mastery of facts or procedural skills that can be taught in a step-by-step manner. However, these practices are thought to be least applicable for teaching involving learning that includes problem solving, higher order thinking, and reasoning, which are the goals for reforming mathematics education (National Council of Teachers of Mathematics [NCTM], 1989, 2000). Hence, it is widely accepted that the change in the practice of teaching mathematics will require more than simply minor adjustments in current ways of teaching (NCTM, 1991).

Typically, the changes in teaching advocated either are drawn from a psychological perspective, which proposes that teachers' knowledge of children's thinking is of primary importance, or from a disciplinary stance, which proposes that teachers' conceptual understanding of mathematics is central for teaching. On these proposals, we do not disagree but maintain that there is another perspective that is essential to consider — the social aspects of learning and teaching. We contend that it is necessary in teaching to take seriously the fact that social learning and the necessity to acquire culturally based cognitive skills is fundamental in children's development. Therefore, we propose to extend the conception of mathematics teaching to include a social perspective that we assert is essential to children's learning of mathematics.

In our empirical examinations of classroom pedagogical situations, we view teaching as an interactive activity and draw on tenets from psychology and sociology for analysis. For us, it is essential to look into the classroom situation to see how teaching is contributing to the mathematical meanings that are evolving and to examine how teachers' actions contribute to children's social learning. In addition to our interest in social interaction and individual learning of mathematics, we also take into consideration the function of social interaction in the establishment of common meaning and the acquisition of cultural knowledge. In this chapter, we first delineate our theoretical argument, in which we claim that social interaction is foundational to children's learning and in our case mathematics. Second, we describe a theoretical framework that is the result of extending our empirical work beyond description to theory. We follow this with examples drawn from our classroom empirical analysis to illustrate the characteristics of teaching. Finally, we argue that not only is the social interaction that exists in classrooms fundamental to children's social learning but also to the "mathematics" that evolves.

THEORETICAL PERSPECTIVE

Three central tenets drawn from psychological and sociological theory influence our analysis of teaching. The first tenet is that to understand teaching one must examine it in conjunction with students' activity as a form of social interaction. Therefore, teaching is situated in school, serves different purposes, and is embedded in different activities and practices. The second principle is that teaching has to do with the development of meaning, both individual and collective. The third assumption is that teaching is about enabling students to acquire accumulated knowledge of a culture. Drawing on these three ideas, teaching practices are thought to have structure and forms of repeatable social interaction that can be identified in the analysis of empirical data from classrooms.

From a sociological perspective, we gain an understanding of social interaction and how it becomes structured among humans. The theorists Goffman (1959) and Garfinkel (1967) both claimed that everyday life consists of normative patterns of interaction and discourse that form the social structure. Once established, these patterns become the reliable routines people depend on in interactive situations. Goffman (1974) created the theoretical construct of *frames* as the organizational and interactional principles by which situations are defined and sustained as experience. Each position within a participation framework is associated with normatively specified conduct (Goffman, 1981). For Goffman (1967), the study of interaction is a study of the "traffic rules of social interaction" (p. 12). Individuals, when they participate, come to anticipate certain behaviors for themselves and for others so that, according to Garfinkel (1967) much of what happens "goes without saying" (p. 8).

Garfinkel (1967), drawing from Mead's emphasis on mind as developing from interpersonal activity, is interested in ways in which knowledge and action are linked and mutually constituted. He contends that participants continually engage in interpretive activity and thus reach understandings as a way of seeking order and normalcy during the course of their everyday conduct. The anticipations to which humans orient and to which their actions are held accountable can be formulated in terms of interactional rules or norms. These norms provide the "cognitive bearings" essential to humans' ability to make continuous sense of situations and to which members are mutually accountable.

Although sociologists are less interested in the internal processes involved in personal construction of meaning per se, nonetheless these meanings are "creations that are formed in and through the defining activities of people as they interact" (Blumer, 1969, p. 5). The sociologists' interest in theory about human living is based on assumptions that humans need to adapt to social existence and to develop a system of shared meanings. Individuals, in this perspective, are seen to construct their meaning in the process of participating in the interactive process of negotiation of meaning that is taken as shared (Krummheuer, 2000).

Cultural psychologists, such as Bruner, hold similar ideas about the importance of social interaction with regard to children's inherent need for a social existence and acceptance into a community as a means for acquiring culturally held knowledge. Bruner (1990, 1996) emphasizes the role of metacognition in thinking but believes that the development of children's capacity for reflective thought originates in social interactions with others. Moreover, Bruner (1990) maintains children need to develop a system of shared meanings in order to participate successfully in human interaction. Along with Rommetveit (1985), Bruner believes that in order to interact and communicate, individuals need to share common understandings that they take as an implicit basis of reference when speaking to one another.

From others such as Tomasello (1999) we gain an understanding of the centrality of social interaction in the cultural learning of children. Beyond those aspects of the mathematical structure, such as quantity and number that infants acquire, there is the concern for the learning of complex forms of mathematics that are socially and historically determined. Tomasello (1999) believes that it is the "social interactions themselves" (p. 200) from which children learn through others about the different ways of looking at and thinking about things that is a central human capacity. He claims that the social processes involved in cultural learning are particularly powerful and distinctively human and consist of three basic forms of social learning (Kruger & Tomasello, 1996).

The theoretical perspectives just discussed take into consideration the uniquely human capacity for sociocultural learning: the notions of the contributions of individuals that enable them to accomplish a commonly shared life; the processes by which individuals mutually negotiate meanings and adapt to various forms of interaction; and, the distinctive social process involved in cultural learning. This point of view that we portray is slightly different from proponents of communities of learners (Rogoff, 1997) and social practice theory (e.g., Lave, 1996; Lave & Wenger, 1991) in that we consider the child as an individual in the process. Including an individual perspective and concomitant mental processes is fundamental to our work of examining the interrelationship of teaching and children's mathematical learning. This perspective forms the basis of our theoretical framework that is discussed next.

THEORETICAL FRAMEWORK

Classroom Investigation

Several researchers have previously analyzed classroom interaction and identified patterns in teaching practice. The early work of Flanders (1970) examined the behavior of teachers' and placed them in levels according to criteria for effective teaching and thus student learning. In his empirical data, he noticed that the more complex the patterns of interaction, the better student achievement. Bauersfeld

(1988), Voigt (1985) and Wood (1994) extended the notion of classroom interaction by identifying reliable and predictable patterns in mathematics classroom interaction. For example, Bauersfeld identified the *funnel pattern*, which consists of a series of teacher questions leading students to producing preferred procedures. Students, he found, needed to only generate superficial procedures rather than meaningful mathematical solutions in order to participate in the interaction. The identification of different forms of interaction drew attention to the existence of classroom routines and the ways these influenced what and how students learned mathematics. Although these studies provide insights into teaching, there remains a need for a fine-grained approach that details the social interaction that occurs between teacher and learners in reform-oriented classes. Given that teaching is most readily observed in action, it is essential to look into the situation to examine the ways that pedagogy is contributing to the mathematical meaning that is developing both individually and collectively. To accomplish this, it is important to examine first the nature of the interaction that evolves between teacher and students and the forms and meanings of these interactive contexts. Second, it is important to examine the content of what is talked about—the topics and themes that emerge. Finally, it is necessary to examine the interactive processes through which the context is established to identify the norms that underlie the interaction (Krummheuer, personal communiqué, September 4, 1998).

The classes that formed the basis of the theoretical framework were the outcome of two earlier projects in second and third grades that used constructivist theory to develop instructional activities for students (cf., Cobb, Wood, & Yackel, 1990; Wood, Cobb, Yackel, & Dillon, 1993). Each of the projects involved collaborating with classroom teachers for 1 year to develop classes that were highly interactive and in which the focus was on children's thinking about mathematics. Although the projects concluded after 1 year, the teachers continued to teach mathematics in this manner and to develop their practice. Nearly 10 years later, we returned to these teachers and gathered extensive data in their classes for 1 year. Although our data included children interacting in pairs and in class discussion, to date we have chosen only to analyze the class discussion. We did this because we found it to be the most complex event and highlighted differences in teaching (Wood & Turner-Vorbeck, 1999). As a general finding for all teachers, discussion was conceived of as a situation in which mathematical understanding was achieved through students' thinking and reasoning. The goal was to come together as a class, after working together in pairs, to present and share personal ideas and thinking for the purpose of promoting individual and common meanings for mathematics. From the combined analysis of these lessons, we were able to describe *teaching* as an activity that included sociological constructs of norms from which social interaction evolved and to connect these to psychological constructs of children's social learning, metacognition, and ultimately to the mathematics that evolved.

EXPLANATION OF THE THEORETICAL FRAMEWORK

The theoretical framework (shown in Fig. 9.1) illustrates a view of mathematics teaching as a complex process that connects the norms that are established to the patterns of social interaction and questioning discourse to the demand on students for reflection and reasoning about mathematics. Condensing the findings from empirical analysis across all teachers, three distinct social interactions or discussion contexts emerged that we label as *Report Ways, Inquiry,* and *Argument.* From these contexts, we identified two dimensions, *participation* and *thinking,* on which teaching varies. The differences that exist in teaching on these two dimensions reveals the ways pedagogy influences the nature of children's mathematical activity

Discussion Context	Mathematical Thinking	Explainers student	Listeners	
			teacher	student
			Responsibility for Participation →	
Report Ways	comparing contrasting	• tell different ways	• accept solutions • elaborate solutions	• compare/ contrast solutions
Inquiry	reasoning questioning	• clarify solutions • give reasons	• ask questions • provide reasons	• ask questions
Argument	justifying challenging	• justify • defend solutions	• make challenges	• disagree • make challenges

(Vertical band between Explainers and Listeners columns, spanning all rows: Responsibility for Thinking ↓)

FIG. 9.1. Theoretical framework for teaching and learning.

and the mathematical meaning that emerges during this event. By generating these two dimensions, we then can make connections from our empirical categories to the theoretical constructs drawn from sociology and cultural-developmental psychology. This process extends the results from the relatively static categories developed for the empirical analysis to the creation of the dynamic axes that represents a return to theory.

PARTICIPATION DIMENSION

The *participation dimension* consists of the extent to which teachers made possible all students' active participation in the social interaction and discourse. Not surprisingly, differences in teachers' expectations for students' giving their explanations varies in each of the three contexts. However, the most noticeable distinctions in teaching are in the specific norms that are constituted for the students participating as listeners in the discussion. From these findings, we can link increases in students' participation to the norms constituted and the social interaction, including language that evolves in accordance to sociological theory. Therefore, we can begin to understand the interrelationship between the differences in teaching as revealed in the participation structures created and the processes by which individual and common mathematical meanings evolve, progress, or both, during discussion.

For example, in a Report Ways discussion, the norms typically constituted for listeners ranged from prompts to "pay attention" to "listen to hear different ways" of solving the problem. In other words, the expectation for listeners was at the least "to listen" and at best to compare their way with that of the explainer in order to know if they should volunteer to contribute a different way or not. Teachers in an Inquiry discussion established expectations for student listeners that included not only that they compare their way with others, but that they also try to understand what the explainer said. Moreover, if they did not understand, the listeners in this context were expected to ask questions for further information or clarification. Finally in the Argument context, listeners were expected to compare their way with that of others, try to understand, and decide if they agreed or disagreed with the student explainer. Furthermore, if they agreed or disagreed, they were to say so and in some cases to tell why.

Responsibility for Participation Axis

The Responsibility for Participation axis on the theoretical framework (represented by the horizontal black arrow in Fig. 9.1) illustrates the increasing responsibility of students to participate in the ongoing discussion. Establishing this axis enabled links to be made from the categorical changes in students' participation to differences in the agreed-on norms teachers establish with their pupils and the connections to sociological theory.[1] Returning to a sociological perspective, the Responsibility for Participation axis exemplifies the finding that teachers' normative expectations for participation were directly related to increasing demands for a more active role from students as listeners as well as explainers. These heightened demands for participation created conditions in which the students who were listening were expected to be increasingly involved in the examination of the thinking of the student giving an explanation.

In order to do this, those listening were progressively expected to follow the reasoning of the one explaining. As the expectations for listeners to participate in the questioning of a student explaining intensified, the demand to engage in complex reflective thinking and reflective judgment also magnified for these students and represented a link to cognitive theory. Thus, as the expectations for students' listening increased so did the responsibility for all students, not simply the pupil explaining, to participate in the negotiation and establishment of mathematical meaning.

THINKING DIMENSION

This brings us to the second characteristic on which teaching differs, that of student thinking. The Thinking dimension consists of the ways in which the type of teachers' questions and students' questions made demands on students to engage in increasingly more complex thinking and reasoning in order to respond. All of the forms of teaching identified represent a shift from a position of telling students information and checking to see if pupils had received it to one of questioning so that it was the children who were providing mathematical information. However, distinctions between the

---

[1] Further details of the findings from the empirical analyses on norms and the evolution of the patterns of interaction are reported elsewhere (c.f., Wood, 1999; Wood & Turner-Vorbeck, 1999).

contexts are further defined by the teachers' questioning that we then can link to an increase in the demand for and the complexity in the reflective activity of the student in accordance with developmental theory. Therefore, we begin to understand the interrelationship between the differences in teaching as exemplified by questioning and the processes by which individual mathematical meanings evolve, progress, or both, during discussion.

For example, in Report Ways, listeners were required to contrast their thinking with that of the explainer in order to determine if they (the listeners) should volunteer or not. In an Inquiry discussion, listeners were to try and make sense of another's explanation and to make reflective judgments about the soundness of the reasoning given. This demand required listeners to follow the thinking and reasoning of the one explaining and to decide if they (the listeners) understood or not. If they did not, listeners were to inquire and ask questions in order to understand better. In this context, understanding was accomplished through processes of questioning, clarifying and using mathematical reasoning in making sense of mathematical ideas. Finally, in an Argument discussion, listeners were not only to follow the reasoning and make sense of it, but also to make reflective judgments about the validity of the reasoning. In this context, children listening were not only to find the error in the explainer's reasoning but also they were to determine why, in order to challenge it, the reasoning was logical to the explainer. Subsequently, in addition to the Responsibility for Participation axis on the theoretical framework, we included a Responsibility for Thinking axis that represents the teaching dimension related to student thinking.

Responsibility for Thinking Axis

The inclusion of the Responsibility for Thinking axis (represented by the vertical black arrow in Fig. 9.1) enables links to be made among
1. The shifts in the teaching activity of questioning;
2. to categorical changes in the demands for children's mathematical thinking;
3. to hypothesized differences in learning.

Moreover, the inclusion of this axis allows for these somewhat static categories to be viewed as dynamic movement by relying on the theoretical considerations. Connecting the empirical findings on distinctions in teachers' questioning and the resulting differences in students' explanations to cognitive development theory deepens the understanding of the interrelationship of the interactive and discursive activities of teaching and students' thinking and reasoning, which are foundational to conceptual understanding of mathematics. The interrelationship between norms, interaction, and students' thinking and reasoning are the basis on which meanings, individual and common, are negotiated in the classroom that represents the link to sociological theory. Individuals, in this perspective, are seen as constructing meaning in the process of participating in the interactional process of negotiation of meaning that leads to the attainment of meaning that is held as common knowledge.

Reflective thinking, as used in this research, is defined as those situations in which children are observed engaged in reflecting on their mathematical ideas, either through physical or mental action. This construct is related to Piaget's (1985) notions of reflective abstraction and Dewey's (undated) ideas of reflective thinking. Several, such as von Glasersfeld (personal communication, April, 1989) suggest that one of the simplest ways to induce individual reflection is through making a comparison, such as that of asking students to rethink their strategy in order to provide more information to others. Moreover, Rogoff (1990) described the knowledge constructed in situations of comparison and contrast as the ways in which skills and/or understanding develop in young children.

The second way reflection occurs is in situations in which confusion, complexity, or ambiguity arises. In these situations, individuals are involved in thinking that involves inquiry, questioning, and reasoning, in order to make sense of the situation. The research of Entwistle (1995), albeit with university students, indicated that deeper meaning and understanding of content occurs as students act to reduce complexity and confusion through thinking, which creates coherence and integration among ideas.

The third way reflection occurs is in situations in which conflict or disagreement arise and is resolved through reasoning that involves critically examining and justifying one's existing conceptions. In their research, Kuhn, Garcia-Mila, Zohar, and Anderson (1995) found that knowledge transformation occurs when individuals reflect on contradictions in their own thought. Kuhn and colleagues describe this as the only situation in which transformations in knowledge conceptions occur.

Teaching also differs importantly in the extent to which teachers make demands on the thinking of those listening. These differences in demands for students thinking are linked to the specific norms that are constituted in each context for children's role as listeners in the discussion. The increasing complexity in participation for the listeners carried with it a demand to follow the thinking of those explaining. In other words, listeners were expected to understand the alternative theories that others gave for solving a problem. In doing so, they were engaging in a process of evaluating whether the reasoning of others made sense or not (Samarapungavan, 1992).

In summary, in each of the forms of discussion, Report Ways, Inquiry, and Argument, we claim that teachers' create distinct forms of social interaction for learning and contribute in a characteristic way to the mathematical meanings that evolve individually and collectively in the class. The types of questions teachers ask were different in each context and this influences the demand made on students for thinking and reasoning about mathematics. Teachers also differ noticeably in their expectations for children's participation during the discussion in each of the three contexts. Moreover, the specific norms teachers initiate and establish with their students at the beginning of the year are directly related to the manner of questioning and the extent of student participation in the three different discussions. We describe these differences in teaching that occur in each of the three discussions and give examples in the next section of this chapter.

CHARACTERISTICS OF TEACHING

Report Ways Discussion

The first form of discussion, Report Ways, is one in which students tell the other members of the class how they solved the assigned mathematical problems. In these classes, the primary emphasis was on students reporting their individual strategies for solving a problem. Teachers established with the children that, when explaining, it was expected that the children would tell different ways to solve problem and provide detail about their strategy if asked by the teacher. In these classes, "different way" meant a way that had not been shared in class discussion yet. In some cases, different way meant that for a given problem each student had a different way. In other cases, different way meant each student had multiple strategies for solving a single problem. Often, the discussion consisted of students giving one strategy for each problem and several problems would be discussed, thus different problem—different way. In other classes, discussion consisted of many student solutions for one problem and only a few problems would be discussed, therefore single problem—many different ways. In these classes, the teacher identified confusion, error, or both, and students were asked to rethink how and/or what they were doing as they solved the problem.

The following episode that occurred during a whole class discussion provides an example of the pattern of interaction and teachers' questioning.

Illustrative Example[2]

The problems being discussed are shown in Fig. 9.2. The problem that Hannah discusses is the third one on the page, 52, 33/empty box. However, she refers to the previously discussed problem 52, 30/empty box; and the last problem 52/empty box, 33.

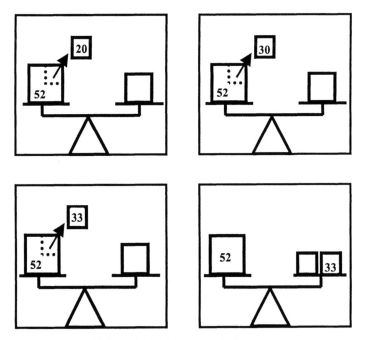

FIG. 9.2. Balance problems.

---

2 All of the examples used to illustrate the three contexts are taken from the empirical classroom data.

Teacher: Hannah, what was your strategy?

Hannah: They're kind of like the same. Um well, this one's the answer so, 52, so . . .

Teacher: What did you do? Did you use the 22 up there to help you?

Hannah: No. We used (pause).

Teacher: Which one did you use to help you?

Hannah: We did this one first . . . We did the last one first. (writes 19 on the overhead)

Teacher: How did you get 19 for that one?

Hannah: Well, I added up (pause) well, 33 and then with that 10 it would be 43 and (pauses as she counts up to 52 by ones on fingers) so 9.

Teacher: So 19 and 33 make 52?

Hannah: (Nods yes).

Teacher: Okay. How did you do the one we are working on now?

Hannah: Well there's 33 here so with that one it could be like right here (points to 33 in last problem). Like that one here so both answers are 19.

Teacher: So it is 19?

Hannah: (Nods head yes)

Teacher: Okay. Nicole did you do it a different way?

Pattern of Interaction and Questioning Discourse

The pattern of interaction that occurs consistently and reliably in a Report Ways context is as follows:
- A child tells how she or he solved the problem.

- Teacher asks how, what, where questions for the purpose of acquiring more information from the child explaining about the strategy used.
- Child tells more information about his or her strategy.
- The exchange continues until the teacher is satisfied with the explanation or agreement is negotiated.
- Teacher asks other children for another way either to do the same problem or a different problem.

The teachers' questioning during the exchange consists of requests for more information for the explanation with queries such as, "How did you do it?" "What did you do?" "Where did you get 20 to add to 32?" The students' explanations consist of providing descriptions of their thinking and strategies for solving the problems. The detail of the children's descriptions varies depending on the extent to which teachers, through their questioning, demand comprehensiveness and clarity in the explanations from the children. This situation can be depicted as one in which students "tell how they solved the mathematics problem."

One other characteristic of teaching defined this context: the children seldom participated in the question asking. The exchange was between the teacher and the child explaining, while the others listened. In addition, at the beginning of the year, the teachers' emphasis when establishing the norms was on the expectations for the children when they were explaining. The teachers' norms for those listening were to simply pay attention or, in more complex situations, the expectation was to compare their strategies to the one being given in order to know if they had a different solution to volunteer when the teacher asked.

INQUIRY DISCUSSION

In other classes, the discussion initially began as a Report Ways with students telling their strategies to those listening. The difference that characterized teaching in an Inquiry discussion was that the children were also expected to clarify their meanings and to give reasons for their thinking in response to inquiry questions from the teacher and the other students. In such classes, the primary emphasis was on trying to understand and to make sense of mathematics by understanding not only an individual's strategy, but also the reasoning behind the solution to the problem. In these classes, the discussion moved back and forth from a Report Ways discussion to an Inquiry discussion. The Inquiry discussion served the function of creating a setting in which personal ideas were open for examination and questioning by the teacher or, in some classes, the other students, with the underlying understanding that it was important to make sense of the mathematics being explained. In these classes, confusion and complexity were viewed as situations for learning.

The following episode that occurred during a class discussion provides an example of the pattern of interaction and teachers' questioning in an Inquiry discussion.

Illustrative Example

The problem is 72 – 39 =___.

> Teacher: My gosh we've got three different ways already. What did you get, Sarah and how did you do it?

> Sarah: Um, 33. I almost did it like Kyle except I did 72 minus 30. And then I um, then I took off 10 and then I got 42. And then, I took off 10 and I got . . . Wait.

> Teacher: You took 72 minus 30 and you got 42. Then you took off 10. Why did you take off 10? Do you remember why you took off 10?

> Sarah: Yes, because it was easier. It was close to 9.

> Teacher: What do you mean it was close to 9?

> Sarah: Because 9 is close to 10 so then 32.

> Teacher: 32? But how did you get 33?

> Sarah: I added 1.

> Teacher: Why did you add 1?

> Sarah: Because you were only taking off 9 instead of 10, so I had to add a 1 back on.

> Teacher: Okay. I understand now. Is there another way we can do this problem?

Pattern of Interaction and Questioning Discourse

- A child tells how she or he solved the problem.
- Teacher (or other children) ask questions or make statements asking for understanding or clarification.
- In some classes, the teacher asks other children if they have any more questions and/or if the explanation makes sense to them.
- The exchange continues until the members of the class (including the teacher) ask no more questions and everyone seems to understand.

In an Inquiry context, the expectation is that students not only tell how they solved the problem, but also are frequently asked to give reasons for solving the problem in a certain way and to clarify their thinking. The teacher asks the same information questions listed in the Report Ways context, but also makes inquiries into the children's meanings by asking, "What do you mean? I don't understand." They also expect children to provide reasons for their thinking, asking questions such as, "Why did you add 20 to 32?" The teachers' *meaning-probing* questions require children to clarify their thinking in order to be understood, while the *why* questions require students to give reasons for their ideas. This situation can be depicted as one in which students understand and reason about mathematics.

In an Inquiry discussion, the children were often seen participating in the question asking. Therefore, the exchange extended beyond an interaction with only the teacher and the child explaining and included those children listening. The norms established that underlie the interaction were more complex for not only the child as explainer but also as listener. The role of listeners was to understand and to make sense of what was said. If the listeners did not, they were to ask questions in an attempt to make sense of an individual's strategy and the reasoning behind it. The expectation that listening students would also participate in questioning was important not only for their learning but this participation also created the possibility for public discourse. That is, there was an opportunity for personal or private thinking to be examined and questioned for the purpose of understanding and establishing common meanings. Public understanding of personal meanings is thought to be an important process in the development of shared meanings, or public knowledge; that is the basis of culture (Goodnow, 1989; Edwards & Mercer, 1987).

ARGUMENT DISCUSSION

As in an Inquiry context, the discussion in these classes began as Report Ways with students reporting their strategies, followed by opportunities to clarifying their meanings and give reasons for their thinking. However, what distinguished an Argument discussion from an Inquiry discussion was that challenges about the validity of an answer or someone's reasoning occurred. In an Inquiry discussion, the teacher and the children asked questions for further understanding and clarification that may have also provided opportunities for errors to be realized, but they never made statements to the effect that something was wrong with the answer or the thinking of the explainer. In an Argument discussion, processes of justification and argumentation involving what might be called informal "proof" occurred—students were expected to justify their reasoning if challenged by others. In these classes, the discussion moved back and forth among Report Ways, Inquiry, and Argument. Moreover, the movement between the Inquiry and Argument discussions was extremely fluid. Thus, classes in which Argument existed also had the most complex forms of interaction and discourse and the more extensive norms for children's participation as explainers and listeners (cf., Wood, 1999). This was mainly due to the active role that the children listening were expected to take in making challenges and providing rationale for their disagreements.

The following episode that occurred during a class discussion provides an example of the pattern of interaction and teachers' questioning.

Illustrative Example

The problems being discussed are shown in Fig. 9.2.

> Teacher: What did you get for an answer to this problem? (Points to problem 3). David?

> David: 19.

> Class: Agree.

> Teacher: (Writes 19).

> David: Our number sentence was 52 take away 33 equals 19.

Teacher: Okay. Anyone have anything different? (to the class). Okay David. How did you solve this problem?

David: (Comes to the front of the room). I knew that 20 plus, (pause) no 19 plus 33 was 52, so I knew that if you took [away] 33 it would be 19.

Teacher: David, I agree with your answer but I don't agree with how you solved it. You said you knew 19 plus 33 equals 52. How did you know that?

David: Because that and that (points to 3 tens and 1 ten) equals 40 and add that and that (points to 3 ones and 9 ones) equals 50 and 2, equals 33.

Teacher: Yes. But where did you get the 19? Nineteen is not given in the problem.

David: I already knew it because the first problem was 52 take away 20 was 32, so 52 take away 33 had to be 19.

Teacher: Ah ha. Okay. Now I agree with what you did.

Pattern of Interaction and Questioning Discourse

- A child provides an explanation of her or his solution to the problem.
- Teacher (or other children) who disagree with the solution or answer presented issue a challenge. The challenger may or may not tell why he or she disagrees.
- The child explaining offers a justification for her or his explanation.
- At this point, the challenger may accept the explanation or may continue to disagree by offering further explanation or rationale for his or her position.
- The child explaining continues to offer further justification for her or his solution.
- This process continues and other listeners may contribute in an attempt to resolve the contradiction.

- The exchange continues until the members of the class (including the teacher) are satisfied that the disagreement is resolved.

In the Argument discussion, teachers questioned pupils about how they solved the problem, asked them to clarify their thinking and give reasons, but also asked questions that were challenges and required responses that provided justification. Therefore, along with asking the questions identified in a Report Ways and an Inquiry discussions described previously, the teacher asked questions such as, "How do you know that?" and "Can you prove that?" This situation can be depicted as one in which students provide justifications and challenges.

In the examples of Inquiry and Argument discussions just given, the interactions consist of an exchange between the teacher and student for the purpose of making evident the activity of teaching. However, much of the time, teaching is not apparent as the students as explainer and listeners dominate the interaction. The following example taken from a whole-class discussion, characterizes student interaction and the dynamic nature of the movement between the Inquiry and Argument discussions.

Illustrative Example

The problem is the third one shown in Fig. 9.2.

Teacher: What did you get for an answer for this problem?

Fred: 25.

Sarah: 19.

Adam: 21.

Teacher: Any other answers? Okay. Fred tell us how you got 25.

Fred: We used the unifix cubes. 52 and then we took away 33. First I took away the tens. 42, 32, 22. Then I counted back the ones, 21, 20, 19.

Karen: But you said it was 25.

Fred: I know, but now I think it is 19, because I counted it again with the cubes.

Teacher: John what do you want to say? (He has his hand raised).

John: I went back to 52 take away 30 is 22 (points to second problem on the paper). And I took away 3 more and that was 19. So I think it is 19.

Teacher: Okay. But why did you take away 3?

John: Because 52 take away 30 is 22, and 33 is 3 more than 30 so it was 19.

Teacher: How did you know that it was 19?

John: Because if 52 take 30 is 22, 52 take away 33 is 3 more than 30, so then I had to take away 3 more from 22, and that would be 19.

Teacher: That makes sense. Sarah what would you like to say?

Sarah: Well if you take 30 from 50, then you would have 20. Then you would have 2 and that 3, so you could take 1 from 20, and that would be 19.

Mark: This is too confusing for me. Sarah, I don't understand why you took the 1 from 20.

Sarah: Because you have 2 minus 3 and so you need 1 off the tens.

Mary: But if you took 1 from the 20, what happened to the 2 and the 3?

Sarah: I took 1 from the tens and added it to the 2 to make 3. [Then] 3 minus 3 is 0. So then I had to take 1 from the tens-20 and that makes the answer 19.

Ryan: Well if you check it by adding 19 and 33, you get 52, so 19 is the answer.

Karen: I think the answer must be 19, because we did it so many different ways to figure it out. And we got 19.

Class: Agree. It is 19.

Although the teaching in this episode appears to be nominal, nonetheless, the pedagogy necessary to establish this context is far more complex than that of traditional teaching. In situations such as this, the endeavor of teaching lies in the norms for student participation established at the beginning of the year and the ways of questioning instigated by the teacher. Now this is embedded in the well-established patterns of interaction and discourse such that the children are actively involved in and responsible for their learning and teaching is less visible.

CONCLUSION

Instances of the teaching described in the three discussion contexts we have described in this chapter can be observed in other reports of classroom interaction and discourse such as Ball (1993), Hiebert et al., (1997), and Schifter (1997). Moreover, those such as Aubrey (1997) and Boaler (1998, 2000) showed that these differences in classrooms affect students' achievement in mathematics. However, we contend that differences in teaching require more of teachers than merely acquiring pedagogical content knowledge of mathematics (e.g., Ma, 1999) or knowledge of children's mathematical thinking (e.g., Carpenter, Ansell, & Levi, this volume). Instead, we believe teaching involves creating modes of social interaction in which students' bring their individual thinking to the fore, but in some instances also engage in the processes of inquiry and validation of ideas through the mathematical practices of explanation, clarification, challenge, and justification of their ideas. These negotiated and validated meanings then become the common ground from which a class is able to progress in their mathematical thinking.

The examples given illustrate teaching that is composed of the interpersonal exchange that leads to the attainment of mathematical meaning through a social learning process involving negotiating meaning and collaboration that are central to the acquisition of both individual and cultural knowledge. But, more importantly, we contend that within each of the modes of social interaction the mathematics realized by children is itself different (Wood, 2000). This is the reason we believe the conception of mathematics teaching needs to be extended to include a social perspective and to take seriously the need of children to adapt to a social existence, to develop a system of shared meanings, and to acquire the accumulated knowledge of their culture.

ACKNOWLEDGMENTS

This research is supported by the Research on Teaching and Learning (RTL) program of the National Science Foundation under award RED 925-4939. Some preparation of this chapter was accomplished while the first author was an Academic Visitor in the Department of Educational Studies, University of Oxford. All opinions are those of the authors.

REFERENCES

Aubrey, C. (1997). *Teaching mathematics in the early years*. London: Falmer Press.
Ball, D. (1993). With an eye on the mathematical horizon: Dilemmas of teaching elementary school mathematics. *Elementary School Journal, 93*, 373-397.
Bauersfeld, H. (1988). Interaction, construction, and knowledge: Alternative perspectives for mathematics education. In T. Cooney & D. Grouws, (Eds.), *Effective mathematics teaching* (pp. 27-46). Reston, VA: National Council of Teachers of Mathematics and Lawrence Erlbaum Associates.
Blumer, H. (1969). *Symbolic interactionism: Perspective and method*. Berkeley: University of California Press.
Boaler, J. (1998). Open and closed mathematics: Student experiences and understandings. *Journal of Research in Mathematics Education, 29*, 41-62.
Boaler, J. (2000). Exploring situated insights into research and learning. *Journal of Research in Mathematics Education, 31*, 113-119.
Bruner, J. (1990). *Acts of meaning*. Cambridge, MA: Harvard University Press.
Bruner, J. (1996). *The culture of education*. Cambridge, MA: Harvard University Press.
Cobb, P., Wood, T., & Yackel, E. (1990). Classrooms as learning environments for teachers and researchers. In R. B. Davis, C. Maher, & N. Noddings (Eds.), *Constructivist views on teaching and learning of mathematics* (pp. 125-146). (Journal for Research in Mathematics Education Monograph Series No. 4.) Reston, VA: National Council of Teachers of Mathematics.
Dewey, J (undated). *Essays in experimental logic*. New York: Dover Publications.
Edwards, D. & Mercer, N. (1987). *Common knowledge*. London: Methuen.
Entwistle, N. (1995). Frameworks for understanding as experienced in essay writing and in preparing for examinations. *Educational Psychologist, 30*, 47-54.
Flanders, N. A. (1970). *Analyzing teaching behavior*. Reading, MA: Addison-Wesley.
Garfinkel, H. (1967). *Studies in ethnomethodology*. Englewood Cliffs, NJ: Prentice-Hall.
Goffman, E. (1959). *The presentation of self in everyday life*. Garden City, NY: Anchor.

Goffman, E. (1967). *Interaction ritual: Essays on face-to-face behavior.* New York: Anchor.

Goffman, E. (1974). *Frame analysis: An essay on the organization of experience.* New York: Harper and Row.

Goffman, E. (1981). *Forms of talk.* Oxford: Basil Blackwell.

Goodnow, J. (1990). The socialization of cognition: What is involved? In J. Stigler, R. Shweder, & G. Herdt (Eds.), *Cultural psychology. Essays on comparative human development* (pp. 259-286). Cambridge, MA: Cambridge University Press.

Hiebert, J., Carpenter, T., Fennema, E., Fuson, K., Human, P., Murray, H., Olivier, A., Wearne, D. (1997). *Making sense: Teaching and learning mathematics with understanding.* Portsmouth, NH: Heinemann.

Kruger, A., & Tomasello, M. (1996). Cultural learning and learning culture. In J. Bruner & D. Olson (Eds.), *Handbook of education and human development* (pp. 369-387). Oxford: Blackwell.

Krummheuer, G. (2000). Mathematics learning in narrative classroom cultures: Studies of argumentation in primary mathematics education. *For the Learning of Mathematics, 20,* 22-32.

Kuhn, D., Garcia-Mila, M., Zohar, A., & Andersen, C. (1995). Strategies of knowledge acquisition. *Monographs of the Society for Research in Child Development, 60* (4, Serial No. 245). Chicago: University of Chicago Press.

Lave, J. (1996). Teaching, as learning, in practice. *Mind, Culture and Activity, 3,* 149-164.

Lave, J. & Wenger, E. (1991). *Situated learning: Legitimate peripheral participation.* New York: Cambridge University Press.

Ma, L. (1999). *Knowing and teaching elementary mathematics.* Mahwah, NJ: Lawrence Erlbaum Associates.

Meserve, B., & Suydam, M. (1992). Mathematics education in the United States. In R. Morris & A. Manmohan, (Eds.), *Studies in mathematics education: Moving into the twenty-first century* (pp. 7-20). Paris: UNESCO.

National Council of Teachers of Mathematics (1989). *Curriculum and evaluation standards for school mathematics.* Reston, VA: Author.

National Council of Teachers of Mathematics (1991). *Professional standards for teaching mathematics.* Reston, VA: Author.

National Council of Teachers of Mathematics. (2000). *Principles and standards for school mathematics.* Reston, VA: Author.

Piaget, J. (1985). *The equilibration of cognitive structures.* Chicago, IL: University of Chicago Press.

Rogoff, B. (1994). Developing understanding of the idea of communities of learners. *Mind, Culture, & Activity, 1,* 209-229.

Rommetveit, R. (1985). Language acquisition as increasing linguistic structuring of experience and symbolic behavior control. In J. Wertsch (Ed.), *Culture, communication, and cognition* (pp. 183-205). Cambridge, MA: Cambridge University Press.

Samarapungavan, A. (1992). Children's judgements in theory choice tasks: Scientific rationality in childhood. *Cognition, 45,* 1-32.

Schifter, D. (1997). *Learning mathematics for teaching.* Newton, MA: Center for the Development of Teaching.

Tomasello, M. (1999). *The cultural origins of human cognition.* Cambridge, MA: Harvard University Press.

Voigt, J. (1985). Patterns and routines in classroom interaction. *Recherches en Didactique des Mathematiques [Research in Mathematics Education], 6,* 69-118.

Wood, T. (1994). Patterns of interaction and learning in mathematics classrooms. In S. Lerman (Ed.), *The culture of the mathematics classroom* (pp. 149-168). Dordrecht: Kluwer.

Wood, T. (1999). Creating a context for argument in mathematics class. *Journal for Research in Mathematics Education, 30,* 171-191.

Wood, T. (2000). Differences in teaching and opportunities for learning in primary mathematics classes. *Zentralblatt für Didaktik der Mathematik [International Reviews on Mathematical Education], 32,* 149-154.

Wood, T., & Turner-Vorbeck, T. (1999). Developing teaching of mathematics: Making connections in practice. In L. Burton (Ed.), *Learning mathematics: From hierarchies to networks* (pp. 173-186). London: Falmer Press.

Wood, T., Cobb, P., Yackel, E., & Dillon, D. (1993). *Rethinking elementary school mathematics: Insights and issues.* (Journal for Research in Mathematics Education Monograph Series No. 6.) Reston, VA: National Council of Teachers of Mathematics.

Making Sense of Mathematics Teaching in Real Contexts

Betsy McNeal
The Ohio State University

My interest in how students' learning is constructed in particular ways in particular communities (McNeal, 1991, 1995) has brought me to thinking about teaching as well. I am convinced that students construct mathematical ideas in the course of interactions with their teacher and classmates, and so my work as a teacher educator has focused on encouraging prospective teachers to listen to their students' mathematical thinking. In 6 years of working with prospective elementary teachers, however, I have repeatedly observed that beginning teachers who seem determined to focus on children's mathematics find this difficult to do under the pressures of practical concerns such as proficiency tests, expectations of parents, colleagues, administrators, evaluations, and scheduling. Eisenhart et al. (1993) offered a case study of one student teacher who shifted from teaching for conceptual to procedural knowledge due to mixed messages from the teacher education program and placement school. This clearly must have affected this student teacher's ability to develop an understanding of and a focus on children's mathematics. Working with an experienced and excellent mathematics teacher has provided me with an even more pressing example that tensions can exist for any teacher between addressing practical concerns and focusing on children's mathematics.

The work of Lampert (1985, 1992) and Ball (1993) provide us with an image of teachers as managers of dilemmas, or as negotiating the tension between multiple and often competing goals. Both Lampert and Ball point out the dual pressures facing mathematics teachers. On one hand, a major goal of schooling is to have students emerge from mathematics instruction familiar with, and being able to use, conventional mathematical procedures and notations. This is not a capricious or arbitrary goal; the procedures are efficient, and a consistent "language" is necessary in order for people to be able to communicate mathematically. On the other hand, effective mathematics teaching builds on what students know, and honors the construction of ideas and concepts, given their experience and knowledge. The teacher discussed in this chapter is committed to this form of teaching, and to helping her students negotiate the difficult pathways between their developed understandings and the standard procedures. This chapter adds to our understanding of how teachers negotiate the tensions inherent in engaging students meaningfully in this way and suggests that these tensions arise, in part, from the multiple contexts in which teachers work.[1]

Like Lampert and Ball, the teacher in this chapter focused her teaching on helping her students construct mathematical ideas that build on what they know. Students in her classroom generated a number of different and effective computational strategies. However, the teacher felt pressure to introduce the conventional addition algorithm to her third graders in preparation for the fourth-grade proficiency test. This is what I refer to as the *societal context* of her work. In this example, I illustrate how the teacher's efforts to help her students connect the standard addition algorithm to their self-generated strategies were constrained by her knowledge of the students' mathematical understandings and backgrounds. This is what I call the *classroom context*. The two contexts discussed here are defined from the perspective of an individual teacher and differ in at least one important way: The societal context is taken as static by the teacher, whereas the classroom context is seen and experienced by the teacher as dynamic. Because the teacher took the societal context as something that she could not change, this context may fade into the background for the reader, but it is critical to our understanding of the competing goals this teacher was trying to negotiate.

---

[1] In this chapter, I use the term *context* to refer to the working environment, both physical and cognitive, experienced by an individual teacher. This environment includes the teacher's goals and her interpretation of the actions, words, and goals of others around her, as well as the teacher's perception of the physical setting.

There are some important differences between the case reported here and other work in this volume. First, I discuss what I learned from working with one teacher rather than with a group of teachers. Second, this was a collaborative research project in that the teacher and I worked together to attempt to resolve a pedagogical dilemma of concern to both of us. Finally, this teacher was already an outstanding mathematics teacher[2] and so our joint inquiry focused on her efforts to refine her teaching practice in order to make sense of this particular dilemma.

BACKGROUND

Betty Tilley is a third-grade teacher at the Miquon School just outside of Philadelphia. She and I met when student teachers placed in her classroom were taking my mathematics methods course. The student teachers spoke of compatibility between their observations in Tilley's classroom and the ideas about teaching that we were developing in our university class.[3] When I visited her classroom, I found that Tilley was not just a fan of the work of Kamii, having read some of her books (Kamii, 1989, 1994), but her classroom looked like the classrooms described by Kamii. Tilley's fascination with children's mathematics was evident in every aspect of her instructional style.

Arguing from personal observations as well as her reading, Tilley had convinced the K–3 teachers, the parents, and the principal of her school[4] that the children should not be taught the conventional addition and subtraction algorithms until third grade, and only then in order to help prepare them for the fourth-grade proficiency test. The delay, Tilley argued, was to allow for the fostering of students' development of place value concepts. When we met, Tilley believed that her students had a firm foundation in place value, but was not sure whether they were learning the conventional algorithms with understanding. She also felt that her teaching of the addition and subtraction algorithms was not consistent with her philosophy of

---

[2] Tilley was known among faculty and parents for her ability to engage students in learning mathematics with meaning, and was nominated by her school for a Presidential Award for Excellence in Science and Math Teaching. My classroom observations over an extended period of time support these views.

[3] Course ideas are compatible with the National Council of Teachers of Mathematics (1991).

[4] The Miquon School was founded on the philosophy of John Dewey and so was already inclined to focus on children's understandings of subject matter.

respecting the children's mathematics and promoting their independent thinking.

Tilley and I designed a project in which we looked closely at what the students were learning when she introduced the conventional addition algorithm and at the role instruction played in that learning. This provided a way for Tilley to reflect on and refine her teaching and for me to learn about the issues that she considered in making her instructional decisions. Tilley made all instructional decisions throughout the year, and she and her assistant teacher were responsible for all instruction. I served primarily as a sounding board for Tilley's ideas and concerns. I also took responsibility for collecting and organizing our data, and I provided an observer's insight into students' learning. The data I draw on in this chapter includes transcripts of video recordings of all instruction on the addition algorithm, transcripts of weekly meetings with Tilley, and her journal writing about classroom observations, concerns, and ideas for instruction.

In the following pages, I first provide an example of Tilley's typical teaching. Then, against this background, I tell the story of instruction in the conventional addition algorithm from the point of view of a teacher whose goal is development of children's mathematical understanding. In presenting this case study, I hope to illustrate how one mathematics teacher negotiated the multiple tensions of her work.

TILLEY'S TYPICAL TEACHING

Each year, Tilley and her students construct a mathematics community characterized by inquiry. She guides the creation of this community by posing mathematical challenges through problems and games and by encouraging students to validate their own solutions. Furthermore, she facilitates discussions in which all students are expected to make sense of each other's mathematical thinking[5], and in which she makes a major effort to understand the children's thinking herself. Tilley's typical style of teaching allows her to take great pleasure in the act of teaching, which she defines as working with children. In the lesson presented, it can be seen that her role was primarily to record the individual children's methods for

---

[5] Students were required to indicate their agreement or disagreement by using silent hand signals that Tilley introduced.

all to see and examine. Typically, she focuses her teaching on helping students develop their capacity for independent reasoning and, toward this end, she emphasizes the natural role of errors and the importance of examination of errors by students and teacher in the learning process. Instructional planning, for Tilley, therefore includes searching for ways to engage students in figuring things out for themselves.

Example Lesson -- January 15[6]

While half of the class was at physical education, Tilley explained to the remaining 10 students that they were going to do some "adding in their minds." She worked with half of the group while her assistant teacher worked with the other half.   Tilley asked the students to add the numbers she had written on the chalkboard (see Example 1).   She wrote the numbers this way in order to allow students to use either horizontal or vertical alignment. Tilley then waited until all students had signaled that they had completed the problem.

132

75   12

Example 1. The problem as written on the chalkboard.

Ms. Tilley: Who's ready to give answers?

Will: 219.

(Ms. Tilley writes 219 on the board, other students signal agreement, except Adam.)

Ms. Tilley: Do you agree, Adam? Or did you get something else?

---

[6] In the transcript, "Ss" stands for unidentified students when several call out responses in chorus. When several unidentified students call out separate responses, they are designated by number (e.g., "S5") to indicate that it may not be the same student who is calling out. Text is added to the transcript for two purposes: text added in brackets should be read as part of the classroom discourse, although it is added for clarification; text added in parentheses might be thought of as stage directions — nonverbal actions or information about where the comments are directed.

Adam: (Shrugs) I had 121.

Ms. Tilley: (Writes 121 on board next to 219) Okay, who wants to
          prove?

Will: (Says quietly to Adam who is next to him) [Did] you leave off
          the 132?

Adam: (to Ms. Tilley) I mean, *two* hundred twenty-one. (She erases 121
          and writes 221.)

Tilley recorded all answers with the intention that the students would
figure out the reason for the discrepancies as they "proved" their
answers. The children are accustomed to this expectation and have
learned that their answers will be accepted, so usually give their
answers even when they may be wrong. She encourages her students
to talk with each other about their work and so was pleased that Will
addressed Adam directly as he tried to figure out the discrepancy
between Adam's answer of 121 and his answer of 219.

The discussion continued:

Ms. Tilley: Okay, who wants to prove? (Hands up: Ruth, Will) Okay,
          Ruth.

Ruth: Well, 132 . . .

Ms. Tilley: Let's see, let me write it. (Writes vertically as shown in
          Example 2a)

Ruth: Plus 10, from the 12, is 142, is 144 with the 2, then add the 5 from
          75, is 149, and then you add the 70 [inaudible].

Ms. Tilley: So you counted by tens? (Ruth nods) So you did plus 10
          plus 10 plus 10?

Ruth: (Nods again) And I got 219.

Ms. Tilley: (Writes the tens as in Example 2b) So you got 219.

Will: Can I prove?

Ms. Tilley: (To the group) Okay. Everyone agree with [*Ruth's*] proof? (Students signal agreement)

132	149
+ 10	+ 10
142	+ 10
+ 2	+ 10
144	+ 10
+ 5	+ 10
149	+ 10
	+ 10
	219

Example 2a. Ruth's solution.   Example 2b. Ruth's solution, continued.

Tilley's questions indicated her desire to understand how Ruth added the 70. Asking if everyone agreed before considering another student's "proof" was a reminder to Will of the expectation to check with the others.

The discussion continued with Will volunteering again:

Will: Can I prove it?

Ms. Tilley: You want to prove it, Will? Okay. I just want to go up by those tens. (counts the 7 tens in Example 2b before erasing) Okay, how did you do it, Will?

Will: Okay, what I did was I switched the 32 and the 75, so that's 175, and then I took the 32.

Ms. Tilley: So you switched that, so it was 175 and 32?

Will: No. Then I took the 30 and put it with the 70 so it was 205.

$$5 + 2 + 2 = 9$$

100	200
+ 75	+ 9
+ 30	209
205	+ 10
	219

Example. 3a. Will's solution.   Example 3b. Will's solution, continued.

Ms. Tilley: (Writes as in Example 3a) So you got 205 there, right? So you still had the 2 [in 132] and the 12.

Will: And then I added the 5, the 2, and the other 2 together.

Ms. Tilley: Now, wait, I'm confused.

Will: (Stands up and points) I didn't use the 5 [in 75] yet.

Ms. Tilley: Oh! You didn't use this 2 yet. (circles 2 in 132)

Will: I didn't use that 2, that 2, or the 5 (pointing to 132, 12, and 75, respectively).

Ms. Tilley: And the 5.

Will: So 5, 2, and 2, that's 9 . . .

Ms. Tilley: Okay. (Writes as in Example 3b)

Will: And then I knew I had 10 left, so I took that so it was 219. (Ms. Tilley hesitates, not writing anything) Because 10 plus 9 equals 19. (Adam, Elizabeth, Jessica, Ruth give agree signal; Elizabeth's hand goes up.)

Ms. Tilley: Oh, that 10 there [in 12] you mean! Ah! Okay, oh no the 5 was gone (Fixes Example 3a then completes Example 3b.) Okay.

Adam: [I probably miscounted.]

Ms. Tilley: Did you? You did it the same way, but you lost track of something, do you think? Okay.

Tilley believed students should decide the correctness of answers on the basis of examination of their solution processes, rather than on teacher evaluation. She was pleased that Will felt free to "teach" her by showing her the 5 he did not use. This allowed her to admit being confused herself, signaling to the students that uncertainty and errors are a natural part of learning. When Tilley hesitated, students appeared to take this as an indication that she did not understand what they were saying, rather than that their answer was wrong: They offered clarification for their thinking, rather than immediately changing their answers. Tilley's response to Adam shows her belief that thinking together can help one recognize one's error and understand what might have caused the error. Adam's comment, "I probably miscounted," shows that he realized his answer was wrong and, listening to the others, speculated as to the reason on his own. Tilley's response showed she values this thinking.

Tilley then called on two other students to prove. After the group had signaled agreement with each of their solution methods, she turned for a final comment to Adam.

> Ms. Tilley: I'm wondering if you left out one of the twos because . . . look, yours is just 2 less than, 2 more than the others (pointing to the 219 and 221). Or if you added one of the twos twice? You think maybe that's what happened? (small nod from Adam, then Ms. Tilley turns to the others) What do you think, do you think maybe that's what he did? (small nods from the others).

By returning to analysis of Adam's answer and inviting group participation, Tilley indicated that sorting out errors is part of what is to be figured out by a mathematical community.

As well as illustrating how Tilley's teaching practice fits with her stated philosophy, these excerpts show how the children were thinking about addition of two- and three-digit numbers prior to instruction in the standard algorithm. Their methods did not begin with adding the ones' digits neither did their strategies always move sequentially from hundreds, to tens, to ones. Although Ruth decomposed the 12 and 75 into tens and ones, she began with the 132 in its entirety. Will, like Ruth, decomposed the addends into hundreds, tens, and ones, but pieced these back together by first using the 100, then some of the tens (70 + 30) to make another hundred, then the ones, and then another ten. Throughout the year, all but one of the children in the class provided proofs of their calculations that combined hundreds, tens and ones in ways that showed a clear understanding of place value. All strategies also showed the children seeking relationships among the addends that would aid them in adding efficiently and keeping track of their total.

The next day, one child, Jane, used a strategy that Tilley thought might provide a useful connection to the standard algorithm. An example of Jane's strategy is shown in Example 4. Jane added 358 + 471 by first adding 300 + 400 and writing a 7 in the hundreds' column, then added 50 + 70, erased the 7 in the hundreds' column and wrote an 8 followed by a 2 in the tens' column, then finally added 8 + 1 for a 9 in the ones' column. Jane's "erasing strategy" appeared to be very close to the standard addition procedure.

$$
\begin{array}{ccc}
358 & \text{becomes} & 358 \\
+\ 471 & & +\ 471 \\
\hline
7 & & 8\ 729 \\
\end{array}
$$

Example 4. Jane's method.

Although Tilley had not planned instruction on the algorithm for another 2 weeks, she noted in her journal:

> Jane did her problems in an interesting way. She put them in columns and added each column, starting with the thousands. Then she erased and regrouped as she needed to. I think I'll share that method with that . . . group . . . It might tip over into people sharing the algorithm. (January 16)

About 2 weeks later, Tilley began a unit of study that led up to, introduced, and practiced the standard procedure for addition. For instruction in the algorithm, she felt that the class fell roughly into two groups -- those who were "nearly there" (some had already begun to find it easier to line their addends up vertically) and those who would probably need more assistance. We follow Tilley's instruction in the standard addition algorithm for the first group. This story is organized to illustrate the development of instruction: laying the foundations, trying to connect the procedure to the students' mental strategies, and then to the students' prior experiences.

INSTRUCTION IN THE STANDARD ADDITION ALGORITHM

Although the conventional addition procedure has become institutionalized precisely because it is an efficient series of steps that can be performed to compute answers without thinking, Tilley felt that to teach this procedure in a step-by-step manner would defeat her goal of fostering the children's autonomy and undermine her implicit message that the children's thinking and ideas are important. Tilley did tell children factual information on occasion, but she typically restricted the "telling" to those ideas that she believed children could not figure out for themselves. She particularly attempted to avoid imposing sanctioned adult ways on children when she thought they would contradict what the children already understood. This fundamental tension is reflected in Tilley's teaching and is explored in the following pages.

While we, as observers with the benefit of hindsight, may have better ways to make the connection, suggestions, or both for the teacher, the following episodes are offered as an empirical basis for discussion of the role played by the two kinds of contexts, societal and classroom, in mathematics teaching.

Laying the Foundations

Tilley began instruction that was intended to lead children into meaningful use of the standard addition procedure by having them play the "rod trading game" (referred to simply as "rod trading") for 2 days.[7] In this game, each child rolls a pair of dice, counts out as many cubes as the sum of the dice, and puts them in the ones' column of her trading board (a paper with columns for hundreds, tens, and ones). The child must trade ten cubes for a rod, and ten rods for a flat whenever possible. The goal is to reach 1,000, and many students turned this into a race. Tilley used the game to introduce the idea and terminology of "trading," which she planned to use to explain the recording process known as "carrying." She then introduced another game called "make the biggest number" (MBN) in which two teams compete to create the bigger four-digit number by deciding where to place a digit obtained on each turn by rolling a die.[8]

Two issues that emerged repeatedly over this instructional period are considered in Tilley's following journal entry:

> The kids really got engaged in the MBN game. I am wondering if I should introduce the idea of naming the places (ones, tens, hundreds, etc.) or if I should just work without it. Last year the kids got very dependent on [a labeled grid] and always wanted it up [on the

---

[7] These are the rods (tens) found among typical base-ten materials. Other items in the materials include small cubes (ones), flats (hundreds), and large cubes (thousands).

[8] Variations used include playing for the largest 6-digit number and for the largest sum of two 4-digit numbers.

[9] Cobb & Wheatley (1988) described a common misconception that "2 tens" refers to "2 rods" or "2 orange things" where a "ten" is different from a "one," but not necessarily by a factor of ten.

chalkboard] so they could remember what to call each place. But I wonder if I could do the whole thing by continuing to talk about the 20 or the 200. (written after February 8 and 9)

One issue expressed here was how to refer to the digits in a numeral in a way that would indicate their value. Tilley's students generally referred to the 2 in 294 as 200 where traditionally taught students will refer to it as a 2, perhaps specifying that it is in the hundreds' place. Tilley and I took the 200 as an indicator that the children understood the meaning of the digits in a numeral and the value of the number as a whole.[9] Tilley was concerned that the children maintain this understanding. The second issue was whether to label the places in a grid on the chalkboard. Tilley frequently expressed concern over the selection of instructional devices that would assist the children's developing understanding without making them dependent on the devices.

Trying to Connect the Procedure to the Students' Mental Strategies

As she observed the children engaged in rod trading, Tilley continued to ponder the best way to teach the standard addition procedure to the group. She wrote in her journal:

> I really think some of them could learn the algorithm just with a simple explanation and I hope I can keep the process fairly short for them. . . . I really want to try to hook it to what they already know and so I think I'll start by doing some of the addition we did mentally and write it vertically and start at the left as they do in their proofs and just write out 400 or 20 etc. on different lines and add them up at the bottom [see Example 5]. I need to think about it some more and try it myself and see how it works. (February 9)

hundreds	tens	ones
3	2	7
1	9	3
+ 2	4	6
	1	6
1	5	0
+ 6	0	0
7	6	6

Example 5. The long cut way.

February 12. Tilley planned to introduce the conventional procedure by recording the students' solutions in an expanded version of Jane's strategy (see Example 4). She hoped to draw the students' attention to the fact that these intermediate sums were the same obtained by starting with the ones' column. She would then introduce "carrying" as a shorter way of recording what students were already doing. Tilley felt this would help the students see the addition algorithm as reasonable rather than arbitrary.

After reminding the children of their prior experiences with mental sums, Tilley opened the lesson, "I'm gonna show you a way that actually is a way that some people [in this group] did it before to add them." She then had the children mentally compute the sum of 327, 193, and 246 written on the chalkboard in no particular order (similar to that shown in Example 1). When one student asked her to "put them in a column," she replied, "I'll put them both ways [horizontally and vertically] so you can work the way you want to." The three children who provided proofs of their answers all began by collecting the hundreds. However, as before, each of their strategies then moved back and forth collecting tens, combining ones to make a ten (7 + 3), or creating subtotals that did not fit with Tilley's intent to record these methods in her expanded version of Jane's strategy.

Having failed to help the children see the intended connection between their methods and her recording system, Tilley decided to show them this transitional recording system directly.

Ms. Tilley: Let me show you a way to do it. (Rewrites 327, 193, 246 as shown in Example 5) You know how sometimes when you do these numbers in your head and they get really big up in the thousands, you sort of lose track of the numbers?

Sam: No.

Ms. Tilley: Well, sometimes that happens when people are working with big numbers and they're working without pencil and paper . . . Yeah? I'm gonna teach you a way, it is a pencil and paper way, but it helps you keep track of the numbers, and it's kind of a short cut way to do it. Okay? And it's sort of like [rod] trading, okay? Do you want me to show you?

Student: Yeah.

Ms. Tilley: It's sort of like rod trading, okay? (Draws lines between the columns) Some of you might know this way. Somebody might have taught you this already.

Will: My sister taught me. Whenever she does it, she messes it up. I can do it better than her.

Ms. Tilley: (Labels each column) First I'm gonna do it the long cut way then I'll show you the short cut way. Now in this way, it's different than the way you usually do it. You know how when you add very often you start with the hundreds or the thousands, you start with the big numbers? It's just like rod trading, you know how when you do rod trading you start with the ones? Everyone agree with that? And so for this method, to make it easier to write down you always start with the ones. (Records steps as shown in Example 5) So if you add up the ones here how many would you get? Yeah, Elizabeth.

Elizabeth: 16.

Ms. Tilley: 16. So I'll write 16. (Writes the 1 under the tens, 6 under the ones) Now, add up the tens, how many would you get? Yeah, Jane?

Jane: You could put the 1 up where the tens is and then you just add them all together.

Ms. Tilley: (Pointing above the tens' column, and nodding) Could we do that next time? Okay. Adding up the tens. Chris.

Chris: 150.

Ms. Tilley: 150. (Writes 150) Okay, then we add the hundreds.

Nancy: 600.

Ms. Tilley: (Writes 600) Okay, 600. Now add them all up. Let's start at the ones again, shall we? How many ones?

S2:   16.

S3:   6.

Ms. Tilley: (Writes 6) Do you agree? Then how many tens?

Ss: (Mixed responses) 10, 6.

Ms. Tilley: From down here. (Gestures over the tens' column of lower sum) I know what you're doing, Jane, you're thinking ahead with it. Okay, 6. (Writes 6) How many hundreds?

Ss: 7.

Ms. Tilley: And the answer is . . .?

Ss: 766.

In the aforementioned, Tilley took an intermediate route to the standard addition algorithm by showing the students a procedure that none of them actually use, but that seemed in her estimation to be in tune with their own methods. Further, she used the familiar experience with rod trading as the reason for starting with the ones. Tilley then attempted to use this to illustrate a parallel to the conventional algorithm that she demonstrated next. Tilley began, "Can I show you the way that Jane knows? And some of you may have seen this," referring to Jane's earlier suggestion to "put the 1 up there where the 'tens' is." She had the children give her 3 three-digit numbers, which she wrote in a place value grid (see Example 6).

hundreds	tens	ones
	1	
5	4	9
9	9	9
+ 1	0	1
1, 6	4	19

Example 6. The short cut way.

The discussion continues:

Ms. Tilley: Okay. Now. On this way of doing it, you start with the ones first. How many ones do we have? Elizabeth?

Elizabeth: 19.

Ms. Tilley: Everyone agree? (Pauses) Okay, now. (Writes 19 in ones'
            column) I can't write 19 ones down there, can I?

Ss: Uh uh. (Quietly indicating no)

Ms. Tilley: So, Jane says write the 9 and put the ten part of the 19 right
            up there [over the tens' column]. Everybody agree with that?

Josh: Oh yeah, I [know this].

Ms. Tilley: (To Josh) You know this way? (To class) Okay, can we add
            up the tens?

Ss: (Mixed responses) 140, 114.

Ms. Tilley: 140. Who wants to prove how you got 140? Jessica?

Jessica: 10 plus 90 equals 100 plus 40 equals 140.

Ms. Tilley: So we have 140, I'm getting confused. Oh, 140! Right.

Jessica: Yeah!

Ms. Tilley: So we have 14 tens, right? Do you agree? So, what should I
            write?

Jane: Put 4 in the tens' column . . .

Ms. Tilley: And what does that mean?

Jane: and 1 in the hundreds'.

Ms. Tilley: So does that mean 140? Do you all agree?

Nancy: Oh, I know what the answer is.

Ms. Tilley: Nancy?

Nancy: One thousand . . .

Ms. Tilley: Wait, let's give people time to add up the hundreds.   Why don't you add up the hundreds, folks?

Josh: One hundred and fifty, I mean and forty-nine.

Jane: One thousand sixty, six hundred forty-nine.

Nancy: No. One thousand five hundred forty-nine.

Ms. Tilley: Okay, some say 5, some say 6. Who wants to prove? Okay, Jane?

Jane: See, we have 2 ones which is 11, (correcting herself) plus nine is 11.

Josh: So that's one thousand five hundred.

Jane: No, no. Look, wait plus 5.

Josh: Six hundred, six hundred.

Jane: One thousand, 100 plus 100 is 200, plus 900 is one thousand one hundred, plus 500 is 1,600.

Ms. Tilley: Is 1,600. So we really need a thing for thousands here, don't we? (Adds another column to the grid) All right, so you have 1,649. Great.

Tilley felt the students followed this new procedure, but considered her attempt to help them build a connection to their own mental algorithms to have been unsuccessful, due to the lack of a smooth way to record their mental processes in a way that looked like the standard algorithm. The detailed account that she gives below in her journal is completely from her memory of the episode.

I am really interested in trying to keep some element of "figure it out yourself" in there but it's not at all clear to me how to do it. I somehow had thought I could write down Jane's [erasing] proof in that form, but she didn't follow a strict hundreds, tens, ones sequence, but put the numbers together by first making the hundreds, then adding some of the tens to get another 100 or close to it, then I think, did the ones and came back and picked up the other tens later. I tried to write it in a way that would make the algorithm clear -- I did suggest adding the ones first, I think . . . but Jane said, as I was writing down the numbers (for the ones I think) that I could just put the one (I don't remember if she called it a ten) up with the other tens in the problem rather than writing it down below. So I used that to just teach them how to do it. I think they knew what it was all about. They did keep calling the numbers by their right names (e.g., 40 instead of 4), which made me confused since when I was writing I forgot that the 140 was the same as 14 tens and I temporarily didn't know what to do with the numbers. Fortunately, it came back quickly. A number of the kids said they'd seen the method before and I think they basically understand it. (February 12)

Trying to Connect the Procedure to the Students' Prior Experiences

<u>February 13</u>. Having decided that perhaps a direct connection between the children's mental methods and the conventional procedure still did not exist, Tilley's next strategy was to help the group connect the standard algorithm with their rod trading experiences and, for some, with their prior exposure to it through parents, siblings, or friends.

Tilley opened with, "When you write down the problems, you know how sometimes you write . . . addition problems this way [sideways]?" She then showed the class how to set up a place value grid, telling the students to write down the numbers that she rolls[10], "And if you want to, you can do this [write them in a grid], but you don't have to." Sam says, "I'm gonna do that without writing numbers at the top. It doesn't really help you." After reminding the children which dice represented hundreds, tens, and ones, she rolled the number 368 ,which they wrote down. Tilley wrote the numbers in her grid.

Ms. Tilley: But, when I roll the next one, you have to write it underneath it to do it this way that I'm teaching you.

S4:   I know how to do this.

---

[10] "Rolling a number" means creating a number from the digits that appear on color-coded dice, so if 2 and 3 are rolled using dice designating tens and ones respectively, the number is 23. Similarly, "rolling problems" refers to rolling numbers to add.

Ms. Tilley: (Rolls just two die) The next one's gonna be a two-digit number.

Ss: 99.

Ms. Tilley: ... Now. 368 + 99, then you draw a line under there (makes Example 7a). And that line really means the same thing as equals. It means that what's up here when you add them together will be the same as what's down there [below the line].

Sam: How do we do this on the lines?

S5:   Can I say it?

Ms. Tilley: Hang on. This way of doing it, Chris, is very much like [rod] trading.

hundreds	tens	ones		hundreds	tens	ones		hundreds	tens	ones
					1			1	1	
3	6	8		3	6	8		3	6	8
+	9	9		+	9	9		+	9	9
						7		4	6	7

| Example 7a | Example 7b | Example 7c |

Without a direct question having been asked, Will volunteered that, "It would be 17." After he explained how he got 17, Tilley continued.

Ms. Tilley: So it's 17 ones, so you're gonna write it down. Now, can I write 17 down there in the ones?

Will: No. You write 7 in the ones and you add one more to the tens.

Ms. Tilley: So I put 7 from the 17 there [under the ones]. (See Example 7b.)

Sam: I don't get it! How could it be 17 when [the sum's] gonna be at least a hundred?

Ms. Tilley: Oh, would you write it this way [vertically], please, Sam?

Jane: I know what the next step is!

Ms. Tilley: He said to put the ten part of the 17 up here (makes mark above the tens). I'm gonna show you how to act this out with the rods.

Sam: I don't get it!

Ms. Tilley: You will (pats his knee). You'll get it.

Sam: It's not 17!

Ms. Tilley: (To Sam) You know what he did? He didn't add up the whole number. He just added up the ones part of the number. And he got 17 ones. Do you agree with that, Sam? (To the group) Now what? Nancy.

Nancy: Well, 9 plus 1 is a hundred, plus 6 equals a hundred and sixty.

Ms. Tilley: So 90 and 10 is a hundred, so it's a hundred and sixty, so what do you write down? I always get confused about that.

Jane: 6.

Ms. Tilley: So that's 16 tens, right? So what do I write here [in the tens' column]?

Jane: 6.

Ms. Tilley: Does everyone agree?

Ss: Yup.

Sam: But what happened to the 17?

Ms. Tilley: The 17, the 7 part's there (pointing to the ones' place in the answer), and the ten part's up there (pointing to top of the tens' column).

Sam: (Starting to cry) I don't get it!

Ms. Tilley: You know what Sam? If you can just be a little bit patient I'll work with you on this. Can you just give me a minute? (to rest of group) Okay. What was the other, what happens to the hundred part?

Jane: You put it up there [over the hundreds].

Ms. Tilley: (Writes as shown in Example 7c) And then what?

S7:   400.

Ms. Tilley: And the answer is . . . ?

Ss: 467.

Ms. Tilley: Now, I think right now some people have seen this before and some people have an idea how to do it this way, and some people still need to have some more explanation. Here's what you can do now. If you feel as if you're ready to . . . do some on your own, then you may get some dice . . . and roll yourself some problems. If you would like to work with me, then stay right here . . . (Sam says something inaudible.) I know. It's very hard to get used to, if you're used to the other way.

Sam: It's a lot harder!

Chris: What's so hard about it?

Sam: Where is the answer? Where does everything go?

This incident with Sam was quite upsetting for Tilley. Sam was one of the brightest math students in the class and so she found it painful to be in the position of asking him to adopt another procedure "just because." Later, watching the videotape of this lesson, Tilley was unhappy with the way she responded to his question, "How could it be 17 . . .?" with a correction, "write it this way." She described this as an "uncharacteristically grim" response to a child's frustration.

This group received no further official instruction on the standard addition algorithm. For the rest of the lesson, a few students worked with Tilley, while the others rolled themselves numbers to add. Practice of this kind continued for several days.[11]

DISCUSSION

Tilley worked within a classroom context defined by the needs and understandings of her students, and her personal goals as a teacher. She also worked within a societal context in which she was expected by the school administration, parents, and the fourth-grade proficiency test to teach her students a specific computational procedure for addition. In this section, I discuss the role these contexts played in Tilley's mathematics teaching.

Classroom Context

The classroom context was defined by Tilley's instructional goals and by the particular students with whom she worked (their current mathematical understandings as well as their personal confidence and ways of learning). Instruction in the addition algorithm was accompanied by a shift in the teacher's goals from supporting students' exploration of number to requiring that students know a specific procedure. This created quite a different context from Tilley's customary teaching (as typified by the January 15 lesson). The preceding excerpts also demonstrate that Tilley's instruction on the conventional algorithm differed from that typically found in classrooms in her emphasis on helping students connect the new algorithm to their self-generated addition strategies and on trying to maintain some cognitive space for their autonomous thinking.

Teaching Goals

In Tilley's typical teaching, she worked to create a classroom in which she could encourage students to identify themselves as mathematicians participating in a community that figured things out together. Her teaching focused on responding to and building on her students' ideas, and she took it as her primary role to pose problems that would encourage children to develop their capacity for independent reasoning.

---

[11] For an analysis of the children's learning, see McNeal and Tilley (1998).

In her instruction in the standard addition algorithm, Tilley had two goals. She wished to continue fostering her students' sense of autonomy, their understanding of numerical relationships, and teach them the conventional addition algorithm. Although she had some personal doubts about the feasibility of achieving both goals simultaneously, Tilley expended an enormous amount of thought and energy in trying to find the best method for accomplishing both goals. As she commented in an interview:

> What I've done in the past is I have not tried to make [the algorithm] relate to how they know to do it in their heads. I've just said, "I'm gonna show you another way to do it, and this is how." And then I start at a very simple level and I get a fair amount of kids knowing how to [add] in their minds, and then you have to do this thing of asking them not to do it in their minds, and I really hate that! (February 21 meeting)

A major theme in Tilley's story is her struggle to find ways to help her students connect the algorithmic procedures to what they already knew. This was particularly important to her because she thought such a connection would help her reconcile the need she felt to teach this adult idea to the children with her desire to continue supporting their mathematical autonomy. Tilley tried to build a direct connection to Jane's and other students' personal mental arithmetic strategies. When this did not seem to flow as smoothly as she expected, Tilley resorted to demonstrating an intermediate method. Finally, she taught the algorithm directly, but all the while looking for a way to connect her instruction to their experience of rod trading, their existing knowledge of the algorithm, or both from outside sources, such as siblings or parents.

Tilley's observations of the children throughout the lessons on the algorithm showed that her two goals conflicted with one other, and caused her to seriously question whether it was necessary to insist that the students practice "her" method when their own methods were perfectly accurate, sensible, and effective. For example, she noted Jane and Nancy's continued use of their own methods even after the conventional procedure had been demonstrated (lessons on February 14 and 23). Similarly, she was aware that one of her most capable mathematics students, Sam, became extremely upset when he had trouble understanding the new procedure she introduced (February 13 lesson).

Along with these attempts to ground the new procedure in familiar mathematical ideas, Tilley struggled to make the new procedure problematic for the students. Repeatedly, she searched for ways to leave something about this new method for them to figure out. This is illustrated by the dilemma in which she found herself when she had to choose between using small numbers to simplify the procedure and using larger numbers so that the procedure could be seen as a reasonable alternative to their mental strategies. She referred to this in the comment cited (February 21 meeting). Tilley repeatedly expressed frustration that the new method offered her students: ". . . nothing to think through. In most of what we do in math, there's some way to think it through." (February 21 meeting).

Students' Understandings

Throughout her instruction, Tilley combined her observations of several students into informal hypotheses about what the group was ready to learn and what was still difficult for them. In particular, the many instances of confusion (both her own and the students') that arose when children attempted to maintain their place value language (referring to adding 358 + 471 as adding "300" and "400" rather than "3" and "4") caused Tilley to wonder whether becoming efficient in the regrouping procedure required the students to change to single-digit language in order to focus on the steps of this algorithm as conventionally understood. She commented,

> I never realized you had to hold two things in your mind at the same time. You have to think of them as what they are (units of tens, hundreds) and then you have to think of them as ones. If you're thinking of it as 150, then you don't know what to write down. (February 21 meeting)

She thought that their understanding of place value and their mental methods were so unlike the steps recorded in the conventional procedure that being required to learn them hindered the children's ability to develop skill in the use of the standard algorithm.

> [I]f you teach it at this age after they have more understanding, it's harder for them to learn, 'cause they have to set aside thinking . . . that it's 90 and 40 and think it's 9 and 4 . . . it's interesting that I have . . . deliberately stopped, saying to them, "And what is this?" in [a few] instances because I think they need a little time to set that aside. . . . I'm only very, very occasionally saying . . . "By the way, what was this 1 here?" (February 23 meeting)

Differences in Teaching Across Classroom Contexts

In both classroom contexts, Tilley reflected on and responded to her students' mathematical ways of thinking. Still, Tilley's teaching is quite different in the context of her instruction in the conventional algorithm. In trying to ensure that students knew a specific procedure, her primary role had become that of presenting mathematical ideas that the children were to know, rather than responding to their ideas. She thought her attempts to connect the conventional algorithm to the children's existing understandings were largely unsuccessful because she was making connections that made sense to her rather than continuing to foster the students' construction of personally meaningful connections.

In the end, Tilley decided she had to simply tell the students the steps of the procedure. She was distressed, however, to find that, as her teaching focused more on showing the steps, she tended to give the children answers to questions she formerly would have asked them to figure out through discussion. She also felt that she was more apt to put aside children's comments and questions so that she could make her point. For example, when Sam complained during her lesson, "I don't get it! How could it be 17 when [the sum] is going to be at least 100," Tilley responded, "Oh! Would you write it this way please, Sam?" Conversely, she felt that at times she clung to her usual style of eliciting thinking from the group or expecting them to be autonomous in their thinking when it was not appropriate to the teaching of a specific procedure. In retrospect, Tilley felt that her discomfort with this didactic instruction had as much to do with her uncertainty about whether it was a good idea to teach the procedure at this point (or at all) as it had to do with the direct instruction she felt the procedure demanded.

Interestingly, new tensions seemed to arise for Tilley in looking across the two classroom contexts. She wondered if children were losing confidence in their own mathematical thinking as she asked them to substitute the conventional procedure for their own, and even began to question her own goals.

SOCIETAL CONTEXT

Given the two goals of schooling mentioned earlier, it is not unusual to find conflicts between children's invented mathematics and conventional adult mathematics. Ball (1993) described an instance in which a student in the class spoke of a number as both even and odd. Ball resolved this dilemma by encouraging her students to explore this invention under the name of "Sean numbers." When a student in her class used the phrase "eight minus one-half" to describe the relationship between 8 and 4, Lampert (1992) found that the goal to provide students with the freedom to explore mathematical ideas and connections conflicted with the goal to teach children the language of mathematics as it is used by "good mathematicians." Both of these examples show students engaged in mathematics that is personally meaningful and valued by their teachers, but the children's mathematics is incompatible with the conventions of adult mathematics. According to conventional definitions, a number cannot be both even and odd (hence Ball's renaming of the subset of numbers that Sean had discovered), nor is "eight minus one-half" equal to four.

Tilley's dilemma could also be described as a conflict between respecting children's mathematics and introducing them to conventional mathematics; in this case, a conventional procedure. Although Tilley's dilemma has much in common with those described by Lampert and Ball, the difference, as I see it, is in the source of the convention — is the "carrying" procedure a convention of mathematicians or of a more general society? Unlike the mathematics in the examples given by Lampert and Ball, the children's self-generated addition algorithms are used and understood by "good mathematicians" and do not contradict any conventional mathematics. For Tilley then, thinking about her work within a societal context required her to consider goals other than her own. That is, society (as represented by the school administration, parents, and the fourth-grade proficiency test), wished her to teach her students a specific computational procedure for addition that she did not consider necessary to the children's mathematical development.

Tilley's case thus illustrates the powerful effect of societal expectations on a teacher's choices. Though she had earned a reputation beyond her own school as an expert mathematics teacher, she described "losing her judgment," "feeling tentative," and having to change her language in order to teach the conventional addition algorithm. She also described her lessons as increasingly "boring" and "dispirited." Despite this unhappiness with her own teaching and the students' learning, Tilley felt unable to simply abandon this procedure without a convincing argument to offer the parents, administrators, and other teachers in her school.

Although Tilley and I often debated whether or not this procedure should be taught, we never focused long on this question because it was clear that the conventional addition procedure was an essential skill in the eyes of parents and fourth-grade teachers, and was still an expectation for instruction at other schools. Instead, our discussions focused on when and how we should teach this procedure if we want to be sure that students understand the mathematics involved and maintain their intellectual autonomy. Before our inquiry, Tilley's tentative answer had been to delay introducing the new method as long as possible, hoping that students would invent procedures that would be very close to the standard algorithm. This happened with Jane and her erasing method. Although a few other children in the group had begun to write their addends vertically as they discovered this to be helpful, most of the children in the second group (not described here) were not inventing such procedures, and yet the fourth-grade teacher would be expecting all of the students to know the standard addition procedure.

FINAL THOUGHTS

Tilley's story is one of a growing body of examples of the complexity of teaching that focuses on children's thinking. Tilley, in her practice, engaged in a variety of intellectual activities before, during, and after her teaching. This included (but was not limited to): (a) analyzing the mathematics that she wished to teach; (b) assessing her students' current understandings of related mathematics; (c) attempting to balance the needs of those who were ready to move on against the needs of those who were not; and (d) evaluating the effects of her method of instruction on the children's autonomy and interest in mathematics, as well as their understanding. These activities were highlighted by the fact that our observations and discussions about Tilley's teaching did not focus on lessons that proceeded smoothly and stayed in tune with her goals. In fact, her struggles to create meaningful instruction seem to define what Tilley meant when she talked about "child-centered" mathematics instruction. For her, this kind of teaching focuses on finding instructional activities that engage children in figuring out some of the mathematics for themselves (even if they do not invent their own procedures) and for which children can find a genuine purpose (the activity must seem reasonable, useful, interesting, or both to them).

As the mathematics education community becomes increasingly critical of conventional teacher-centered instruction, Tilley's experience is an important reminder that didactic instruction can result from situations other than a teacher's instrumental beliefs about mathematics, or behaviorist views of teaching and learning. This particular case suggests that instruction can be constrained by societal expectations about what should be known and thus taught, by a teacher's goal, and by her understandings of the students and their ways of knowing.

ACKNOWLEDGMENTS

This project was funded by the Spencer Foundation Small Grants Program, but the opinions expressed in this essay are solely those of the author. Portions of this chapter were reported in an earlier paper presented at the 1997 annual meeting of the American Educational Research Association.

REFERENCES

Ball, D. L. (1993). With an eye on the mathematical horizon: Dilemmas of teaching elementary school mathematics. *The Elementary School Journal, 93*, 373-397.

Cobb, P., & Wheatley, G. (1988). Children's initial understanding of ten. *Focus on Learning Problems in Mathematics, 10* (3), 1-28.

Eisenhart, M., Borko, H., Underhill, R., Brown, C., Jones, D., & Agard, P. (1993). Conceptual knowledge falls through the cracks: Complexities of learning to teach mathematics for understanding. *Journal for Research in Mathematics Education, 24*, 8-40.

Kamii, C. (1989). *Young children continue to reinvent arithmetic: Second grade.* New York: Teacher's College Press.

Kamii, C. (1994). *Young children continue to reinvent arithmetic, Third grade.* New York: Teacher's College Press.

Lampert, M. (1985). How do teachers manage to teach? Perspectives on problems in practice. *Harvard Educational Review, 55*, 229-245.

Lampert, M. (1992). Practices and problems in teaching authentic mathematics. In J.F. Oser, A. Dick, & J. Patry (Eds.), *Effective and responsible teaching* (pp. 295-314). San Francisco: Jossey-Bass.

McNeal, B. (1995). Learning not to think in a textbook-based mathematics class. *Journal of Mathematical Behavior, 14*, 205-234.

McNeal, B., & Tilley, B. (1998). Learning the standard addition algorithm in a child-centered classroom. In S. Berenson, K. Dawkins, M. Blanton, W. Coulombe, J. Kolb, K. Norwood, & L. Stiff (Eds.), *Proceedings of the Twentieth Annual Meeting of the North American Chapter of the International Group for the Psychology of Mathematics Education, Vol. 2* (pp. 819-825). Columbus, OH: Eric Clearinghouse for Science, Mathematics, and Environmental Education.

McNeal, M. (1991). *The social context of mathematical development.* Unpublished doctoral dissertation. Purdue University, West Lafayette, Indiana.

National Council of Teachers of Mathematics. (1991). *Professional standards for teaching mathematics.* Reston, VA: Author.

Commentary 3

Questions and Issues

Barbara Jaworski
University of Oxford

In this section our attention is drawn toward sociological characteristics of teaching, their relation to desired learning outcomes, and ways in which approaches to teaching can be developed.

1. In what ways does the social dimension need to be made explicit in defining teaching?

Betsy McNeal introduces her study of teaching with reference to the social and societal expectations that cannot be ignored by teachers, whatever their personal pedagogical preferences. She recognizes that "teachers who seem determined to focus on children's mathematics find this difficult to do under the pressures of practical concerns such as proficiency tests, expectations of parents, colleagues, administrators, evaluations, and scheduling."

For many teachers, such societal expectations control pedagogy through reductionist practices whose outcomes, far from being the success story the expectations demand, show ineffective learning resulting in inadequate growth of students' mathematical knowledge. Thus, teachers and teaching become the butt of societal criticism. The inherent paradox is that the practices seen to result from the external pressures lead to the opposite, in learning terms, of what the external agents are demanding.

Somehow, attention needs to be given to the complexity of social and societal demand, within social settings of classroom, school, society, and culture. Without such recognition and attention, teaching will fail, as has been widely demonstrated. With this attention there is still no guarantee of success, as McNeal's chapter shows.

The teacher, Betty Tilley, McNeal's partner in research, shifts from building on students' own ways of thinking mathematically to presenting a standard algorithm due to perceived external pressures. As part of this shift, her approaches to classroom interaction change in a fundamental way, from encouraging to suppressing children's participation. Children are bewildered and upset. Tilley is guilt-ridden. Yet she is knowingly aware of the reasons for her transition, and McNeal highlights the inherent tensions.

Focusing on children's mathematics is an element of pedagogic strategy espoused by many of the authors in the sections of this book. Research has provided evidence of the value of such focus in terms of children's development of mathematical understanding. Although not made explicit, we might suppose that students whose mathematical thinking has been enhanced through such teaching will be well able to contend with standardized tests, provided that they are socialized into the expectations of such tests. Yet, if they are not able to use standard algorithms in tackling such tests, is this to be seen as a deficiency in their understanding? There is the question of what the tests are actually testing. The McNeal chapter is salutary in making clear that idealised approaches to learning and teaching, such as working on children's misconceptions, will not be effective in classrooms unless some of these wider social issues are simultaneously addressed. This poses a challenge for research and development.

The chapter by Terry Wood and Tammy Turner-Vorbeck takes social factors of classroom interaction to be a prime consideration of teaching alongside the more traditionally recognized psychological factors. This is not a concern with the wider social factors as addressed by McNeal, but a detailed attention to sociological dimensions of constructing activity within the classroom.

Their contention is that if focusing on children's mathematics is to be seriously valued as a pedagogical process, it needs to be understood through an analysis of classroom activity that clarifies the social and psychological dimensions of the teaching-for-learning process. The social dimensions studied here are those involved in creating a classroom ethos conducive to fostering students' high level thinking: largely the ways in which classroom norms are developed and students encouraged to interact for successful learning. The analysis stops short of consideration of wider societal influences and concerns such as political pressure and cultural differences, but it could be that establishing social norms in the classroom is but a first step to addressing wider issues.

The analyses in this chapter take a sociological frame, looking closely at dialogue and interpreting interactions in terms of teaching intentions and students' sense-making. This brings us to our next question.

2. What is involved in a sociological analysis of teaching?

Teaching in this book seems to mean teaching that focuses on children's thinking about mathematics. Studies of children's thinking have often been psychological in focus as research tries to analyse the ways in which students make sense of mathematics. Where teaching is concerned, a focus on children's sense-making would be psychological, but the creation of opportunity for such sense-making shifts into a social domain. In the book so far, teaching has been seen to encompass aspects of classroom interaction such as discussion, negotiation of meaning and inquiry, to involve contextual problem solving, and to engage students in areas of mathematics identified within an expected elementary curriculum — a complex agenda. The chapter of Wood and Turner-Vorbeck seeks to identify characteristics of such teaching and to develop theory relating modes of teaching, social structures developed in the classrooms and students' learning.

The research described is a study of teaching where the participating teachers are trying to develop their practice in the terms outlined, and cope with issues and tensions on the way. The research sought to characterise both the practices observed and their ongoing development by the teachers. One part of this involved a scrutiny and classification of interactions between teachers and students and their effects on children's developing thinking. It involved a study of transcripts of dialogue between teachers and students, as well as recorded reflections from the teachers. It takes whole statements from teachers and students, and interprets them against wider evidence — observations of researchers, and teachers accounts of their activity. The resulting characterisations are exemplified with relation to extracts from the data from which they emerge.

The study offers two kinds of outcome that are of value to other researchers and practitioners: First, it describes a set of practices and processes that might be seen as germane to a wider variety of settings where further research can explore and confirm or challenge what is proposed here; second, its emergent categorisation of interactions as "report ways," "inquiry," and "argument" provides a framework against which to scrutinise dialogues we have read in different parts of this book. We can recognize, for example, that where dialogues involve only report ways, they are valuable in encouraging students' articulation and description, and enable teachers to get access to students' thinking. But they do not overtly encourage students to express why their processes work or to question whether they work, as do modes of inquiry and argument. These latter two modes seem crucial to mathematics and mathematical development in encouraging students to move toward explanation, justification, and proof. However, to handle student engagement in inquiry and argument, teachers have to be mathematically confident. Otherwise, they will have difficulty in handling students' questions that take them outside their own [the teachers'] knowledge boundaries. This shows an important linkage with issues raised in the last section. It is not surprising if inexperienced mathematicians often leave their students in the report ways mode.

The authors' characterization of the three modes led to the emergence of theoretical constructs of participation and thinking. In these two dimensions, analysis shows that students became more active participants or thinkers as the mode shifted from report ways to argument. In the argument mode, students were taking more responsibility for their thinking and the thinking became correspondingly more critical. In the resulting theoretical framework these dimensions form axes against which students' activity in the classroom might be judged and, potentially, teaching modified to enable students' mathematical understanding to become more conceptual.

Such analysis links a close study of the practical approaches in the social domain to the intellectual goals of mathematical learning and the psychology of children's thinking. In doing so, it provides a framework within which teaching can be seen to develop and through which such development can be promoted. But how might such promotion be possible?

3. What are the areas of research/scholarship into teaching and its development in which "we" can provide enlightenment? How do "we" enable teaching to develop?

In the "we" in the question above, I count the authors in this book, but I also count all professionals who are engaged in the education of mathematics teachers and in research into the education of mathematics teachers. I have asked the following question elsewhere: "In all of this complexity, what is it that mathematics educators do, or can do, to promote, enable, facilitate, support, or engender (or even *recognize*) effective mathematics teaching in classrooms?" (Jaworski, 1999, p 184). The theoretical perspective just discussed charts a teaching process through which children have been seen to become more effective thinkers. What has been done and what can be done to enable such a process to develop? How can we learn more about the process and the issues that are raised in its implementation by teachers?

First of all, in recognition of the process and awareness of issues, the theoretical perspective can be used to observe teaching, learning, or both interactions in classrooms. Observations would note teachers' development of report ways, inquiry and argument, and some understanding of the issues such development raises for teachers. The reported study has undertaken some such observation and analysis already. Such analysis documents manifestations in practice of the theory employed, and leads to some proficiency of recognizing theory in practice. Teachers familiar with such research can promote it in their own practice, as is happening with the participating teachers.

If we are teaching mathematics ourselves, we can work overtly with students toward creating the classroom environment in which students engage in the three modes of participation and thinking. As researchers also, we can observe critically the resulting thinking of our students: what levels of responsibility students are taking, what degrees of critical awareness they are developing, whether they are moving into generalization and proof, or staying in particular description. A cycle of teaching and research would result: teaching leading to research observations; research leading to enhanced teaching.

However, we are usually not teaching mathematics ourselves, but participating in the development of those who do teach mathematics — the teachers. In what ways can we work with teachers to enable them to develop the practices we would try to develop ourselves? Martin Simon's chapter has hinted at the answer to this, particularly in its final comments. The process is not one of somehow finding out what teachers know and "topping up" that knowledge, but one of engaging teachers in the thinking and activity that in our own experience as researchers leads to learning.

As teachers ourselves, we would enable development by engaging in research and learning from our observations and critical analyses as described. Can we not, therefore, mobilize our experience as researchers to working with teachers for their enhancement of teaching through a research process? (Jaworski, 1999). These are complex ideas, but as Martin Simon says, "We as researchers find that it is impossible to conduct productive research on mathematics teacher development without ongoing, explicit modification of our conceptual frameworks with respect to mathematics learning and teaching." (p. 168)

The processes involved in the Wood and Turner-Vorbeck study include both research elements and developmental elements, and research into the developmental elements. Although complex, it is a small step to turn such research into a developmental tool.

4. To what extent do the generalizations we are making apply to preservice and inservice educators?

In all the chapters of this book, teaching development relates to the practices of experienced teachers. Thus the teacher education considered is inservice education. However, much of the theory and practice that these chapters have addressed has potential for the education of beginning teachers. In many preservice programs, teachers are asked to study children's mathematical learning. From this, ideas about children's reasoning and alternative conceptions become evident to the novice teachers. Such knowledge then becomes available for planning lessons. If the novices also have access to ways in which they can work to expose children's thinking, and have children themselves express their thinking, then this too can become a part of lesson planning. The methods described by Deborah Schifter and others for making teachers aware of the possibilities for students to articulate, discuss, and negotiate mathematical ideas can all be used with beginning teachers. An advantage here is that beginners do not have a barrier of existing practices to impede their learning of new approaches, although their past experiences of being learners of mathematics themselves might be one barrier. Thus, the development of a methodology for the development of teaching for experienced teachers can be extended to beginning teachers. However, this is another story and another book.

REFERENCES

Jaworski, B. (1999). The plurality of knowledge growth in mathematics teaching. In B. Jaworski, T. Wood, & A. J. Dawson (Eds.), *Mathematics teacher education: Critical international perspectives* (pp. 180-209). London: Falmer Press.

Part V

WHAT DO WE KNOW ABOUT
TEACHING THAT SUPPORTS
STUDENTS' CONSTRUCTION OF
MATHEMATICAL KNOWLEDGE AND
WHAT IS STILL UNDER DEBATE?

OVERVIEW

This section contains three essays of commentary on the previous chapters. The first, by Barbara Scott Nelson, pulls together much of what has been said earlier and raises questions for further research. The second, by Virginia Richardson, sets this body of work on new forms of instruction in elementary school mathematics in the context of research on teaching, more generally. The third is a short set of remarks from the editors of this volume, arguing for continued development of theory.

Constructing Facilitative Teaching

Barbara Scott Nelson
Education Development Center, Newton, MA

This chapter synthesizes ideas from the earlier chapters to illuminate what is known about teaching that supports students' construction of mathematics knowledge and what questions remain to be investigated. Although the authors of several chapters have offered insights on such teaching from their chosen theoretical and methodological positions, my goal is to use their work to synthesize an emergent view of teaching that is consonant with a constructivist view of learning, and make connections among the views provided by the authors to create a more complete description. In doing so, we see that there are points at which these lines of work overlap — where researchers may be looking at similar phenomena from quite different points of view. These points of overlap offer the opportunity to explore the interconnections between quite different theoretical orientations, to reveal the instances where differing points of view and inconclusive evidence remain, and to articulate current points of contention and debate. Because the theoretical orientations taken by the authors lead them to focus on quite different aspects of facilitative teaching, some of the most interesting and productive lines of work for the future may occur at these points of overlap.

CHARACTERISTICS OF FACILITATIVE TEACHING

I have chosen to use the term *facilitative teaching* in this chapter, referring to instruction that is compatible with a constructivist view of learning, because it aptly describes the relationship between the teacher and the student in this kind of learning/teaching interchange. Facilitative teaching is teaching that is designed to support the process of students' individual construction of knowledge. In doing such teaching, the teacher attends to the students' mathematical ideas, makes an assessment of the nature of those ideas in relation to the mathematical concepts under consideration, and makes an intervention—asking a question, suggesting an activity. The teacher, in effect, has bifocal vision, with one eye on the students' mathematical understanding and one eye on the mathematics as cannonically understood (Ball, 1993). The teacher is continually moving back and forth between these two, working to bring students' mathematical understanding into closer alignment with mathematics as conventionally understood.

There are a number of characteristics of such teaching that distinguish it from classical pedagogy. Among the most central are (a) what teachers attend to while they are teaching; (b) the hypotheses that teachers develop about their students' mathematical understanding; (c) how teachers decide what the next good question or activity will be; (d) patterns of classroom discourse and participation; and (e) the nature of teachers' learning while teaching. The authors of chapters in this book have identified and analyzed these characteristics in different ways. In this section, I take these up, one at a time, discussing what we can learn about them from the several perspectives represented here and what questions remain to be investigated.

It should be noted that these characteristics of facilitative teaching are my analytic constructs drawn from the previous chapters, and are not meant as linear steps taken, one after the other, in the act of teaching. In fact, they all occur together, in a seamless web, in any particular circumstance of teaching. I have disentangled them here, in order to be able to look more closely at what can be said in detail about each of these aspects of facilitative teaching.

Refocusing Attention During Teaching

Facilitative teaching begins as the teacher pays attention to students' mathematical thinking. This is the hallmark of this kind of teaching, as teachers are enjoined no longer to attend only to whether the student has the correct answer, or to simply ensure that students are engaged in the mathematical activities suggested by one or another curriculum—doing practice worksheets, working out a problem with base-ten blocks, or working with other students in a small group to solve complex mathematics problems. The several perspectives on facilitative teaching taken by the authors in this book illuminate quite different aspects of teachers' attention to student thinking.

Carpenter, Franke, and colleagues argue that teachers need to attend to the strategies or procedures that children use in solving mathematical problems. For a host of addition and subtraction problems with identified semantic structures, over a period of months or years children will typically move from direct modeling of the problem structure, to more efficient counting strategies, and finally to the even more efficient and abstract use of known number facts and invented algorithms (Carpenter, 1985). Carpenter, Franke, and colleagues argue that teaching that facilitates children's construction of mathematical knowledge entails attending to children's use of such strategies. Franke quotes a teacher who knows the trajectory of strategies that has been established by research on the nature of children's mathematical thinking:

> . . . I definitely think there's a framework with CGI that's made a big difference for me. Strategies have been identified, there's definitely a hierarachy. That's helped . . . How do you decide why [some] problems would be more difficult than others for children to solve? You know, what makes this problem difficult? And with CGI, that has been researched, and I think accurately researched, and it enables me to know why certain kids are struggling, what I can do to facilitate that. (p. 52)

Rather than looking at the mathematical meaning the students are making, Carpenter, Franke, and colleagues suggest that teachers infer what students understand mathematically by attending to and understanding the strategies that they use.

Those scholars who focus on the mathematics of children's thinking would have teachers pay attention directly to the mathematical meaning that students are making. As Deborah Schifter notes in her chapter, teachers pay attention to many aspects of their students' behavior when attending to their mathematical thinking—the clarity of their speech, the emotional tone, classmates' responses, how the numerals are written. But, Schifter argues, attending to the mathematics in what one's students are saying is a different, and essential, thing. If teachers are to support children in their building of mathematical knowledge, Schifter argues teachers need to think through and reconnect with the basic mathematical principles that their students use. She provides the example of Liz Sweeney, who is interested in Jamea's procedure for finding the answer to 29 x 12 (in which Jamea made the 29's into 30's because 30 was an easier number to work with, multiplied 30 times 12, and then took away the extra 1 twelve times). In this example, Liz has attended to Jamea's mathematical ideas about the nature of numbers and the way she was using the operations of multiplication and addition to work out this problem.

Schifter notes that teachers need to learn to listen to the mathematics in what children say, and she suggests a number of things that can help them develop a sense of what to attend to — writing down in exquisite detail what children say when they explain how they did a piece of mathematics, examining print and video cases in which children explain their mathematical thinking, and so on. These are ways that teachers can practice attending to the mathematics in what children say off-line, so to speak, out of the hurly-burly of classroom life in which they are called on to be making decisions about what to do next.

Miriam Sherin makes a similar point, in her story of David Louis. She notes that in watching video clips of his mathematics classroom, David at first tended to focus on the pedagogical strategies that he had used, or failed to use. ("How could I have done that differently?" "What could I do next time to make that a better lesson?" "What could I have done . . . to start some discussion on what she did and why that was useful?"). Sherin notes that David is not unusual in this — and many teachers, whose professional responsibility is to decide what to do next, focus on these features of videotaped classrooms. But Sherin also tells the story of how David's perspective changed. He began to look at the videotapes with an eye to discerning what had happened in the classroom, not what should have, or could have, happened. This led him to attend far more carefully to the mathematical ideas that the students were discussing noticing, in one case, that the students had changed the meaning of the mathematics question posed in the problem from "Which swimmer has the fastest and slowest initial speed" to "Which swimmer has the quickest reaction time." For David, trying to understand what had happened during the lesson came to mean making sense of the students' mathematical ideas from the video recording.

Attending to both the ideas of the subject and to what we know about how children learn it probably is essential for good facilitative teaching, and might be considered the requisite pedagogical content knowledge (Shulman, 1986). Warfield makes this point quite specifically in her paper, arguing that mathematical knowledge in addition to knowledge of patterns in the development of children's mathematical thinking allows teachers to pose questions differently, understand mathematical thinking that differs from that described by the research-based taxonomy, examine the mathematical validity of children's mathematical thinking, and create tasks that enable students to extend their understanding. However, beyond Warfield's case study, we do not yet have research on the effects of teachers' attending to both the mathematics and the well-known patterns in children's learning. There is substantial research on the development of children's ideas about a range of mathematical topics that are part of the terrain of elementary school mathematics instruction--irrational numbers, proportional reasoning, spatial reasoning and geometry, prealgebraic thinking, and so on. We do not yet have easily available research on how knowledge of such research helps teachers attend to children's mathematical thinking, as we do in the CGI case, nor do we have research that shows how teachers' own mathematical knowledge affects how they attend to children's mathematical thinking in these areas.

Simon takes us to a different level in our examination of what facilitative teaching requires teachers to attend to, and why. He argues that teachers' ideas about what it means to construct new mathematical ideas also affect what they attend to and what they do. Simon suggests that teachers consider the possibility that students are making very different meanings of the ideas than they themselves make. Facilitative teaching, from this perspective, entails asking the question, "What are my students' understandings related to this particular mathematical idea and how might those understandings be transformed?" Thus, according to Simon, the teacher is interested in how students who think and act in particular ways might build on those ways of thinking and acting to develop more powerful mathematical conceptions.

To illustrate the impact of the teachers' ideas about what it means to construct mathematical ideas, Simon gives the example of the use of base-ten blocks in teaching students about place value. A teacher who thinks that children need to construct the "same" mathematical idea as is generally understood tries, probably in vain, to emphasize what the children should be seeing when they look at the base-ten blocks. She asks, "How many tens are there? How many ones are there?" She writes the tens numeral to the left of the ones, "So what number is that?" However, given the perspective that, until mathematical ideas have been constructed, they literally cannot be "seen" in the base-ten blocks, the analysis of the situation is quite different. The students' inability to see the place value relationships indicates that the students do not have concepts that would afford that seeing. This leads to the teacher's investigation of the students' number conceptions and further inquiry into the conceptual field of place value.

We note that Sherin, Schifter, Simon, and Franke and Kazemi are careful to tell us that teachers need to learn how to attend to their students' mathematical thinking in the ways they [the students] describe. Most teachers are not accustomed to attending to their students' mathematical thought at the requisite level of detail and may not initially see why it is useful or necessary. Given the way that mathematics teaching has traditionally been understood, the variety and ingenuity of children's mathematical thinking has not been visible to most teachers. But if teachers are to help children construct new mathematical ideas, teachers must become skilled at examining these ideas in detail. Research on how this interest and skill develops would be useful.

Wood and Turner-Vorbeck's sociological treatment of teaching adds a new dimension to the picture we have been building of what teachers attend to when doing facilitative teaching. Wood and Turner-Vorbeck identified three different sets of norms and expectations for mathematical discourse that may obtain in classrooms—norms and expectations that have very different implications for how children's mathematical thinking is regarded by the teacher and the kinds of participation in mathematical discussion that are likely to occur. In their taxonomy, teachers in the *report ways* discourse pattern appear to listen for a step in a procedure, anticipating the next step that will follow; teachers in *inquiry* discourse patterns listen to see if the child has clearly explained his meanings and reasons; in the *argument* discourse pattern, teachers seem to listen for (and actually provoke) justifications for children's mathematical assertions. Wood and Turner-Vorbeck report that in all three cases, classroom discussion was conceived of as providing a context in which students would develop mathematical understanding through thinking and reasoning. But the nature of the discourse between teacher and students becomes cognitively more complex and demanding in the inquiry and argument forms of discourse.

The sociological, psychological, and mathematical perspectives suggest that teachers attend to quite different aspects of children's mathematical learning. To understand how these perspectives relate to each other, it would be particularly important to probe phenomena that appear in all three, looking for relationships between what can be seen from each theoretical orientation. To take one example: Is a teacher's capacity to initiate and maintain a discourse pattern based on mathematical argument, in which particular mathematical challenges are raised (and students' mathematical challenges of each others' thinking supported), dependent on the teacher's understanding the mathematics and attending to the mathematics in children's ideas? Does the challenge come from the structure of the question (that is, that it requires the student to give a justification), or from its mathematical content in relation to the student's mathematical thinking? Or both? To take another example, can discourse based on mathematical argument be done by attending to typical patterns of misconceptions or problem-solving strategies or does it depend on attending to the students' mathematical meaning? What about teachers who are in the inquiry pattern of discourse? Are they attending to the mathematics of children's ideas or may they be attending largely to patterns? And are conception-based teachers, in the Simon construct, more likely to attend to the mathematics or the patterns in children's mathematical work, and do their classrooms move back and forth between all three types of discourse patterns or only some? In general, what are the relationships between these theoretical orientations toward what teachers attend to when doing teaching that facilitates children's construction of mathematical knowledge?

Forming Hypotheses About What Individuals and Group's are Ready to Learn

All of the authors agree that in teaching that supports students' construction of mathematical knowledge, once teachers have attended closely to some aspect of children's mathematical thinking, they form hypotheses or conjectures about what mathematical concept or idea individual children, or the group as a whole, currently understand, do not understand, or are ready to work on. This is subtly different from the earlier concept of *readiness to learn*, which involved ascertaining if students were conceptually ready to learn a lesson that the teacher wanted to teach. In a constructivist view, students are continually in the process of understanding ideas and deepening their understanding. Teaching that is consonant with this constructivist view of understanding entails intervening in this process in order to focus students' attention on central aspects of the ideas they are working on. Unsurprisingly, our authors have subtly different things to say about the nature of such hypotheses, which are extensions of their basic positions.

First, we can see the difference between the psychological and mathematical perspectives, in what these scholars think teachers develop hypotheses about when thinking about what their students need to work on next. Carpenter, Ansell, and Levi and Franke and Kazemi suggest that teachers make hypotheses about where their students are in the taxonomy of problem-solving strategies established by research, and whether their students are ready to use more advanced problem-solving strategies; that is, strategies that are more efficient (e.g., involving counting rather than direct modeling of the problem) or that abstract from the circumstances of the problem and involve use of number facts or invented algorithms. Hypotheses about strategies are taken also to be hypotheses about the children's underlying mathematical understanding. For example, Ms. Gehn (Carpenter, Ansell, and Levi, this volume) regularly probed individual students to determine whether they could use more advanced strategies and, in February, thought a number of children in her class were ready to start to use invented algorithms and that they might do this in the domain of money, where their familiarity with combinations of coins would allow them to think about numbers more abstractly without the support of the blocks or other physical materials. This turned out to be the case.

Schifter and Warfield, coming from a mathematics perspective, argue that teachers build hypotheses on the basis of their assessment of the mathematical validity of the students' ideas. Within this frame, Schifter would have teachers listen for the sense in children's mathematical ideas, even when the logic has gone awry, asking, "What is the child doing, mathematically?" Using the example of Thomas, Schifter suggests that faced with a problem he did not know how to solve, Thomas thought he saw an analogy to something he did know, and so he tried it (adding numbers to both numbers in a multiplication problem in order to make them easier to work with, and then subtracting them from the answer). Schifter's hypothesis is that he (and the class as a whole) now needs to consider how addition and multiplication differ and why the shift from addition to multiplication changes the computation strategies one can employ.

McNeal also focuses on mathematical issues when she tells of Betty Tilley's hypothesis that the children's comfort with the place value language they had developed during the year, as they solved three-digit addition problems in their own ways (using the language of 100s), got them confused when they had to switch to the language of single-digits, which is stressed in the standard algorithm. While Tilly's hypothesis looks to be about language, it is really about what the children thought that addition problems were about. They understood very well that there were hundreds, tens, and ones in any three-digit number and that such numbers could be broken up and recombined in many ways. Their language reflected this. But the standard addition algorithm treats every digit as though it had simply the value of that digit (when you add 327 and 248 you add the 7 and the 8, write down the 5 and carry the 1, writing it next to the 2, making 12). The children understood how the number system worked, but the language of the standard algorithm didn't reflect what they understood about numbers.

We can see that the psychological and mathematics perspectives lead to subtlely different views about the kinds of hypotheses that teachers might make in the course of facilitative teaching. The psychological perspective requires that teachers know the research literature on the development of children's mathematical thinking and be able to recognize specific strategies when they see them in their classrooms, in order to be able to infer what students are understanding mathematically. The mathematical perspective requires understanding of mathematics on the part of the teacher, together with a sense of what ideas children often have difficulty with.

These authors do not tell us much in these chapters about how such hypotheses might be tested in facilitative teaching. However, Simon steps back and provides a longer-term, more iterative view of the relationship between developing and testing hypotheses in the classroom and using hypotheses to guide instruction. In his view, there is an interaction phase, in which the teacher assesses the student's relevant mathematical understandings and poses mathematical questions or facilitates mathematical activities; followed by a reflection phase, in which the teacher interprets the student's mathematical activity, perhaps modifying his understanding of the student's mathematical knowledge, and develops a hypothetical learning trajectory consisting of the goals for student learning and a plan for the next mathematical intervention. The cycle then repeats. Such hypothetical learning trajectories, argues Simon, need to include both a model of the mathematics at issue and a model of the student's mathematics. Simon reports that the teacher's model of the student's mathematics has less predictive value when the planned context differs from the contexts in which the learner was observed earlier, difference being defined from the perspective of the learner, not the teacher. Therefore, teachers must regard their models of students' mathematics as necessarily incomplete.

All authors agree that developing a hypothesis about what the student knows, does not know, or is ready to work on, is a critical step in teaching that aims to support students' construction of mathematical knowledge. However, they have subtlety different views regarding what these hypotheses should be about, and give somewhat different emphasis to the contingent nature of teaching that is created by the need to continually develop hypotheses to guide action.

Questioning

If children build their mathematical knowledge by thinking through puzzling mathematical questions, how do the different perspectives on teaching that supports students' construction of knowledge — psychological, mathematical, and sociological — treat the mathematical content of the questions that teachers pose in the course of such teaching? This is, perhaps, the least addressed issue in this set of papers but we can tease out some sense of this from most of the chapters. Once again, we see that each perspective illuminates a different aspect of teacher questioning and has different things to say about intentionality in facilitative teaching.

Carpenter, Franke, and colleagues consider that choosing challenging questions entails identifying what problem-solving strategies a student is using; that is, what mathematical understanding the child has, and which problems he might be ready to explore. So, for example, a child who is still solving one type of addition problem by direct modeling, but is using counting for other types, might be ready to try counting on the more difficult addition problems.

Schifter illuminates the mathematical nature of teachers' questioning in the discussion of Thomas, in which she hypothesizes that the next challenging question will be one that helps Thomas (and his classmates) think about the difference between addition and multiplication. According to Schifter, once teachers have identified the conceptual issue that is hanging a student up, a new question or problem can be posed to help the student see the situation in a new way. It is worthy of note that Schifter phrases this in terms of the ideas that Thomas is already working on. That is, she has not provided us with an analysis of what Thomas did not know (though some of the teachers said that he was lacking in good number sense and Schifter, herself, later notes that Thomas did not apply the distributive property). Rather, Schifter wants teaching to be based on what Thomas is doing; teachers should ask themselves, "From what mathematical perspective would this have been a sensible thing to do?" This orientation is both affirming of children's thinking and, as also argued by Simon, an attempt to see the mathematics from the child's perspective and not only from the teacher's own perspective. It also joins the teacher in the child's efforts to understand.

In Simon's view, whatever is chosen as the next, challenging, question should be viewed as the test of a working hypothesis about what the child is working on mathematically. This gives us an image of teaching as a very dynamic enterprise, in which the teacher is continually exploring the terrain of children's mathematical thinking.

Wood and Turner-Vorbeck look at the teacher questioning that occurs in reform teaching from a different perspective. They argue that in asking their questions teachers are participating in a conversational exchange with students. In the process of finding out about students' thinking—asking them to describe their thinking, asking them to clarify the meaning of something they said, or challenging a student's explanation—teachers are contributing to the interchange in ways that result in children deepening their mathematical understanding. Wood and Turner-Vorbeck focus on the characteristics of teacher questioning that promote thinking and reasoning, whatever the mathematics topic might be. The effects of such questioning need not be intentional, according to Wood and Turner-Vorbeck. For example, some teachers may not realize that their questions function to deepen understanding; they are simply trying to clarify meaning the child is expressing.

Patterns of Discourse and Participation

Facilitative teaching is characterized by very different patterns of discourse and participation from classical pedagogy in elementary mathematics. Classrooms in which facilitative teaching occurs are characterized as mathematics-doing communities, in which both teacher and students are engaged in the exploration of mathematical ideas. Although the teacher is not viewed as the dispenser of mathematical ideas, the teacher's mathematical and pedagogical expertise informs the ebb and flow of mathematical discourse and the mathematical problem solving that occurs. Students, too, contribute to the emergent patterns of discourse and participation, as they learn how to articulate their thinking and develop ways of working together with other students. At issue here is the kind of community that a mathematics class is, or becomes, under the direction of the teacher.

All of our authors describe this dimension of facilitative teaching to some degree, but the importance they give it in their analyses varies. One position, illustrated by Sherin, Warfield and Schifter, characterizes as primary the mathematical ideas that students have and the attention that teachers pay to these ideas. The responses teachers make to students' mathematical ideas have consequences for the interaction patterns that develop but the interactions themselves are not the primary object of investigation for these scholars. A second position, illustrated by Carpenter et al., and Simon, conceives of the cognitive work that students and teachers do and the social processes through which that work is constituted, as coemergent. That is, as students and teachers work together on mathematical ideas, individuals' mathematical ideas and the classroom as a mathematics-doing community are constructed. A third group, consisting of Wood and Turner-Vorbeck, takes the patterns of discourse themselves to be central rather than peripheral in determining how teaching unfolds in the classroom.

We can see this play out by examining how discourse and participation patterns in facilitative teaching are represented by each position. Sherin treats them as consequences of what teachers are attending to. She notes that when David Louis began to listen to what was happening, mathematically, in his classrooms, he slowed down the pace of the class so that he could follow the different ideas that came up and decide how to proceed. He also added new instructional strategies to his repertoire, including asking probing questions and rephrasing students' ideas. All of our authors portray this attitude of respectful listening on the part of teaching that supports the development of student thinking. Several (Sherin, and Franke & Kazemi) note that when teachers begin listening carefully to their students' mathematical thinking, students, too, begin listening to each other in this way.

Carpenter et al. treat the expectations and norms of classrooms in which teachers engage in facilitative teaching as co-emergent with teachers' attention to children's problem-solving strategies. They describe classrooms in which teachers do not show students how to solve mathematics problems or model particular solution strategies. Rather, students work on three or four given mathematics problems and then three or four children are called on to share their strategies with the class. The teacher might ask additional questions, for example, "Could you say that one more time?" "Did anyone solve it a different way?" but she generally lets the students do most of the explaining. The norms for sharing are clearly established. Carpenter et al. also describe the function that students' articulation of their ideas plays both for individual students and for the class as a whole, when they note that by regularly explaining how they solved problems and negotiating how solutions were alike or different, individual children became more reflective and more articulate in explaining their thinking. Further, sharing strategies appears to play a critical role in enabling students to develop more advanced strategies and connecting them to existing strategies. The more advanced students model strategies for other students, and, in explaining the strategies, make the underlying cognitive processes visible.

McNeal gives considerable attention to the norms and participation patterns in Betty Tilley's classroom, describing them as being that of a mathematics community characterized by inquiry. Betty Tilley guides the creation of this community by posing challenging problems and games, encouraging students to validate their own solutions, and facilitating discussions in which all students are expected to make sense of each others' mathematical thinking, indicating their agreement or disagreement by using silent hand signals, and in which she makes it a major point to understand the children's thinking herself. She defines her teaching as working *with* children. Her teaching focuses on helping her students develop their capacity for independent reasoning and toward this end, she emphasizes the natural role of errors (theirs and her own) and error analysis in the learning process. She was willing to be seen as "in error" or confused herself and have the students "teach" her, signaling to the students that mistakes are a natural part of learning.

Simon does not talk much about discourse and participation patterns in the chapter here (though he does elsewhere; Simon, 1997), saying merely that the current knowledge of the individuals, the shared knowledge of the group, and the norms for mathematical activity of the group all influence how mathematical situations are understood and the potential transformations that the students' knowledge might undergo in the process of dealing with that situation. In general, Simon characterizes his theoretical framework as built on an emergent perspective (Cobb & Yackel, 1996; Cobb, Yackel & Wood, 1993) – a socioconstructivist perspective on mathematics learning that involves the coordination of cognitive analyses with an interactionist analyses.

Wood and Turner-Vorbeck, on the other hand, view the norms and expectations for participation in facilitative classrooms as central aspects of learning and teaching, not secondary. They look at the characteristics of discourse, itself, for indications of the opportunities provided for students to construct mathematical knowledge. Their research reveals three different patterns of classroom interaction, distinguished by the kinds of questions that teachers ask of students. In the report ways context, teachers ask students *how*, *what*, and *where* questions; in the inquiry context, teachers ask questions that require students to explain what they meant or why they did something. That is, students were asked not only how they solved a problem but also were asked why they solved it that way and to clarify their thinking. In the argument context, teachers also ask the additional question, "How do you know that?," which is a challenge and requires a response that provides justification.

Further, in different kinds of teaching context, student responsibility for examining the thinking of the explainer increased (from listening to see if their way of solving the problem was different from the explainer's, to trying to understand what the explainer said and asking questions, to deciding if they agreed or disagreed with the student explainer), and the thinking that was required of students grew cognitively more complex. All forms of thinking (comparing one's own thinking with another's, trying to understand what another means, and critically examining another's thought) require reflection on the part of students, but this reflection becomes increasingly complex. In the end, Wood and Turner-Vorbeck argue that the patterns of participation established in the classroom support different kinds of private knowledge construction by individual students and thus constitute a central, not peripheral, role for discourse in determining the nature of the mathematical thinking that is available for students.

As in the case of the difference each perspective provides vis à vis what teachers should attend to, analyzed earlier in this chapter, the difference in orientation between those who focus primarily on the cognitive content of teacher/student interactions and those who focus primarily on the patterns of the discourse in the classroom is both significant and rich in possibilities for future research. Clearly, all classrooms have both subject matter content and patterns of interaction. One characteristic of the current discipline-based reforms in mathematics education and the corollary research on learning and teaching is the attempt to keep analysis of the two integrated. An earlier tradition, the process–product program of research on teaching, divorced research on teaching from consideration of the content of what was being taught. Dimensions of teachers' behavior of interest included such actions as the pacing of instruction, the presence of wait time after questions were asked, the structuring of lessons, frequency of praise or criticism, use of lower or higher order questions, and so on (Brophy & Good, 1986). These characteristics of teaching behavior were studied quite independently of the intellectual content of the lesson.

However, teaching in which the effort is to help students construct specific ideas in mathematics (or other subjects) cannot be examined independently of the content of the ideas under consideration. The ways in which students and teachers work with the ideas matters (Shulman, 1986). It is important that studies of the interaction patterns and patterns of participation in such classrooms include consideration of the ways in which such patterns promote mathematical thinking itself. Wood and Turner-Vorbeck have made a substantial contribution to our ability to do that, with their linkage between the kinds of questions asked, the kind of participation those questions afford, and the nature of the reflective thinking that such questions require on the part of students. In an earlier section of this chapter, I identified a number of questions for further research that would forward the integration of mathematical, cognitive, and sociological perspectives. Such work is also important because it would contribute to the further development of sociological analyses of mathematics classrooms that are deeply rooted in consideration of the mathematical ideas at play in those classrooms.

Teaching As Learning

It has been argued (cf. Lampert & Ball, 1999) that teaching is fundamentally and essentially an ambiguous and uncertain enterprise. It requires knowing things in the situation—things that one cannot know in advance of any particular encounter. Because, in teaching, that supports students' construction of knowledge, teachers are attending to the mathematical ideas of the particular students in their classes, and that student thinking is to some degree unpredictable. Such teaching necessarily requires continual inquiry into students' thinking on the part of the teacher. I examine what the authors of these chapters have to say about this in this section, examining their views on how teachers continue to learn in the context of their classrooms.

Franke and Kazemi provide the most systematic and theoretical analysis of teachers' continual learning while teaching through their construct of *generativity*, by which they mean teachers' ability to continue to add to their understanding. Drawing on earlier papers, Franke, Carpenter, Levi & Fennema (1998) described as generative those teachers who listen carefully to the details of their students' mathematical thinking, use what they learn to make ongoing instructional decisions, and regularly test and revise their knowledge about student problem solving. Such teachers see themselves as learners about children's mathematical thinking. They see the knowledge they have as their own to create, adapt and change.

> And so every time you interact with a child, you're gaining more knowledge of how to interact with other children. Every time they show you, and tell you, what they're doing and thinking, you just learn more about what's going on in their head[s]. (Franke, Carpenter, Levi & Fennema, 1998, p.17)

Citing the taxonomy of students' problem-solving strategies, Franke and Kazemi note that teachers who have developed a framework for analyzing students' mathematical thinking use that structure as they assimilate what they hear from students. The framework helps them know what to listen for and how to connect what they hear to their other knowledge. If teachers view the knowledge embedded in that framework as something they can add to and change, then the framework provides the connections that allow knowledge to become generative. When Schifter notes that knowledge acquired through interactions with students informs the teaching of the same content with other students, one imagines that she is viewing the situation similarly, but with a focus on the nature and structure of teachers' mathematical knowledge. One could also read Simon's description of conception-based teaching as involving the continual generation, and revision, of hypothetical learning trajectories that guide teacher decision making and interactions with students as in the same, general, line of thought about how teachers continue learning.

Further, and this is the focus of the analysis of the Franke and Kazemi chapter in this volume, generativity develops within the context of communities of teachers. Teachers who engage in generative change shape both the form and content of their collaborative relationships to permit practical inquiry about children's mathematical thinking (Franke, Carpenter, Levi & Fennema, 1998). Franke and Kazemi show how a working group of teachers, all engaged in trying to understand in considerable detail the strategies that students in their classroom use, supplements and extends the learning about children's thinking that those same teachers do in their own classrooms. The view that teachers continue to learn about children's mathematical thinking finds support in the work of other scholars as well (Richardson, 1990; Warren & Rosebery, 1995; Russell et al., 1995)

ISSUES

In this section I take up several issues that emerge from the consideration of teaching presented by the authors of this book. These include

- The tension between a view of mathematics teaching that is child-centered and developmental, and a view of mathematics teaching that takes into account societal expectations;
- the tension between looking at the mathematics in what a child says and looking at general patterns of children's mathematical thought; and
- the need to develop more detailed and refined descriptions of pedagogy.

Mathematics Teaching as Child-Centered Versus Social Expectations

The current mathematics education reform movement is noted for its suggestion that teaching build on careful attention to children's mathematical thinking and take as its goal the development of strong mathematical thinkers. In this, it extends a long line of progressive thought about the possibilities of schooling (Cohen, 1995). However, there is a tension between studies of teaching that focus on the teaching/learning interchange in decontextualized fashion, and studies of teaching that view it as a process that simultaneously represents society's need for an educated populace, according to a possibly wide range of values.

In this book, Carpenter and colleagues introduce the child-centered perspective in a radical form when they suggest that in classrooms where teaching occurs, whose purpose is to support individual students' construction of mathematical ideas, there need be no instructional objectives for the class as a whole, at least not in the familiar form of a curriculum or set of lesson plans that lay out the order in which mathematical concepts will be addressed. Rather, in facilitative teaching, as Carpenter and colleagues envision it, the point is to have each student moving along a problem-solving trajectory that is challenging for him or her.

McNeal provides the social expectations side of this tension through the story of Betty Tilley, who needed to meet the social expectation that her students would be able to do the standard addition algorithm by the end of third grade. Mastery of the conventional addition procedure was an essential skill in the eyes of parents, the fourth grade teacher, and other schools. McNeal offers this example in order to remind us that teaching can also be viewed as a social practice embedded in a web of school and community values. In this view, the teacher's job is to balance what she understands as best for her students with what she knows that society expects of her (see also Lampert, 1985).

Some would view the mathematics curriculum or textbook as a mediating force—an expression of society's expectations that takes into account, to a greater or lesser degree, what is known about the development of children's mathematical thinking. However, from the point of view of the teacher who is listening carefully to children's mathematical thinking and building instruction on her judgment about what they are ready to think about, the curriculum or text, in laying out lessons and units in linear fashion, simply brings directly into the classroom the basic tension between staying with the children and accommodating societal expectations. The presence of curriculum or text tacitly poses to the teacher every day the question, "Are you going to stay with what the children are ready to think about, or are you going to move on to the next lesson?"

In this book are presented analyses of teaching from a psychological–constructivist position, in which the focus is on how teachers influence the development of individual children's mathematical thought and analyses of social interaction, in which are examined the effects of classroom norms and patterns of behavior on the nature of mathematical thinking that is made possible.

Integrating these perspectives on teaching with a perspective that would situate teaching in a particular time and locale is a job yet to be done. Cobb and Yackel (1996) began this work in their conceptualization of the "sociocultural" perspective as useful for understanding how established cultural meanings in the larger society become enacted in the classroom. The poignancy of Betty Tilley's story reminds us how important it is to find conceptual ways to join the child-centered and societal perspectives.

Looking at the Mathematics in What a Child Says Versus Looking at General Patterns of Thought

As noted earlier in this chapter, there is a subtle difference between the psychological and mathematical perspectives in their identification of exactly what it is that teachers should pay attention to when they attend to children's mathematical thinking. The psychological perspective, at least as represented here, suggests that teachers attend to the evolution of children's mathematical thought as indicated by the developmental trajectories of problem-solving strategies. These strategies have been shown to function over many different mathematical ideas and appear to be considered more general and powerful features of children's thought than the mathematical content of the thought itself. The mathematics perspective, on the other hand, emphasizes the mathematical content of the ideas children have and what is mathematically puzzling or difficult about those ideas. The mathematics perspective acknowledges that children will have different understandings of mathematical ideas than will adults, but focuses on the mathematical meaning that the student is making, rather than viewing it as an example of a more general characteristic of children's mathematical thought.

This difference, while subtle, affects what these researchers think teachers should attend to when they listen to children's mathematical thinking, and what they think teachers need to know in order to teach. As noted earlier, any single instance of mathematical thinking on the part of a child can be examined from both psychological and mathematical perspectives. While each theoretical perspective throws different aspects of the phenomenon into focus, what remains to be worked out is whether these perspectives can be coordinated, so that the psychology and the mathematics of the event are related. One can imagine a series of research question that would explore this relationship. For example, one might pose the question as follows: in an instance where a child is solving a Join Change Unknown problem by using known math facts (*Connie had some marbles. Jim gave her 5 more marbles. Now she has 13 marbles. How many marbles did Connie have to start with?*; the psychological perspective); what is the mathematical meaning that the child experiences (mathematical perspective)? And is there more than one kind of mathematical meaning for each of the structures on the taxonomy?

The Need to Develop More Detailed and Refined Descriptions of Pedagogy

In an earlier section of this chapter, I noted the relative sparseness of the authors' discussion of what would constitute a challenging question, once one had developed a hypothesis about what the student understood and didn't understand. This is emblematic of the striking absence of analysis of the pedagogy of facilitative teaching among the authors in this volume. With the exception of the Wood & Turner-Vorbeck chapter, in which the nature of the teacher's questioning is carefully analyzed, there has been very little discussion in these chapters of the instructional moves involved in facilitative teaching. Further, most of the images presented are of interchanges between the teacher and an individual student, or a small group of students. We do not see images of entire classrooms, we do not have discussions of the relative merits of such organizational arrangements as cooperative groups and whole-group configurations; nor is there significant discussion of the materials that might be available to aid instruction—textbooks, mathematics manipulatives, problem sheets, and so forth.

The fact that our authors' focus on children's ideas and the ways in which teachers can learn what those ideas are and analyze what the next important idea to wrestle with would be, represents an important shift in considering the essence of teaching. In the view of the authors in this book, the next useful instructional move depends entirely on the adequacy of that move for bringing the next idea into focus in a useful form. Whether the next question should be "Why did you do that?" or whether a different representation of the mathematical problem would make it accessible to a particular group of students depends entirely on the adequacy of the teacher's analysis of what the students are currently thinking about and what they might usefully think about next. In that respect, our authors have focused on the core of the issue when considering what is fundamental about facilitative teaching.

However, it would be useful to begin to specify how particular pedagogical moves relate to increased opportunities for students to stretch their mathematical thinking. Wood and Turner-Vorbeck begin this work in their analysis of the qualitatively different kinds of student responsibility for thinking and reflection that are associated with different kinds of questioning on the part of the teacher. Much more work of this kind would be very useful. For example, what are the different ways in which a particular mathematical problem could be represented and what are the characteristics of each representation, from the point of view of making the core mathematical idea accessible to students? How might a teacher think through the ways in which a number of students in her class might respond to a particular mathematics activity, and how might she adjust the activity so that it posed legitimate mathematical challenges for a group of students whose mathematical understanding varied? How would a teacher think through the circumstances in which she might want students to work in small groups as opposed to working on their own? We expect that the answer in all cases would be, "it depends," but specifying with some precision on what the choice would depend would take us a long way toward a pedagogy of facilitative teaching.

CONCLUSION

The chapters in this volume provide very rich analyses of the nature of teaching that is compatible with a constructivist view of the nature of learning. They employ different disciplinary foci and different analytic methods. Nonetheless, a coherent view of such teaching emerges. For the most part, these scholars seem to be talking about the same fundamental act of teaching.

As we have seen, there are subtle differences in what the authors in this book think teachers should pay attention to when they listen to children explain their mathematical thinking. They view different aspects of the classroom as central (e.g., what is happening inside children's heads vs. the nature of discourse and participation patterns). And they appear to have slightly different views about the degree of uncertainty that may be entailed in the fact that this teaching fundamentally rests on making hypotheses about student thought. But one is struck more by the sense of an underlying similarity of vision about teaching than by the quite subtle differences among these authors.

Most important, however, is the need to begin to transcend the differences in views about teaching that are artifacts of the methodological and disciplinary perspectives that our authors have taken. In several sections of this chapter, I have pointed toward questions and investigations that would examine the overlaps and relationships between aspects of the practice of teaching that are thrown into relief by particular analytic lenses. This, together with the theoretical work recommended in the last chapter of this book, constitute an agenda for future work.

ACKNOWLEDGMENTS

This writing of this chapter was supported by the Research on Teaching and Learning (RTL) program of the National Science Foundation under award RED 925-4939. All opinions are those of the authors.

REFERENCES

Ball, D. L. (1993). With an eye on the mathematical horizon: Dilemmas of teaching elementary school mathematics. *The Elementary School Journal, 93*, 373-397.

Brophy, J., & Good, T. (1986). Teacher behavior and student achievement. In M.C. Wittrock (Ed.), *Handbook of research on teaching* (3rd ed., pp. 328-375). New York: Macmillan.

Carpenter, T. P. (1985). Learning to add and subtract: An exercise in problem solving. In E. A. Silver (Ed.), *Teaching and learning mathematical problem solving* (pp. 17-40). Hillsdale, NJ: Lawrence Erlbaum Associates.

Cobb, P. & Yackel, E. (1996). Constructivist, emergent, and sociocultural perspectives in the context of developmental research. *Journal of Educational Psychology, 31*, 175-190.

Cobb, P., Yackel, E., & Wood, T. (1993). Learning mathematics: Multiple perspectives, theoretical orientation. In T. Wood, P. Cobb, E. Yackel, & D. Dillon, (Eds.), *Rethinking elementary school mathematics: Insights and issues.* [Journal for Research in Mathematics Education Monograph Series, No. 6 (pp. 21-32).] Reston, VA: National Council of Teachers of Mathematics.

Cohen, D. K. (1995) Teaching practice: Plus ca change... [the more things change the more they remain the same] In P. Jackson (Ed.), *Contribution to educational change: Perspectives on research and practice* (pp. 27-84). Berkeley, CA: McCutcheon.

Franke, M. L., Carpenter, T. P., Levi, L., & Fennema, E. (1998, April). *Capturing teachers' generative change: A follow-up study of professional development in mathematics.* Paper presented at the Annual meeting of the American Educational Research Association, San Diego, CA.

Lampert, M. (1985). How do teachers manage to teach? Perspectives on the problems in practice. *Harvard Education Review, 55*, 229-246.

Lampert, M., & Ball, D. L. (1999). Aligning teacher education with contemporary K–12 reform visions. In L. Darling-Hammond & G. Sykes (Eds.), *Teaching as the learning profession: Handbook of policy and practice* (pp. 33-53). San Francisco: Jossey-Bass.

Richardson, V. (1990). Significant and worthwhile change in teaching practice. *Educational Researcher, 19*, 10-18.

Russell, S. J., Schifter, D., Bastable, V., Yaffee, L., Lester, J. B., & Cohen, S. (1995). Learning mathematics while teaching. In B. S. Nelson (Ed.), *Inquiry and the development of teaching: Issues in the transformation of mathematics teaching* (pp. 9-16). Newton, MA: Center for the Development of Teaching, Education Development Center.

Shulman, L. S. (1986). Those who understand: Knowledge growth in teaching. *Educational Researcher, 57*, 4-14.

Simon, M. (1997). Developing new models of mathematics teaching: An imperative for research on mathematics teacher development. In E. Fennema & B. S. Nelson (Eds.), *Mathematics teachers in transition* (pp. 55-86). Hillsdale, NJ: Lawrence Erlbaum Associates.

Warren, B., & Rosebery, A. S. (1995). Equity in the future tense: Redefining relationships among teachers, students and science in language minority classrooms. In W. Secada, E. Fennema, & L. Adajian (Eds.), *New directions for equity in mathematics education* (pp. 298-328). New York: Cambridge University Press.

Constructivist Mathematics Instruction and Current Trends in Research on Teaching

Virginia Richardson
University of Michigan

The chapters in this book represent an approach to research on teaching that has become more prevalent in recent times. This form of research is conducted within an well-articulated frame that represents a strong commitment to a particular theory about or stance toward the phenomenon being studied. In the chapters in this book, the commitment is to a theory of learning, *constructivism*, that is being extended, in part, through research, to considerations of teaching and teacher education practices. One could say that all research is conducted within a specific theoretical frame such as constructivism. However, for a number of years in the study of teaching, the lens being used was not well articulated. In many cases, it was neither acknowledged nor always known or understood as a frame or lens. What is different and helpful about the approach to research in this volume is that the constructivist frame is both acknowledged and communicated.

I have been asked to place the work that is represented in this volume within a larger consideration of research on teaching. I plan to do this with reference to a publication that is in press at this time, the *Handbook of Research on Teaching* (4th ed.; Richardson, 2000). More recent work in research on teaching carefully specifies the lens through which a phenomenon is being observed and analyzed; however, as just suggested, this was not always the case. An historical look at research on teaching across the four editions of the

Handbook takes us from a view of teaching as transmission of knowledge and skills to teaching as the facilitation of meaning making. Each approach includes a vision of effective teaching, a delineation of what students should be learning, the stance toward the research that is undertaken, and the nature of teacher education and change. But the individual research on teaching frames may also be placed within much larger currents of social thinking. The transmission view, for example, was located squarely within the behaviorist traditions of thinking about control of human behavior, and within strong quantitative traditions of research. However, most contemporary educational research has been influenced by two "revolutions": one, cognitive, and the second, postmodern. Thus, we see the work in this volume—an exploration of facilitative teaching of mathematics—within a larger frame of research on teaching, which, itself, is buffeted and often influenced by trends in social thinking such as social cognition and postmodernism.

TWO VIEWS OF TEACHING

The Earlier Transmission View

Research on teaching came into its own as a field of study during the late 1960s and early 1970s with process–product research. Large-scale studies attempted to tie teacher behaviors to student achievement. In these studies, teachers who were identified as more or less effective on the basis of their students' scores on achievement tests were observed and their behaviors recorded. Correlation analysis identified significant differences between more and less effective teachers, leading to the concept of time on task and the direct instructional model (Berliner, Fisher, Filby & Marliave, 1978; see also Brophy & Good, 1986, for a thorough summary of this literature).

These studies were conducted within a vision of the teacher as transmitter of knowledge and skills. Transmission was accomplished through specific teacher behaviors designed to maintain students' attention to the material at hand, and to provide tasks that would allow them to practice skills so that the students would remember them. At that point, there were no alternative views of teaching that were well articulated and accepted; thus the direct instructional model was developed in a seemingly theoryless and singularly objective view of the effective classroom.

We now know that the transmission model represents a strong image of teaching and student learning—one that affected not only the research conducted on teaching, but also our thinking about and research on teacher education and professional development.   For example, professional development within the transmission model consisted of the provision of information on effective behaviors to teachers. The research that was conducted on this process, by and large, was classic experimentation with both teacher behaviors and student achievement as the outcomes of interest (Gage, 1978).

Mathematics was one of two subject matters of interest in the process–product research, primarily because the outcomes that defined the effectiveness of teachers consisted of scores on standardized achievement tests in which mathematics and reading were subjects tested. It should be pointed out that, like the studies in this book, most of these studies were conducted at the elementary school level.   However, the findings of these studies often became an integral element of professional development for secondary school teachers. These professional development sessions often began with such statements as: "Research says that these are the behaviors you should employ in your mathematics teaching."

Process–product research led to a model of mathematics teaching best represented by the work of Good and Grouws (1979). They began with a correlational process–product study in which they compared behavior of effective and less effective fourth-grade teachers when they were teaching mathematics. *Effective teachers* were defined as those whose students gained more on standardized mathematics tests than students of the less effective teachers. They then used the findings in an experiment designed to change teacher behaviors in the direction of the results of the correlational study. The model of teaching was designed for whole-class mathematics teaching, and provided teachers with guidelines for conducting a lesson, including the time to be spent on each activity. The professsional development consisted of a manual for teachers and two, 90-minute workshop sessions. In a series of studies, Good and Grouws found that teachers changed their behaviors and student achievement gains were substantial as measured by standardized tests.

Lest we think that this type of research has been completely replaced with a newer form, Floden (2000) has made a strong argument that much of the process–product approach to research on teaching is still with us. He calls it the *effects of teaching model* that involves the search for causally relevant connections between teaching and student achievement. He suggests that this model is operating today, even within constructivist frames. For example, he cites Cobb and colleagues in their study of a professional development program designed to develop teachers' understandings of a new teaching role. They compared the teachers' students' scores on several tests to those of students in classrooms in which the teachers did not participate in the inservice (Cobb et al., 1991; Cobb, Yackel & Wood, 1989). As we move to the more contemporary approaches to conducting research on teaching, it is best to realize the legacy of this approach.

Toward a Postmodern, Constructivist View of Teaching

Concerns about the nature of the achievement measures (product), research methodology, and potential context effects in process–product research (e.g., Fenstermacher, 1979) led to the development of quite different approaches to studying classrooms. Disciplinary frameworks and research methods other than those typically found in educational psychology were applied in the study of classrooms. These included anthropology, sociolinguistics and sociology. Research employing qualitative methods and case study approaches began to appear in well-established journals. The influence of the cognitive revolution turned the attention of researchers away from teacher behaviors toward teachers' thought processes and their knowledge as they planned, implemented their lessons, and reflected on their practices. By the late 1980s and early 1990s, this movement toward teacher cognition affected all aspects of research on teaching, including the conceptions of effective teaching, student learning, and the approach to research used to explore teaching (Carter, 1990).

At the same time, an even more significant social theory was beginning to influence research on teaching: the movement from modern to postmodern thinking. (For a description of this movement in research on teaching, see Hamilton & McWilliams, in press.) This movement has created great turbulence in the field. Postmodernism raises questions that jar the very foundations of our understanding of research. These questions concern the nature of knowledge, who owns it, who produces it, and how it should be used. The conflicts go beyond the old qualitative-quantitative methodology controversy as described by Erickson (1986) in the *Handbook of Research on Teaching* (3rd ed.). They now focus on the very nature of research and knowledge and the uses of research in the improvement of practice.

Postmodernism has brought with it an understanding of the theoretical frame or lens that a researcher brings to the study of teaching, and the influence of these lenses on such research aspects as the research design and stance, observation foci, data analysis, and interpretation. Postmodern philosophy and qualitative research methods encourage authors and researchers to be clear about their biases in conducting their work and writing about it. This may be seen in the chapters in this volume. The theoretical frame is constructivist learning extended to teaching theory within the subject matter of mathematics. This constructivist theory guides the vision of the effective teacher, the nature of the content to be learned by students, the choice of research question, and the approach to research, including what is being observed, and other critical elements of the research. This was also pointed out by Martin Simon in his chapter in this book.

Along with the focus on teacher cognition came a shift to constructivist theory and a significantly altered vision of the act of teaching. The effective teacher was no longer viewed as standing in front of the class transmitting information and skills to students. The teacher became the facilitator of learning or meaning-making by students through creating environments, tasks and dialogues in which students access their prior knowledge, consider alternative premises, alter, and add to their existing understandings with information and ways of thinking that are introduced to them by the teacher and other experts, readings, their peers, and their own research.

Given the constructivist view that each student has unique background knowledge and experiences, the teacher is compelled to keep track of individual differences and to adjust lessons on the basis of this knowledge. This is particularly important in current classrooms with students of diverse backgrounds.

Within this conception, teaching requires complex thought and decision making in situations of uncertainty and variable contexts. Notions of the complexity of teaching and the variability of the context work together to help promote the view of the teacher as a thinking, decision-making, reflective, and autonomous professional. Because teaching is complex and contexts vary, teachers themselves need to make decisions and reflect on their situations and teaching in order to act in appropriate ways.

The work in this volume reflects this view of teachers and teaching. This may be seen in the approaches taken in professional development, and in the conduct of the research. The change and research processes intermingle, and the roles of the researcher and researched come together at times and is often difficult to distinguish. In all cases, the researcher is seen as learning and changing along with the teacher(s) who are engaged in change. The teacher holds knowledge about his or her classroom and students and is continuing to learn about the students. The researcher is learning about the teachers' contexts, the way the teachers think about their classrooms, and the processes of change in which the teacher is engaged. Therefore, what the researcher is learning about this process becomes the findings of the study, and the results are often personalized.

CURRENT TRENDS IN RESEARCH ON TEACHING

Teacher Change and Teacher Learning

The view of teacher change that accompanied the transmission model of teaching was consistent with a view of learning that brought knowledge and skills to the student from somewhere and/or some-one external to the individual who was learning them. The focus of teacher education and professional development was on classroom behaviors; and following the publications of process–product research, these desired behaviors were described as "research-based." Within this view, the desired outcomes were clearly and unambiguously set and the workshop or teacher education class focused on teachers learning and practicing these behaviors.

As the conception of teaching changed from one of transmission to facilitation and the conception of learning from acquisition of behaviors to construction of meaning, the question of how teachers themselves could be encouraged to change their ways of thinking and approaches to teaching became paramount in the research, policy and practice literatures. Recently, there has been considerable work on the development of standards in various subject-matter areas. An example is the mathematics standards for students (National Council of Teachers of Mathematics [NCTM], 1989, 2000). Because these standards call for a very different approach to teaching, research began to focus on processes of teacher change. At first, the new ways of thinking and teaching were taught to teachers in a transmission approach. Large groups of teacher education students were lectured on constructivist theories and how to implement them in the classroom. (Actually, there is still much of this that is going on today.)   However, it soon became apparent that the transmission model was appropriate neither for K–12 students nor for teachers as learners.   The anticipated changes in teachers and teaching were thought to entail more than the acquisition of a new teaching method, but involved changes in beliefs and practices around the nature of teaching.   This form of change itself required the development of conceptions of teacher change and research on processes that would be effective in helping teachers develop these newer teaching roles (Richardson & Placier, in press).

Teacher Education and Professional Development

The current views of teacher change contest the idea that teachers are recalcitrant and do not change (Richardson & Placier, in press).   The recalcitrant label stems from a view of change in which individuals or groups outside the classroom mandate or suggests the changes that teachers should make.   In fact, research suggests that teachers voluntarily change all the time.   They reorganize their classrooms, using reading groups, try different activities and texts, change the order of topics in the curriculum, attempt different interpersonal skills, and so on.   When teachers experiment with new activities in the classroom, the new practices are assessed by the teachers on the basis of whether they work.   When these activities work, it means that they engage the students, do not violate the teacher's particular need for control, and help the teachers respond to system-determined demands such as high scores on standardized tests.   If they work, they are internalized and absorbed into the teacher's repertoire of activities.

This new understanding of naturalistic teacher change led to a considerable number of studies of processes that would help teachers change their beliefs about student learning, the nature of teaching, and the role of the learning environment in student development. These studies often focus on particular subject-matter areas such as mathematics, science, English, and social studies because the learning and teaching standards are usually developed around these subjects. The most productive research-based approach to staff development suggests a long-term effort in which teachers are engaged in inquiry into their own often-tacit beliefs and practices (Richardson & Hamilton, 1994).   This process is enhanced through dialogue, particularly with those who understand practice and the particular context in which the teacher is working.   A certain trust level is important within the community because it is helpful for the participants to accept and talk about practices that do not seem to work, and to accept responsibility for them. Thus, the development of a discourse community is productive in beginning this process of change.

The work in this volume confirms and adds to this newer vision of teacher change and professional development. For example, there is a strong case made for teachers as learners. This is not necessarily a descriptive view; rather, it is normative. That is, teachers should be learners. Thus, great efforts are made in the professional development programs described in these chapters to work with teachers to become learners—in particular, to constantly learn about their students' thinking and learning of mathematics. This is evident in the Cognitively Guided Instruction (CGI) professional development models discussed in the chapters by Carpenter, Ansell, and Levi, Franke and Kazemi, Sherin, and others. Other common elements of professional development processes discussed in this volume are: (a) staff development programs are being conducted over a considerable period of time; (b) the staff developer/researcher is often a collaborator in the process learning about teacher learning while the teacher is learning about her students' learning; and, (c) one goal of the process is working with teachers to make their practice and justifications for their practice their own (Schifter, this volume). Sherin's chapter also makes considerable use of videotaping in her work , a very popular means of providing a different perspective on a teachers' practices (Tochon, 1999). Thus, research on teacher learning that examines changes in knowledge and beliefs as well as practices, has led to the development of a number of different conceptions and forms of teacher knowledge and belief.

New Forms of Knowledge and Knowing in Teaching

As the focus of attention in research on teaching shifted from teacher behaviors to teacher cognition, beliefs and knowledge have become the two most important factors in the explanations of teacher practices and considerations of teacher change. In the traditional philosophical literature, knowledge requires a "truth condition" that suggests that a proposition is agreed on as being true by a group of people (Fenstermacher, 1994). Propositional knowledge has epistemic standing; that is, there is some evidence to back up the claim. Beliefs, however, do not require a truth condition. Beliefs have also been found to be powerful in their effects on teaching practices as evidenced in much of the work represented in this volume.

Within the field of research on teaching, however, the differentiation between beliefs and knowledge is not strongly evident. Many in the field define knowledge as that which is held in the teachers' heads, with or without a truth condition (Kagan, 1990). This psychological view of teacher knowledge has led to the identification of and research on a number of different forms of knowledge. Two forms of knowledge that have been studied extensively are *practical knowledge* and *pedagogical content knowledge.* Practical knowledge differs from *formal knowledge* in that formal or warranted knowledge is much more closely related to the philosophical conception of knowledge. Formal knowledge may be found in textbooks, research articles, and experts' heads. Content or disciplinary knowledge is one form of formal knowledge. However, practical knowledge, often tacit, may be found in teachers' heads and in their actions within their own classroom contexts. Pedagogical content knowledge, on the other hand, combines formal and practical knowledge. These various forms of knowing and believing are now described.

Beliefs, defined as propositions that are accepted as true by the individual holding the beliefs, are of interest in research on teaching in the investigation of the ways in which beliefs may affect teaching practices. Most current studies of teacher beliefs are conducted within the hermeneutic tradition (that is, they focus on how the individual teacher makes sense of the environment in which she or he is operating; Richardson, 1996). These studies suggest a complex relationship between teachers' beliefs and actions. In most current research-based conceptions, the perceived relationship between beliefs and actions is interactive. Beliefs are thought to drive actions; however, experiences and reflection on action may lead to changes in and/or additions to beliefs.

Beliefs are seen as important in teaching and teacher education in several ways. The first suggests that students of teaching bring powerful beliefs into their teacher education classes. These beliefs must be attended to by both the student of teaching and the teacher educator if the student is to move beyond the images of teaching acquired as a student. Another additional and related way is instruction that focuses directly on beliefs. As Green (1971) suggested, one goal of teaching is to help students form belief systems that consist of a large proportion of beliefs based on evidence and reason. Thus, the investigation of beliefs in the teacher education classroom should involve their rejection, alteration, or transformation into knowledge with warrant and evidence attached. Without attention to beliefs, transformational changes in teaching practices have a low probability of success.

Practical knowledge is an account of how a teacher knows or understands a classroom situation (Clandinin & Connelly, 1987; Elbaz, 1983). Practical knowledge is gained through experience, is often tacit, and is contextual or local. This form of knowledge is not, however, synonymous with beliefs because it is thought of as embodied within the whole person, not just in the mind. Embodied knowledge is more than cognitive and relates to the ways in which people physically interact with the environment (Johnson, 1987). It is this practical knowledge that may be used in an improvisational manner in the classroom. This conception of knowledge does not separate the knower from the known, is personalized, idiosyncratic, contextual, and emerges during action.

Pedagogical content knowledge refers to a way of knowing the subject matter that allows it to be taught (Shulman, 1987). It is grounded in the disciplines but adds an understanding of how to transform formal knowledge of the disciplines into the enacted curriculum within a teaching context. This knowledge combines that of the subject matter itself, with knowing how students learn the content, students' preconceptions that may get in the way of learning, and representations of the knowledge in the form of metaphors, examples, demonstrations, and so forth that allow it to be transformed into material that the students may learn. Inquiry into teachers' pedagogical content knowledge has been active since 1985. This research suggests that teacher education students' formal knowledge of the disciplines is quite weak, and that formal teacher education programs are a weak contributor to the formation of pedagogical content knowledge (Zeichner, 1999). However, there is strong evidence that those becoming teachers benefit from the courses that emphasize pedagogical knowledge as compared with those who enter teaching with subject matter background, but no pedagogical education (Grossman, 1990).

Content knowledge. As mentioned, there is strong evidence that the content knowledge held by preservice teacher education students is quite weak. This is particularly the case with the knowledge of mathematics and science held by elementary teachers. It is apparent that "finger-tip" content knowledge is very important in a constructivist classroom. Unfortunately, early views of constructivist classrooms suggested that content knowledge is not important—that the teacher and students create their own knowledge. MacKinnon and Scarff-Seatter (1997) suggested that teacher education students may be formulating a "truncated" view of constructivism, as represented in this alarming quote from an elementary science education student:

> I am very anxious to return to my classroom and teach science. Constructivism has taught me [that] I do not need to know any science in order to teach it. I will simply allow my students to figure things out for themselves, for I know there is no *right* answer. (p. 53)

Research on teachers' content knowledge in mathematics is very well represented in this volume. In fact, this volume takes the importance of subject matter to a new level. Of particular interest, here, is the notion of the need to study teachers' content knowledge as it is used in practice as developed by Warfield in her chapter. However, although attention to the context-specific nature of content knowledge makes considerable sense, it seems to break down the initial differentiation between content knowledge and pedagogical content knowledge. That is, it would appear that formal knowledge is affected by context, suggesting a mix of content with other knowledge that the term pedagogical content knowledge implies. This makes it a more difficult to determine the amount of content knowledge a prospective teacher should be developing in his or her schooling prior to teaching. Warfield also makes an interesting case for using research-based information on children's thinking about mathematics to provide a focus for teachers to expand their knowledge of the mathematics that they teach.

Constructivist Teaching

It should hardly be necessary to have a section in this chapter on constructivism in research on teaching, given the content of the chapters in this volume. However, constructivism has slipped into research on teaching in an amazingly comprehensive way since the last *Handbook of Research on Teaching* (Wittrock, 1986). *Constructivism* is a descriptive theory of learning; and most constructivists would agree on the view that the traditional approach to teaching—the transmission model—promotes neither the interaction between prior and new knowledge nor the conversations that are necessary for internalization and deep understanding necessary for students' learning. The information acquired by students from traditional teaching, if acquired at all, is usually not well integrated with other knowledge and beliefs held by students.

Although these are the common understandings, there are also considerable disagreements, such as the degree of "social" involved in the constructivist conception. Further, and more importantly in this context, there is not a direct relationship between the theory of student learning and the practice of teaching because constructivism is a theory of individual learning. Although constructivist learning theory may speak quite closely to a tutoring situation, it does not direct teaching practice within a "normal" classroom containing a collective of students. Thus, considerable research attention focuses on the constructivist classroom. Some of the questions that are being addressed are: (a) What is the place of formal knowledge in a constructivist classroom?, and How should it be introduced?, and (b) At what point during instruction does it make sense to "tell" students formal knowledge, answers to questions, or both? These issues are being worked out within the different disciplines, and evidence indicates that constructivist classrooms vary depending on the subject matter (Leinhardt, in press).

The chapters in this volume approached many important questions concerning teaching mathematics in a constructivist manner. The depth of understanding of the facilitative role, the understanding of student learning of mathematics, the ability to understand individual students' thinking, and knowledge about the mathematics that is the focus of attention in the classroom at a particular point in time all become extremely important in these findings. The examples of teacher dialogue in these chapters with students may be helpful in providing real-life descriptions of the nature of questioning and explanation in such classrooms.

Teaching to Individual Differences: Gender and Culture

Constructivist learning theory suggests that the background knowledge, beliefs, and understandings that students bring to the classroom strongly affect what they learn within the classroom. Given this frame and the current attempts to integrate students with differing cultural and language backgrounds as well as learning styles and abilities suggests that attention to the background knowledge of students is critical in the teaching process.

Certainly, the work represented in this volume moves toward teachers' deep understanding of individual students' growth, development, and thinking processes in mathematics learning. However, one way of examining an approach to teaching and learning is to determine whether there are groups of students with common characteristics who do not do quite as well as the others. Teachers often have a tendency to blame the child in such situations. However, we can also look at the particular approach to teaching to determine whether there might be a relationship. I wonder about two such possibilities: gender and culture.

Research on differences in the ways teachers approach girls and boys in the classroom has a longstanding tradition in research on teaching (Biklin & Pollard, in press). There is no doubt teachers often treat girls differently from boys and teachers are often not aware of doing so. Examples are the questions asked of boy versus girl students. They are often qualitatively different, and the intellectual follow-up on boys answers is often different and usually more thorough for boys than girls. However, it is also the case that girls act differently in classrooms than boys, and the effort continues to be made to understand teachers' different behaviors as a reaction both to the differences in classroom behavior by boys and girls, and the social forces that may affect these different behaviors. There is also a longstanding research tradition that examines the apparently quite real differences in girls and boys' learning of mathematics. I remain curious about gender differences in constructivist mathematics classrooms.

Multicultural education has received considerable attention in research on teaching as schools and classrooms continue to be more diverse racially/ethnically, linguistically, and economically. Further, it is also the case in many countries, including the United States, that the teaching population itself is dominated disproportionately by teachers of the majority culture (Dilworth & Brown, in press). Knowledge and understanding of various cultures and the culturally informed ways of approaching the tasks of teaching and learning thus become imperative for teachers. Of particular importance in this area is the development of the concepts of *culturally relevant learning* and *teaching* (Ladson-Billings, 1994). Based on research of successful teachers of African-American students, this concept suggests that knowledge of the culture and community of the students is utilized in these classrooms and guides instructional pedagogy and elements of classroom action and interaction such as the classroom management system.

Within the subject matter of reading instruction, Delpit (1986, 1988) has created strong challenges to constructivist and literature-based reading programs. Delpit presents a powerful cultural argument for the problems created by whole language instruction for students of color. Researchers have begun to examine cultural and ethnic differences in scientific world view in relation to the national standards that have been proposed (Eisenhart, Finkel, & Marion, 1996; Lee, 1999). I wonder how culturally influenced ways of knowing and constructing knowledge will be operationalized for students of color, low-income students, or both in these constructivist mathematics classrooms.

Moral Development

McNeal's chapter describes working with a teacher who is faced with an ethical dilemma that causes her to teach in a way that she might not were she able to close the door and block out administrators, parents, state policy makers, and others who have different goals than hers. This ethical dilemma is played out constantly within classrooms, but is often less demanding when the "common culture" of goals for student learning on the part of the teacher matches those of society. The nature of the moral dimensions of classrooms and schools is a growing trend in research on teaching.

For years, research has focused on the teaching of the basic skills and of reading and mathematics. More recently, other subject-matter areas such as science, writing, history, and geography have been included in this research. It is also the case, however, that teachers may have a strong influence on the moral development of students. Current research in this area is investigating the moral dimensions of classroom life and indicates that the moral life of the classroom is robust and powerful (Jackson, Boorstrom & Hansen, 1993; Hansen, in press; Fenstermacher, in press; Richardson & Fallona, in press). Teachers, however, are often unaware of the nature and/or consequence of their actions in relation to the moral development of their students.

As one thinks of the classrooms in which the teacher may consciously and unconsciously deliver this moral development, the mathematics classroom does not come readily to mind. Traditionally, curricula that are felt to be amenable to moral "lessons" are English literature, social studies, and history. However, as pointed out by Ball and Wilson (1996), the moral is embedded in the method — whether it is a history, mathematics, or teacher education lesson.

Subject Matter Studies

For a number of years, particularly at the height of the process–product era, a primary purpose of research on teaching was to identify generic teaching behaviors that would be applicable at any grade level, with any students, and in any subject matter area. Following the lead of Shulman (1974), who called for research on teaching within specific domains such as subject matter, it soon became apparent in this work that the teaching of mathematics may be a little different from teaching reading, just as effective teaching in second grade may be a little different from that in fifth grade (Brophy & Good, 1986).

In a recent chapter, Leinhardt (in press) grapples with the question of whether it may be worthwhile to explore teaching practices across subject matters, at least for some constructs. In order to examine the question, Leinhardt selects teaching "commonplace" instructional explanations within the subject matters of history and mathematics. Leinhardt (in press) concludes the following:

> The explanations, then, are explanations in the context of subject matters and are prompted as part of the justification or clarification of an approach to a problem or a deep issue. Instructional explanations in both history and mathematics have different aspects to them depending on the focus of the explanation, but they are internally self-referential and integrated.

And yet, in this volume about teaching mathematics, there is important work that speaks to researchers, teachers, and teacher educators who are working in other subject matters; just as the work in other subject matters is useful to the researchers in this volume. To give a sort of radical example, as I facilitate graduate students' development of writing skills, I could certainly use Schifter's chapter about mathematical skills that teachers need, by substituting research or research design for mathematics. It is also useful to consider Wood and Turner-Vorbeck's three forms of interactive discussion and their characteristics within the context of facilitating writing as well. That is, Report Ways, Inquiry, and Arguments, are interesting ways of thinking about different forms of discussion in classes in which student work is paramount. While these ways of thinking are certainly not "generic" within their present form, they may certainly, with some adjustment, be useful in other domains.

CONCLUSIONS

I hope that I have been able to indicate how tying the work of research on teaching within a particular subject matter area to trends within research on teaching and, to a certain extent, to even broader social research trends is a helpful exercise. I might also say that it works the opposite way. Reading these chapters in depth has been helpful to me in understanding the details and importance of teaching research within one subject matter and helping to consider the future direction of research on teaching. I do, however, have one set of questions that I believe should be contemplated over the next several years. It begins with a short story.

In the mid 1970's, as I was thinking about the direction of research on teaching and considering the importance of subject matter, I talked with Joseph Schwab, the wonderful and influential curriculum and philosophy professor at the University of Chicago. I asked him how much education was required to be able to think mathematically, and how much was required to teach mathematics. (At that point in time, and continuing today, there is a strong sense that thinking within one discipline is being very different from thinking within another discipline.) He said that one needed more than a Bachelor's degree to think mathematically, but that such a degree was enough for teaching. "You need to see the light at the end of the tunnel" in order to teach mathematics, he said.

After reading the chapters in this volume, I am pretty well convinced that this approach to the teaching of mathematics will lead at least some students to think mathematically well before they pursue graduate education. My questions are the following: Is this what we want? Do we really want all children to think mathematically? If they think mathematically, are they also able to think in other disciplines? Do we also want them all to think historically, scientifically, literarily, philosophically, artistically? Is one person able to do that? I end with this set of questions as yet unanswered.

REFERENCES

Ball, D., & Wilson, S. (1996). Integrity in teaching: Recognizing the fusion of the moral and intellectual. *American Educational Research Journal, 33,* 155-192.
Berliner, D., Fisher, C., Filby, N., & Marliave, R. (1978). *Executive summary of the beginning teacher evaluation study.* San Francisco, CA: Far West Laboratory.

Biklin, S. K., & Pollard, D. S. (in press). Gender. In V. Richardson (Ed.), *Handbook of research on teaching* (4th ed.). Washington, DC: American Educational Research Association.

Brophy, J., & Good, T. (1986). Teacher behavior and student achievement. In M. C. Wittrock (Ed.), *Handbook of research on teaching* (3rd ed., pp. 328-375). New York: Macmillan.

Carter, K. (1990). Teachers' knowledge and learning to teach. In W. R. Houston (Ed.), *Handbook of research on teacher education* (pp. 291-310). New York: Macmillan.

Clandinin, D. J., & Connelly, F. M. (1987). Teachers' personal knowledge: What counts as personal in studies of the personal. *Journal of Curriculum Studies, 19,* 487-500.

Cobb, P., Wood, T., Yackel, E., Nicholls, J., Trigatti, B., & Perlwitz, M. (1991). Assessment of a problem-centered second-grade mathematics project. *Journal for Research in Mathematics Education, 22,* 3-29.

Cobb, P., Yackel, E., & Wood, T. (1989). Young children's emotional acts while doing mathematical problem solving. In D. McLeod & V. Adams (Eds.), *Affect and mathematical problem solving* (pp. 117-148). New York: Springer-Verlag.

Delpit, L. (1986). Skills and other dilemmas of a progressive Black educator. *Harvard Educational Review, 56,* 379-385.

Delpit, L. (1988). The silenced dialogue: Power and pedagogy in educating other peoples' children. *Harvard Educational Review, 56,* 379-385.

Dilworth, M., & Brown, C. (in press). Consider the difference: Teaching and learning in culturally rich schools. In V. Richardson (Ed.), *Handbook of research on teaching* (4th ed.). Washington, DC: American Educational Research Association.

Eisenhart, M., Finkel, E., & Marion, S. (1996). Creating the conditions for scientific literacy: A re-examination. *American Educational Research Journal, 33,* 261-295.

Elbaz, F. L. (1983). *Teacher thinking: A study of practical knowledge.* London: Croom Helm.

Erickson, F. (1986). Qualitative methods in research on teaching. In M. C. Wittrock (Ed.), *Handbook of research on teaching* (3rd ed., pp. 119-161). New York: Macmillan.

Fenstermacher, G. D. (1979). A philosophical consideration of recent research on teacher effectiveness. In L. S. Shulman (Ed.), *Review of research in education* (Vol. 6, pp. 157-185). Itasca, IL: Peacock.

Fenstermacher, G. D. (1994). The knower and the known: The nature of knowledge in research on teaching. In L. Darling-Hammond (Ed.), *Review of research in education* (Vol. 20, pp. 1-54). Washington, DC: American Educational Research Association.

Fenstermacher, G. D. (in press). On the concept of manner and its visibility in teaching practice. *Journal of Curriculum Inquiry.*

Floden, R. (in press). Research on effects of teaching: A continuing model for research on teaching. In V. Richardson (Ed.), *Handbook of research on teaching* (4th ed.). Washington, DC: American Educational Research Association.

Gage, N. L. (1978). *The scientific basis of the art of teaching.* New York: Teachers College Press.

Good, T., & Grouws, D. (1979). The Missouri Mathematics Effectiveness Project: An experimental study in fourth grade classrooms. *Journal of Educational Psychology, 71,* 355-362.

Green, T. (1971). *The activities of teaching.* New York: McGraw-Hill.

Grossman, P. L. (1990). *The making of a teacher: Teacher knowledge and teacher education.* New York: Teachers College Press.

Hamilton, D., & McWilliams, E. (in press). Ex-centric voices that frame research on teaching. In V. Richardson (Ed.), *Handbook of research on teaching* (4th ed.). Washington, DC: American Educational Research Association.

Hansen, D. (in press). Teaching as a moral activity. In V. Richardson (Ed.), *Handbook of research on teaching* (4th ed.). Washington, DC: American Educational Research Association.

Jackson, P., Boorstrom, R., & Hansen, D. (1993). *The moral life of schools.* San Francisco: Jossey-Bass.

Johnson, M. (1987). *The body in the mind: The bodily basis of meaning, imagination, and mind.* Chicago, IL: University of Chicago Press.

Kagan, D. (1990). Ways of evaluating teacher cognition: Inferences concerning the Goldilocks principle. *Review of Educational Research, 60,* 419-469.

Ladson-Billings, G. (1994). *The dreamkeepers.* San Francisco, CA: Jossey-Bass.

Lee, O. (1999). Science knowledge, world views, and information sources in social and cultural contexts: Making sense after natural disaster. *American Educational Research Journal, 33,* 187-220.

Leinhardt, G. (2000). Instructional explanations: A commonplace for teaching and location of contrast. In V. Richardson (Ed.), *Handbook of research on teaching* (4th ed.). Washington, DC: American Educational Research Association.

MacKinnon, A., & Scarff-Seatter, C. (1997). Constructivism: Contradictions and confusions in teacher education. In V. Richardson (Ed.), *Constructivist teacher education: Building new understandings* (pp. 38-56). London: Falmer Press.

National Council of Teachers of Mathematics. (1989). *Curriculum and evaluation standards for school mathematics.* Reston, VA: author.

National Council of Teachers of Mathematics. (2000). *Principles and standards for school mathematics.* Reston, VA: author.

Richardson, V. (1996). The role of attitudes and beliefs in learning to teach. In J. Sikula (Ed.), *Handbook of research on teacher education* (2nd ed., pp. 102-119). New York: Macmillan.

Richardson, V. ·Ed. (in press). *Handbook of research on teaching* (4th ed.) Washington, DC: American Research Association.

Richardson, V., & Fallona, C. (in press). Classroom management as method and manner. *Journal of Curriculum Inquiry.*

Richardson, V., & Hamilton, M. L. (1994). Staff Development: The practical argument process. In V. Richardson (Ed.), *Teacher change and the staff development process: A case in reading instruction* (pp. 109-134). Teachers College Press.

Richardson, V., & Placier, P. (in press). Teacher change. In V. Richardson (Ed.), *Handbook of research on teaching* (4th ed.). Washington, DC: American Educational Research Association.

Shulman, L. S. (1974). The psychology of school subjects: A premature obituary? *Journal of Research in Science Teaching, 11,* 319-339.

Shulman, L. S. (1987). Knowledge and teaching: Foundations of the new reform. *Harvard Educational Review, 57,* 1-22.

Tochon, F. (1999). *Video study groups.* Madison, WI: Atwood Publishing.

Wittrock, M. (Ed.) (1986). *Handbook of research on teaching* (3rd ed.). New York: Macmillan.

Zeichner, K. (1999). The new scholarship in teacher education. *Educational Researcher, 28* (9), 4-15.

Final Remarks

Terry Wood
Purdue University

Barbara Scott Nelson
Education Development Center, Newton, MA

Janet Warfield
Purdue University

FROM DESCRIPTION TO THEORY

Many of the contributors to this book, as well as much of the mathematics education research community in general, take a psychological orientation toward learning, following the constructivist theoretical tenets of Piaget. They take an individual and developmental perspective when looking at children's learning, in some cases integrating concepts from cognitive science and information processing theory. One reason for the reliance on Piaget's theory is that it builds from notions that are fundamental to mathematics (e.g., the role of logic and logical reasoning). It also offers a mechanism to account for conceptual change, in the ideas of assimilation and accommodation. However, this is a perspective that focuses exclusively on the individual and on the mental processes of learning within the individual. Several contributors to this book see teaching as playing a fundamental role in creating conditions that enable children to make changes in their thinking that are necessary to understand the ideas and concepts that form the logic of mathematics.

The recent emergence of social constructivist perspectives that focus on the social and cultural aspects of learning has also influenced thought about mathematics teaching. We see two strands of influence among the authors represented in this volume. Vygotsky's interest in the ways in which young children are acculturated to cultural knowledge has influenced some of the contributors. Vygotsky's interest was in the social and instructional features of learning, particularly language and tools. This perspective brings to the psychological perspective on children's learning issues of culture and diversity. In addition, the microsociologists, who focus on the group and social processes involved in establishing order in everyday life (e.g., on the role of interaction and routine in the conduct of human affairs) have influenced some contributors' views of teaching. These authors also take up the microsociologists' interest in the processes involved in meaning–making among individuals and the process of establishing common knowledge in a group.

Each contributor to this book comes from a theoretical stance that influences his or her view of teaching and most of the chapters in this book are descriptive of pedagogy or are conceptual, in that they help us formulate what mathematics teaching might be that is responsive to a constructivist view of learning. The questions remain: How can the field move forward to the formulation of a theory of mathematics teaching itself? How can we move from the kind of careful descriptive and conceptual work presented in this volume to the development of theory?

In this section, we discuss the importance of moving beyond description to the development of theory in teaching. We discuss three existing theoretical perspectives on mathematics teaching as examples: the work of Guy Brousseau (1997) in France, Barbara Jaworski (1994) in the United Kingdom, and Alan Schoenfeld (1998) in the United States. The work of each of these scholars is rooted in very different intellectual traditions and we are not arguing for any of these theories in particular. Rather, we regard them as examples of theory building that rely on the empirical analysis of teaching situations for its formulation.

Over the past 20 years, Brousseau has written in French about his theory of teaching mathematics, but only recently has his work been edited and translated (Brousseau, 1997). At the center of his work is the articulation between theoretical work and experimental research in elementary school mathematics classes. Central to Brousseau's (1997) theory is the notion that the teacher's work consists of the "double work"(p. 35) of producing "a *recontextualization* and *repersonalization* of the knowledge" (p. 23) in order for it to become the student's mathematical knowledge. This process consists of creating *didactical situations* — mathematical ideas embedded in problem contexts for student exploration. In addition, situations must be created for decontextualizing, generalizing, and abstracting ideas beyond the context of the original problem situation. Further, the teacher endeavors to create situations for *institutionalization* in which ideas constructed or modified during problem solving attain the status of knowledge in the classroom community.

> The teacher therefore must arrange not the communication of knowledge but the *devolution* of a good problem. If this devolution takes place, the students enter into the game and if they win learning occurs (Brousseau, 1997, p. 31).

The didactical situation is viewed as a system of reciprocal obligations between the teacher and students that resembles a contract. But what is of interest is the *didactical contract*, "that is to say, the part of this contract which is specific to the 'content', the target mathematical knowledge." (p. 32). The theoretical concept of interest in *didactique* is not the contract itself, but instead the hypothetical process of how students and teacher find a contract.

Jaworski's (1994) research in secondary mathematics teaching is another example of empirical inquiry extended to theory through development of the construct of the *teaching triad*. From observational research and case studies on teaching, Jaworski created and validated the teaching triad as a way of characterizing teaching. The teaching triad consists of three closely linked categories, *management of learning, sensitivity to students*, and *mathematical challenge*. Management of learning is revealed "in a set of teaching strategies and beliefs about teaching which influence the prevailing classroom atmosphere and the way in which lessons are conducted" (Jaworski, 1994, p.107). The category of sensitivity to students is revealed in the, "teacher-student relationship and the teacher's knowledge of individual students and influences the way in which the teacher interacts with, and challenges, students" (Jaworski, 1994, p. 108).

These two constructs reflect teaching in general, while mathematical challenge is specific to mathematics teaching and "arises from the teacher's own epistemological standpoint and the way she offers mathematics to her students depending on their individual needs and levels of progress" (Jaworski, 1994, p. 108). In commenting on her conceptualization of teaching, Jaworski (1994) noted that the teaching triad is useful as a device that helps to characterize "investigative mathematics teaching" (p. 108). Her analysis of a teacher named Simon, who held a transmission view of teaching, served as a counterexample to investigative teaching. Jaworski's (1994) observations revealed differences in Simon's teaching with regard to Jaworski's constructs, particularly with regard to mathematical challenge that were observed as "almost completely lacking" (p. 183).

Finally, the current work of Schoenfeld (1998) is an attempt to describe the teaching actions of highly competent mathematics and science teachers. He stated:

> Our intention is to provide a detailed theoretical account of how and why teachers do what they do "on line" — that is, while they are engaged in the act of teaching. This theoretical characterization of teaching is embodied in a model of the teaching process. The model describes, at a level of mechanism, the ways in which the teacher's goals, beliefs, and knowledge interact, resulting in the teacher's moment-to-moment decision-making and actions (p. 1).

Schoenfeld's goal is to develop a theory of *teaching-in-context* in order to explain how and why teachers make specific decisions and use specific actions in the process of their teaching with the possibility of predicting teachers' actions. Schoenfeld's model of teaching-in-context is grounded in the tradition of cognitive science and in two theoretical constructs that informed earlier work on students' thinking in context. These are that "the activation levels of beliefs, goals, and knowledge are mutually supportive" (p. 2) and "the actions taken by the teacher will be selected in a way to be consistent with the current highly activated beliefs, goals, and knowledge of the teacher" (p. 2). Schoenfeld (1999a) claims that the model he and colleagues developed provides a general explanatory frame "for understanding teaching-in-context as a function of their knowledge beliefs and goals" (p. 4).

Although, in this volume, some attempts to link empirical findings to theoretical formulations of teaching and student learning exist (cf., Simon, Wood & Turner-Vorbeck) many of the contributions are largely descriptive or conceptual. As Schoenfeld (1999b) commented "to be able to describe and provide detailed theoretical models of such activity, explaining how and why teachers do what they do amidst the complexity of the classroom, is to make significant strides in understanding human thought and action" (p. 13).

To this end, we argue that extending beyond descriptive inquiry and reconceptualization of teaching to generate and debate possible theoretical frameworks for teaching is essential to the progress of mathematics education. Because teaching is situated, that is, it is the exercise of professional judgment in particular circumstances, powerful theory may be hard to come by. However, if this is the case, then with theory would come consistency in conceptualization, evidence, and argument; the possibility of prediction; and principles that can inform such practical tasks as the design of teacher education and professional development programs. The field is currently rich in embryonic theoretical positions about teaching based on a constructivist view of the nature of learning—albeit based on different and sometimes contradictory underlying assumptions. Continuing to engage in the process of theory generation is an important task for the future of mathematics education.

REFERENCES

Brousseau, G. (1997). *Theory of didactical situations in mathematics: Didactique des mathematiques, 1970-1990.* (N. Balacheff, M. Cooper, R. Sutherland, & V. Warfield, Trans. & Eds.). Dordrecht: Kluwer.

Jaworski, B. (1994). *Investigating mathematics teaching: A constructivist enquiry.* London: Falmer Press.

Schoenfeld, A. (1998). Toward a theory of teaching-in-context. *Issues in Education, 4* (1), 1-94.

Schoenfeld, A. (1999a, April). *Dilemmas/decision: Can we model teachers' on-line decision-making?* Paper presented at the Annual meeting of American Educational Research Association, Montreal, Canada.

Schoenfeld, A. (1999b) Looking toward the 21st century: Challenges of educational theory and practice. *Educational Researcher, 28,* 4-14.

AUTHOR INDEX

SUBJECT INDEX

LIST OF CONTRIBUTORS

Ellen Ansell, University of Pittsburgh

Deborah Loewenberg Ball, School of Education, University of Michigan

Thomas P. Carpenter, Wisconsin Center for Education Research, University of Wisconsin-Madison

Megan Loef Franke, Curriculum, Teaching Leadership and Policy Studies, University of California Los Angeles

Barbara Jaworski, Department of Educational Studies, University of Oxford

Elham Kazemi, College of Education, University of Washington

Linda Levi, Wisconsin Center for Education Research, University of Wisconsin-Madison

Betsy McNeal, School of Teaching and Learning, Ohio State University

Barbara Scott Nelson, Center for the Development of Teaching, Education Development Center

Virginia Richardson, School of Education, University of Michigan

Deborah Schifter, Center for the Development of Teaching, Education Development Center

Miriam Gamoran Sherin, School of Education and Social Policy, Northwestern University

Martin A. Simon, Department of Curriculum and Instruction, Pennsylvania State University

Tammy Turner-Vorbeck, Department of Curriculum and Instruction, Purdue University

Janet Warfield, Department of Curriculum and Instruction, Purdue University

Terry Wood, Department of Curriculum and Instruction, Purdue University